COOKING WITH THE NOONDAY CHEF

VOLUME 3

BY
WALTER N. LAMBERT

WITH A SPECIAL CONTRIBUTION BY
ANNE WAYLAND LAMBERT

PUBLISHED BY PULLMAN PRESS
COPYRIGHT HELD BY TASTE MATTERS, INC

COVER DESIGN : SHEILA HART
COVER PHOTOGRAPHS: ERNEST ROBERTSON

To Pat, a very special lady to enjoy. We hope you enjoy. Sincerely, Walter and Anne Lambert 8 '99

INTRODUCTION

On May 1, 1989, we did our first cooking segment on Channel 8 in Knoxville. We worked with an electric skillet on a blue Formica counter. I gave it six months at most. After all, I was not a chef. I was a lobbyist for The University of Tennessee. I had done that for years. I intended to go on doing that for years. I liked my job.

Of course, I had written a cookbook called **Kinfolks and Custard Pie** which had been published by The University of Tennessee Press. I had also been asked to write a restaurant review column for the Knoxville News-Sentinel which I had been doing for about three years. And then there was the fact that I had cooked since I was nine and I knew I enjoyed it, even when things didn't come out just the way I hoped.

But none of that was television. None of that was trying to compress a reasonable recipe into 3 or 4 minutes and hope that you got it done and that it looked reasonably good. None of that was asking folks to take their time and resources to write to get a recipe because it looked good when they saw it on TV. None of that was food processors that quit in mid show or ovens that blew a fuse at a most inopportune time. And so, I gave it six months.

By the time six months came along, many of you were saying very kind things to us. You like the recipes and you loved my wife, Anne's, centerpieces. You made us feel part of your family. With your encouragement we stayed on. After a while, we incorporated the first year's worth of recipes and some bonus recipes into Cooking With the Noonday Chef, Volume 1. You bought a lot of those (We still have some left). After a decent interval, out came Volume 2 and you bought a lot of those as well (We still have some left). We just kept cooking.

On February 1, 1997, Gray Communication introduced WVLT to Knoxville. They were kind enough to ask Anne and me to keep on cooking and to do it even more often. The format was changed and we were suddenly working on a food segment every day instead of every week. It was a whole new world.

We decided that this would be a fine time to wrap up the recipes from the Noonday show and the old format so that you would have a complete set. This book is what came of that effort. It is the longest of the three volumes which we have produced from the show and in our opinion it is the best. Of course, one would hope that one would improve with practice. I suppose that we need to let you be the judge of whether we have.

We would not have made it this far without the help of lots of people. First among those who have made these shows possible is Kroger. This fine grocery chain adopted us some years ago and we have never been treated nicer in our lives. Mr. Curtis Roberts and his crew at Kroger Knox Plaza never met a problem they couldn't solve. A whole series of assistant managers have devoted themselves to meeting our needs. The current one is Brian Knock and he is terrific. We put a special burden on the floral department (well, actually Anne does, but I am trying to be nice about this) and Vivian Norton and Jennie Austin have always risen to the challenge. Our own deli manager, Maurice Phillips, has gotten us involved in wine festival and all sorts of good things. Produce folks and meat and canned goods and all the rest have been there when we needed them.

None of this would have been possible if Mr. Hunter MacWilliams and his able assistant Glenda Jones had not given their support to all that we have done. We cannot say enough good about Kroger and we hope that we will be working with them for a hundred years.

In addition to the good Kroger folks, we have had help from lots of other folks. Proffitt's Department store furnished our kitchen and every once in a while still think of something we might need. The nicest thing they do is allow their fine home economist, Ann Kemmer, to come be part of the show. Ann is a wonder and we enjoy working with her.

We have worked with an array of other folks at Channel 8. The most persistent was Alan Williams. Alan and I picked on each other for years and enjoyed every minute of it. Or at least I did. Alan is now involved in a whole series of exciting activities at Channel 8 and we don't see as much of him, but he was and is a great friend and we are proud that we know him.

There are too many other folks for us to remember all of them. You will find many of them listed in a special index at the back of the book. However, two folks demand some special attention. First, Margaret Lu is a good friend, a delightful person and a fine artist. She did the illustrations in both Volumes 1 and 2. She and her wonderful family continue to give us aid and assistance. Second, we especially need to thank my University colleague and Secretary, Denise Askins. Not only does she put up with me there, but she has taken her own time to lead Anne and me through the mysteries of the computer. We are grateful to both of these folks.

Please do not let this sound as if this were some kind of ending to our involvement with the folks at Channel 8 and all of you. Rather, it is an exciting and new beginning. And it will last a long time if you keep watching and writing and being part of our lives.

Both Anne and I hope that you will find this collection of recipes interesting, helpful, and a good guide to cooking. We sincerely ask that you continue to let us know what you like and what you do not. Only if you do that will being part of Channel 8 continue to be the wonderful experience it has been since May 1, 1989.

Now go cook something and invite us over to share it with you. After all, we feel like a part of the family.

Walter N. Lambert, Noonday Chef

QUICK AND EASY MEAT LOAF (TV 212)

1 lb lean ground beef
1 pkg dry onion soup mix
1 cup (approx) cracker crumbs
1 small can tomato sauce
2 eggs

Mix all ingredients thoroughly. Shape into a loaf. Bake in a 350 deg oven about 1 hour. Some time back, one of the regulars who watches the show asked why I didn't show her how to do a good, simple meat loaf. I think this one is very good and couldn't be simpler. A couple of quick tips: I always wash and quarter potatoes and bake them in the dish with the meat loaf. Good potatoes, one dish to wash. I also use this same mixture to make good stuffed peppers. Simply remove the inside of bell pepper and either leave them whole or halve them. Pack with the meat mixture, and bake about 45 minutes. Always, ALWAYS, remove meat loaf from the pan as soon as it comes from the oven to avoid it reabsorbing a lot of grease.

Now, a word about my personal prejudices about meat loaf: I want it to be soft. I hate meat loaf with the consistency of a hockey puck. If you like it firmer, use more meat to the same amount of other ingredients. You could go up to two pounds of meat with the seasonings above and still get a respectable meat loaf. Remember, cooking is art not science.

Do not be a fanatic about using cracker crumbs. I have made good meat loaf with bread, shredded wheat, oatmeal, rice, and probably some things I don't even remember. Just remember the more the filler will absorb liquid, the less you should use of it.

Also, if you should find yourself without tomato sauce, use about ½ cup catsup. Further, if you think meat loaf should have a sauce, try draining off about 1 TBSP of the grease from the baking pan into a small saucepan. In the grease cook a small onion, which has been chopped fine until it is transparent and starts to brown. Add about ½ cup chopped green pepper and saute for a minute more. Add a can of chopped tomatoes, and allow to cook down until the desired consistency (about 10 minutes). Salt and pepper to taste and serve hot.

Oh, I almost forgot to tell you...this works fine with turkey. You may want to use only half the tomato sauce, otherwise, you can do exactly the same thing and reduce the fat considerably.

Walter N. Lambert, Noonday Chef

FRESH STRAWBERRY MOUSSE (TV 213)

1 quart strawberries, hulled and sliced, divided
1 cup confectioners sugar
½ cup strawberry liqueur
1 envelope un-flavored gelatin
1 pint heavy cream, whipped

Soften the gelatin in the liqueur, and heat just enough to dissolve the gelatin. Reserve. Puree half of the strawberries; blend in the sugar. Mix the gelatin mixture in the pureed strawberries. Stir in the remaining strawberries. Fold into the whipped cream. Turn into a 1 ½ quart mold; chill until firm. Unmold and serve cold.

This is strawberries and cream taken uptown. It is as lovely as it is good. We often pile the mixture into individual crystal glasses to set up. With a fresh strawberry on top, it looks like you worked all day. Now I can hear lots of you saying that you do not want to use liqueur. Fine--use water or milk instead. If you object to alcohol, you may feel that way because in this recipe, the alcohol does not cook out.

Now I can tell you that my favorite way to eat strawberries is just to eat them. I am not crazy about strawberry preserves, strawberry pie, or even strawberry rhubarb pie. I'm sorry, that is just the way I am. That is what makes this such a wonderful dessert for me. The true, fresh taste of the strawberries make it what it is. By the way, this works nicely with the big California strawberries. It is absolutely unbeatable with the better tasting Tennessee strawberries.

If you just must cook strawberries, try the following quick cobbler.

QUICK STRAWBERRY COBBLER

1 quart of strawberries, hulled and sliced
1 cup sugar, divided
4 TBSP butter or margarine
½ cup self rising flour
½ cup of milk

Pour ½ cup of sugar over the berries; allow to stand about 1 hour at room temperature. Bring to a boil. While heating the berries, melt the butter in a 8" square pan. Pour in the strawberries. Mix remaining sugar, flour and milk; pour evenly over the top of the berries. Bake at 350 deg for about 40 minutes or until brown. Serve hot with whipped cream.

Walter N. Lambert, Noonday Chef

STRAWBERRY LIME PRESERVES (TV 214)

4 to 4½ cups strawberries, hulled and crushed
2 tsp grated lime peel
¼ cup lime juice
1 box (1¾ oz) powdered fruit pectin
7 cups sugar

Measure the berries after they are crushed. Place crushed berries, lime peel, lime juice, and fruit pectin in a heavy, large kettle. Stir to mix. Place over high heat and bring to a full boil. Add sugar. Bring to a rolling boil and boil rapidly for 1 minute, stirring constantly. Remove from heat and skim off foam. Allow to cool; stir several times to mix fruit.

At this point, there are several options. You can ladle the preserves into sterilized jelly glasses and seal with about a ¼ in layer of paraffin. Be very careful in heating paraffin. I recommend a double boiler. Also be very careful that drops of water do not get into the hot paraffin. You can also put the very hot preserves into sealing jars and invert them a couple of times during cooling to distribute the fruit. I should tell you that USDA recommends placing the sealed jars into a water bath and cooking them for 5 minutes to sterilize. We just put them into a tightly covered container and keep them in the refrigerator. They are eaten quickly enough that there is no problem.

Now, I should tell you that I am doing this recipe by popular demand. I have said several times that I am not that fond of strawberry preserves (or any cooked strawberries for that matter). Several of you have chastised me for my attitude. I aim to please. I like this recipe because the lime juice and peel cuts the cloying sweetness a little. Now the most popular strawberry preserve recipe in East Tennessee is that of the late **Lucy Curtis Templeton** who was a long time columnist for the **Knoxville News-Sentinel. Louise Durman** who is my editor at the paper tells me that it is still the most requested recipe she has. By the way, DO NOT double this recipe.

LUCY CURTIS TEMPLETON'S STRAWBERRY PRESERVES

1 quart strawberries, washed and stemmed
3 cups sugar

Put 1½ cups sugar with fruit in pan and boil 5 minutes. Add remaining sugar and boil 10 to 15 minutes. Watery fruit must be cooked longer. Pour into a covered non-metallic container, and allow to stand at room temperature for 24 hours, stirring occasionally. Store in refrigerator or seal in jars as above.

Walter N. Lambert, Noonday Chef

STRAWBERRY BREAD (TV 215)

1 cup strawberries, sliced
2 TBSP sugar
1½ cup flour
1 cup sugar
1 tsp soda
¼ tsp salt
½ cup salad oil
1 tsp vanilla
2 eggs, beaten

Sprinkle the 2 TBSP sugar over the strawberries, and allow to stand in the refrigerator several hours or overnight. Blend all dry ingredients. Mix together the oil, eggs, vanilla and strawberries. Mix with the dry ingredients just to blend. Turn into a greased 9x5x3" loaf pan and bake about 50 minutes at 350 deg.

I promise this is the last week for strawberry recipes. But the season for local berries is so short that I cannot resist them. I continue to eat until I break out with hives. A number of variations are possible with this recipe. First, you can add 1½ cup chopped pecans if you like. I think it is nicer without them. You can also add a little cinnamon as well. I personally do not like this at all, but some people love it. Now one last strawberry recipe just for a bonus.

FRESH STRAWBERRY PIE

1 unbaked 9" pie shell
1 quart strawberries
1 cup sugar
3 TBSP cornstarch
½ cup water
2 TBSP lemon juice
3 to 4 drops red food color
whipped cream or whipped topping

Wash, cap, and slice strawberries into the baked pie shell, reserving about 1 cup of berries. Put reserved berries into the food processor with the sugar, cornstarch, water and lemon juice. Using the steel blade, run until strawberries are completely chopped and all ingredients are blended. Place into a heavy saucepan, and cook over medium high heat until the mixture comes to a boil and is clear and thick. Add food coloring. Pour cooked mixture over the strawberries and lightly work down into them. Allow to stand in the refrigerator about one hour before serving with whipped cream. Enjoy.

Walter N. Lambert, Noonday Chef

ROASTED POTATO SALAD (TV 216)

1 to 1½ lb potatoes, cubed and roasted
2 medium onions, peeled, roasted, and chopped
1 cup each, celery and green onions, chopped
½ cup each, dill and sweet pickle relish
½ cup mayonnaise
¼ cup red wine vinegar
2 TBSP dark mustard
Salt and pepper to taste

Roast the onions and potatoes and allow to cool. Toss with celery, green onions, and pickle relish. Beat together the mayonnaise, vinegar, and mustard. Pour over the potato mixture; toss to cover. Place in a covered container and chill for several hours. Toss again and serve.

Roasted vegetables are the newest and, to my mind, one of the best things to come along. First, they are lower in fat and salt and all sorts of bad things. Second, they are amazingly easy. To prepare the potatoes for this recipe, cut the potatoes (I use red ones and leave the peel on) into small cubes. What size doesn't matter so long as they are relatively uniform. Place the cut potatoes into a heavy plastic bag and pour about 2 TBSP olive oil into the bag with the potatoes. Close the bag and toss potatoes to get a coat of oil over them. Pour out onto a heavy cookie sheet, and place in a 400 deg oven for about 45 minutes. Stir about half way through. I roast onions by peeling them, cutting them in half, coating lightly in oil and roasting just like the potatoes. I then chop them after they are cooked and cooled. This sort of cooking works great for squash, sweet potatoes, eggplant and all sorts of other things. It is important to remember that you want only a light coating of oil, and you need to cook them in a hot oven. Keep the pieces far enough apart that air can circulate.

Now, a recipe for roasted potato salad which does not use mayonnaise:

LIGHT ROASTED POTATO SALAD

1 to ½ lb potatoes, cubed and roasted
2 medium onions, roasted and chopped
1 cup each, green peppers, green onions, and celery, chopped
¼ cup olive oil
½ cup red wine vinegar
2 TBSP brown mustard
salt and pepper to taste

Mix the oil, vinegar, and mustard. Toss all ingredients together, and chill in a covered dish for several hours before serving.

Walter N. Lambert, Noonday Chef

BEER BAKED BRISKET (TV 217)

    1 3½ to 4 lb beef brisket
    ½ tsp each salt and pepper
    1 large onion, sliced thin
    3 TBSP brown sugar
    ½ cup chili sauce
    1 12 oz can of beer (not lite beer)

Place the brisket in a lightly greased 13x9" baking dish; sprinkle with salt and pepper. Spread onion slices over the meat. Mix together remaining ingredients. Pour over meat. Seal closed with aluminum foil, and place into 350 deg oven for 2 hours. Remove foil and bake an additional 30 minutes. Slice across the grain; serve hot or cold.

Brisket is one of those wonderful cuts which often gets treated badly. Be sure to cook it long and slow with some liquid. Otherwise, you will have a totally inedible piece of meat. Cooked correctly, you will have meat which is good hot or cold and will be as tender as can be.

By the way, the drippings from this roast make an excellent gravy. Simply pour the drippings into a sauce pan. Skim off as much fat as possible. Because the meat is so lean, there will not be much. Mix about 2 TBSP flour for each cup of drippings with about ½ cup of water until there are NO lumps. Pour into the drippings, and stirring constantly, cook until boiling and thick. Serve hot over the meat or even with mashed potatoes, if you are so inclined.

One of the ways we see brisket most often is as corned beef. I love it. Pick a nice one with as little fat as possible, and then cook according to package directions. When the corned beef is tender, remove it from the pot and add carrots, potatoes, onions, turnips, parsnips, cabbage or whatever vegetables you like best. Boil until vegetables are just tender. Place the sliced corned beef in the center of a platter, and surround it with the vegetables which have been lifted from the stock. Thicken the stock with the flour and water mixture we talked about above, and pass it with the meat and vegetables. By the way, I always serve hot corn bread with this. It's kind of a cross-cultural thing.

Now one last quick way to do a fresh brisket. Put the brisket into the baking dish as we described above. Spread a can of cream of mushroom soup over the meat. Sprinkle with a package of dry onion soup. Pour a cup of water over (or use a can of that leftover beer); seal and cook as above. This is best sliced and served hot.

6

Walter N. Lambert, Noonday Chef

QUICK TOFFEE COOKIES (TV 218)

½ cup butter or margarine
1 yellow cake mix (pudding added kind)
2 eggs
1 TBSP water
1 6 oz pkg bits-o-brickle chips
1 cup (approx) pecans, chopped

With a mixer, beat butter until soft. Add cake mix, eggs, and water. Beat until fully mixed. Stir in brickle chips and nuts completely. Drop by generous teaspoonfuls onto an ungreased cookie sheet. Bake at 350 deg 8 to 10 minutes or until lightly browned.

These little cookies, have absolutely everything. They are quick, they are easy, they are good. In fact, they have one other advantage. If you make them a day ahead, allow them to cool completely, and store in a tightly covered container, they are better after they have stood for a day or two. So if you are looking for something to take along on a trip to keep children's mouths closed, these may be just the ticket.

Now because these cookies were so easy, I started wondering why you couldn't do other flavors. The answer is that you can. The obvious question was about chocolate. While I have not tried it yet, the next experiment will be German Chocolate cake with pecans and coconut. Now, I give you my very own chocolate, peanut butter cookies:

QUICK CHOCOLATE, PEANUT COOKIES

½ cup butter or margarine
1 devils food cake mix (pudding added kind)
2 eggs
1 TBSP water
1 6 oz pkg. peanut butter chips
1 cup peanuts or pecans, chopped

With a mixer, cream the butter until it is soft. Add the cake mix, eggs and water. Beat until fully blended. Stir in peanut butter chips and peanuts. Drop by generous teaspoonfuls onto an ungreased cookie sheet. Bake at 350 deg 8 to 10 minutes until lightly browned.

With both of these cookies, they come out of the oven very soft. It is best to allow them to cool on the pan for a few minutes before removing them to a rack to cool completely before you store them away to mellow a little before you eat them. Enjoy.

7

Walter N. Lambert, Noonday Chef

SUMMERTIME NOODLES (TV 219)

> 8 oz egg noodles, cooked
> 1 cup each, coarsely grated carrot, cucumber and celery
> 1 lb chopped cooked chicken
> ½ cup each, peanut butter and wine vinegar
> 2 TBSP each sesame oil and Durkee hot sauce
> ¼ cup soya sauce

Toss together noodles, chicken, and chopped vegetables. Mix all remaining ingredients, and pour over the noodle mixture. Toss to coat. Place in a covered dish and refrigerate several hours to allow the flavors to mix. Serve cold.

This is an absolutely unparalleled <u>Chinese noodle dish</u> which has become part of summer for us. If you use tabasco sauce instead of the **Durkees** then cut the amount about half. You can use any kind of vinegar, but I really like either white wine vinegar or Japanese rice wine vinegar. I do not like cider vinegar very much. If you happen to not like any of the vegetables I have used, simply leave it out and use more of the others. These however give some flavor and some texture, and I think make a nice blend. Chopped coriander leaves can be added.

Oh, before I forget, the chicken is completely optional. With it, we use this as a main dish. Without it, it makes a nice side dish with grilled chicken. Either way, it is a good summer dish.

You should know that the Chinese were doing pasta before the Italians ever heard of it. In fact, one story, probably not true, is that **Marco Polo** brought pasta back from China when he went to visit and that all the Italians did was add tomatoes. Decide for yourself what you think of this idea. Now in Thailand, they do a similar but slightly different dish:

THAI NOODLES

> 8 oz wide rice noodles, cooked and drained
> 2 cloves garlic, minced
> 2 cups bean sprouts
> 2 TBSP chopped fresh coriander leaves
> ¼ cup each, soya sauce, rice wine vinegar, and sugar
> ¼ cup chopped peanuts
> 1 TBSP Tabasco sauce

Toss together noodles, bean sprouts, coriander and the peanuts. Mix all remaining ingredients; pour over mixture. Toss. Place in a covered dish and refrigerate several hours. Serve with wedges of lime as a side dish with meat.

Walter N. Lambert, Noonday Chef

ALL AMEXICAN BURGERS (TV 220)

 1 lb lean ground beef
 ¼ cup crushed nacho chips
 ¼ cup picante sauce (mild, medium, or hot)
 2 TBSP soya sauce
 4 slices Monterey Jack cheese

Blend beef, chips, soya and picante sauce. Shape into 4 burgers, and grill about 4 or 5 inches from a hot charcoal fire. It will take about 5 or 6 minutes on each side for a medium burger. During the last 3 or 4 minutes, top each burger with a slice of cheese.

My favorite way to do burgers is to put the flavor inside rather than on the outside. This combination is one we particularly like. Sometimes, we shape this into eight patties and place the cheese on four of them and place the other four patties on top. Shape to completely enclose the cheese inside the burger and broil as above.

The burgers are also good with chopped onion, soya sauce, and Worcestershire sauce to added taste. We have been known to blend dry onion soup into the meat with about ¼ cup water and shape and broil as above.

Now a new way to do hot dogs as well:

DRESSED UP DOGS

 8 hot dog buns and 8 franks
 1 8 ½ oz can whole kernel corn, drained
 ¾ cup grated cheddar cheese
 ¼ cup grated onion
 2 TBSP each, **JFG** mayonnaise and dark mustard

In a small bowl, mix corn, cheese, onion, mayonnaise and mustard. Place the franks into buns and spread the corn/cheese mixture evenly in each bun on top of the frank. Wrap each in heavy duty foil, and grill away from the highest heat about 20 minutes, turning frequently. (These may be baked for 20 minutes in a 350 deg oven instead). Serve hot.   We have also used a sauerkraut, Swiss cheese and mustard combination, as well as a pickle relish, onion, cheese and chopped tomato combination with good results on these dogs. By the way, for super quick baked beans to serve with these, pour a large can of pork and beans into a heavy casserole dish. Cover the top with a layer of chopped onions and spread a jar of Heinz chili sauce over the top. Baked covered about 30 minutes. Uncover and bake another 20 minutes to brown. Serve hot or cold.

9

Walter N. Lambert, Noonday Chef

LIME FLAVORED SALMON (TV 221)

        1 lb salmon steaks 1" thick
        3 TBSP lime juice, divided
        2 TBSP each, soya sauce and cooking oil
        ¼ cup butter, melted
        1 TBSP chopped cilantro

Place salmon steaks with 2 TBSP lime juice, soya sauce and oil in a heavy plastic bag and seal the top. Turn to coat the fish. Refrigerate for at least one hour. Blend remaining lime juice with butter and cilantro. Keep warm. Drain marinade from the fish and reserve. Broil the salmon about 4 to 5 inches from the charcoal about 8 or 9 minutes on each side, brushing with the marinade. Serve with the butter.

Although salmon is a fairly oily fish by nature, it can become very dry if broiled without something to seal the outside. This marinade accomplishes that nicely with a flavor which complements the flavor of salmon rather than trying to overcome it. I am afraid that cilantro is not really easy to find, but there is no substitute for this pungent herb. In a real pinch, this dish is okay with flat parsley, but you lose a lot of flavor.

I like to serve salmon with simple broiled vegetables. Cut small zucchini or yellow squash in half lengthwise, brush with olive oil and sprinkle with oregano and broil on the cooler part of the grill. It will take about twenty minutes with you turning only once. Potatoes can also be given a very good flavor and texture if cooked on the grill. I usually do potato kabobs. Cook new red potatoes in the microwave with a little water about 8 to 10 minutes for a pound of potatoes. They should be tender-crisp. Thread potatoes onto soaked bamboo skewers, or metal skewers, and grill on the edges of the grill about 8 or 10 minutes, turning to prevent burning. If you like, you can brush with some of butter mixture you have made for the salmon above. If you plan to do this, be sure to increase the recipe to have enough.

Now a quick, bonus fish to grill:

MUSTARD-HORSERADISH SAUCE FOR FISH

        3 TBSP each, Olive oil and Dijon mustard
        1 TBSP each, sour cream and horseradish
        1 tsp oregano

Mix all ingredients and use to brush any whitefish fillet (orange roughy, etc.) during broiling.

Walter N. Lambert, Noonday Chef

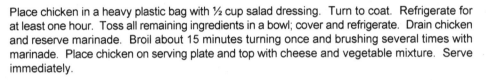

MEDITERRANEAN CHICKEN (TV 222)

    6 chicken breasts, boneless and skinless
    ½ cup bottled Italian dressing
    1 cup feta cheese, crumbled
    1 cup chopped, seeded cucumber
    ½ cup each, chopped seeded tomato and chopped red onion
    1 TBSP each lemon juice and Italian dressing

Place chicken in a heavy plastic bag with ½ cup salad dressing. Turn to coat. Refrigerate for at least one hour. Toss all remaining ingredients in a bowl; cover and refrigerate. Drain chicken and reserve marinade. Broil about 15 minutes turning once and brushing several times with marinade. Place chicken on serving plate and top with cheese and vegetable mixture. Serve immediately.

This dish is a great combination of tastes and textures which will brighten any summer meal. In fact, it can be made into a summer meal by shredding some lettuce and/or spinach and placing on a plate. Cut the chicken breast into crosswise slices and scatter on the greens. Top with cheese and vegetable mixture. Instant Greek chicken salad which would make a perfect luncheon dish. If you do this, you may want to pass a little extra Italian dressing.

If you choose not to go the salad route with this chicken, a good <u>simple mixed vegetable side dish</u> would work nicely. Try mixing about 1 cup each cauliflower and broccoli florets with ½ cup broken snap peas and ½ cup carrots which have been cooked in the microwave for about 3 or 4 minutes. Toss vegetables, and place into the center of a large (approx 18" square) piece of heavy duty aluminum foil. Dot with a couple of tablespoons of butter, and sprinkle with 1 tsp lemon pepper. Roll down foil to seal completely. Broil on medium heat on grill for about 20 minutes turning at least once. Serve immediately. For a different and delightful chicken, try the following:

BOURBON GLAZED CHICKEN

    6 or 8 chicken breasts or a cut up frying chicken
    ¼ cup orange juice
    3 TBSP butter
    1 TBSP bourbon whiskey
    1 TBSP molasses

Cook chicken in microwave for 8 or 9 minutes. Remove skin if using whole chicken. Mix all glaze ingredients, and bring to a boil. Place chicken pieces on a medium grill; broil 8 minutes on a side for the breasts or 10 to 12 minutes for whole chicken pieces, brushing with the glaze.

Walter N. Lambert, Noonday Chef

GRILLED FRUIT (TV 223)

> 2 large, firm bananas, peeled and cut into 1½" pieces
> 4 ½" thick fresh pineapple slices
> 2 oranges, peeled and cut into 4 slices each
> 1 ½ cups vanilla yogurt
> ¼ cup honey
> ½ cup granola (optional)

Mix honey and yogurt; chill. Thread banana pieces onto bamboo skewers which have been soaked in water. Place the fruit onto medium heat on a gas grill or about 6" from the charcoal; broil about 3 minutes on each side. Place the warm fruit in a serving bowl and pour the yogurt mixture over. Sprinkle with granola if desired. Serve immediately.

This is one of those desserts which is so simple and so good that I don't know why I didn't think of it. I think it is the perfect accompaniment to dinner on a hot summer night. If you don't want to use the granola, this is good sprinkled with a little nutmeg. You may of course use any combination of these fruits that you like.

By the way, my favorite dessert of all time is one which requires no cooking at all. Simply pile fresh peaches into individual serving bowls. Spoon on a good dollop of sour cream and sprinkle with brown sugar. If you must, you can substitute vanilla yogurt for the sour cream. It changes the flavor very little and lightens the dish considerably. If you like, mix the peach slices with blueberries. Now one more grilled fruit dessert:

GRILLED PEACH DESSERT

> 2 freestone peaches, peeled, halved and pitted
> 2 TBSP brown sugar
> ½ tsp nutmeg
> 1 ½ tsp rum flavor
> 2 tsp butter, melted
> ½ pkg (10 oz) frozen raspberries in syrup
> 2 tsp lemon juice

Combine raspberries with lemon juice in food processor; process until smooth. Strain to remove seeds and set aside. On an 18" square of heavy duty foil, place peach halves cut side up. Divide brown sugar into center of each. Sprinkle with remaining ingredients. Fold foil down to seal. Cook over hot coals about 20 minutes. Place one peach half on each serving dish and pour raspberry puree over.

Walter N. Lambert, Noonday Chef

BANANA BROWNIES (TV 224)

   ½ cup butter
   2 1 oz squares unsweetened chocolate
   ½ cup each, granulated and brown sugar
   1 egg
   1 large banana, mashed (about ⅔ cup)
   1 tsp vanilla
   1½ cup all purpose flour
   ½ cup coconut

In a medium saucepan (or a Pyrex mixing bowl in the microwave), melt butter and chocolate together. Remove from heat and beat in the sugars and then the egg, banana, and vanilla. Stir in the flour. Turn into a greased 8" square pan, and bake about 30 minutes in a preheated 350 deg oven. Allow to cool in the pan and cut into squares.

If you are the sort that thinks brownies must be iced, go right ahead and ice these. However, let me suggest a slightly different solution: While the brownies are still hot from the oven, sprinkle the top lightly and evenly with powdered sugar. Then melt another square of the unsweetened chocolate and drizzle it over the top. Be sure to let the brownies completely cool, and let chocolate set up before you try to cut them. Now let me say just a word about the melting. Anytime you are melting chocolate you need to be careful about not overheating it. For this recipe, I place the butter and chocolate in a heat proof, non- metal, mixing bowl and run it at high speed in the microwave for about 45 seconds. I then stir the mixture and continue stirring in 15 second increments until both are melted. Proceed as above. The following is an interesting variation on this recipe:

MARBLED BANANA BROWNIES

   ½ cup butter
   1 1oz square unsweetened chocolate, melted
   1 cup brown sugar, packed
   1 egg
   1 large, ripe banana, mashed
   1 tsp vanilla
   1 ½ cup plain flour
   ½ cup shredded coconut

Melt the butter. Stir in brown sugar. Add egg, banana and vanilla and mix. Add flour and mix completely. Pour about ⅔ of the mixture into a greased 8" square pan. Add coconut and melted unsweetened chocolate to the remaining batter. Drop spoonfuls of chocolate batter over plain batter; cut through with a knife to produce marbled effect. Bake 30 minutes in a preheated 350 deg oven. Allow to cool in the pan and cut into squares.

13

Walter N. Lambert, Noonday Chef

COOL AS A CUCUMBER SALAD (TV 225)

    1 3 oz pkg. lemon or lime gelatin
    ¾ cup boiling water
    6 oz cream cheese
    1 cup mayonnaise
    1 tsp grated horseradish
    2 TBSP lemon juice
    ¼ tsp salt
    ¾ cup cucumber, peeled, seeded and chopped fine
    ½ cup finely chopped onion

Dissolve gelatin in hot water. Blend mayonnaise, cream cheese, lemon juice, horseradish, and salt until all lumps are gone. Fold into gelatin. Stir in cucumber and onion. Pour into a lightly oiled gelatin mold or into individual dishes. Turn out onto lettuce to serve.

I am not much for gelatin salads or desserts. **Anne** tells me that I shouldn't let my prejudices cloud what I do for you. So here you are. A good creamy cucumber salad. I personally always use sugar free gelatin for this (and almost everything else). Not only do you not get the sugar, but I think the flavor is better. Be sure your cream cheese is at room temperature before you start this, or it will be very hard to get it to mix with the mayonnaise. I generally start the process with a wooden spoon and then switch to a French whisk to finish the process. I have to tell you that the only problem with not completely mixing it is that you get lumps of cream cheese, which you may think of as a reward not a punishment. Since we are into molded salads, let me give you this one which I like to serve with a dollop of sour cream rather than mayonnaise:

MOLDED GAZPACHO SALAD

    2 envelopes unflavored gelatin
    3 cups tomato juice (or V-8 juice)
    ⅓ cup red wine vinegar
    1 tsp salt
    2 tomatoes, peeled, seeded and chopped
    1 cucumber, peeled, seeded and chopped fine
    ½ cup each, bell pepper, onion and celery, chopped
    2 TBSP chopped chives
    ½ tsp Tabasco (optional)

Sprinkle gelatin over tomato juice and allow to sit for a few minutes to soften. Heat and stir over medium heat until gelatin has dissolved. Remove from heat and add vinegar, salt, and Tabasco (if used). Allow to partially set. Add vegetables, pour into a 2 quart mold, and allow to set.

Walter N. Lambert, Noonday Chef

QUICK CHICKEN FLORENTINE (TV 226)

4 boneless chicken breast halves
1 10 oz frozen chopped spinach
½ tsp each, chopped garlic and salt
1 can cream of chicken soup
½ soup can of white wine
¾ cup hot and spicy Cheez-it crumbs

Coat an 8x8" pan with cooking spray. Sprinkle the garlic in the pan. Place chicken in a single layer over the garlic. Thaw spinach and squeeze dry. Sprinkle over chicken. Sprinkle with salt. Mix soup and wine; pour over the spinach. Sprinkle the top with cracker crumbs. Cover with foil and bake 30 minutes in a preheated 350 deg oven. Uncover and cook an additional 30 minutes until top is brown. Serve hot.

Here we go again! A complicated- looking dish with an interesting sauce which requires almost no work at all. Somehow, I have always looked on anything done a la Florentine as being particularly elegant. In case you don't know, all that fancy title indicates is that the dish is prepared with spinach. By the way, squeezing the spinach is important. Otherwise, the dish has far too much liquid. Now if you happen to be a purist, you can squeeze the spinach into the soup instead of the wine. It will give it a strange color but a very good taste.

Remember, the use of wine is a matter of taste. If you are forbidden any trace of alcohol, simply use water instead of wine. Again, if I want to remove the wine from a recipe and still want to give a little extra flavor, I have been known to use ginger ale or even **7up.** If you decide to do this, don't tell anyone I suggested it.

QUICK FISH FLORENTINE

1 lb fish fillets (use turbot, orange roughy, or cheap flounder)
1 can cream of celery soup
½ cup sour cream
1 TBSP flour
1 10 oz pkg chopped spinach
¾ cups cracker crumbs

Spray an 8" square pan with a cooking spray. Cook spinach until about half done. Allow to cool and squeeze dry. Arrange fish fillets in a single layer. Mix soup, sour cream, and flour. Sprinkle spinach over the fish, and spread soup mixture evenly over the spinach. Sprinkle with cracker crumbs and bake in a preheated 350 deg oven about 30 minutes. Serve hot.

Walter N. Lambert, Noonday Chef

CHESS SQUARES (TV 227)

1 yellow cake mix
1 stick butter (or margarine) melted
4 eggs (divided)
8 oz cream cheese
2 tsp vanilla
1 lb powdered sugar

Combine cake mix, butter, and 1 egg. Press into a 9X13" pan. In a food processor or blender, mix the 3 eggs, cream cheese, and vanilla completely. Add powdered sugar; mix until blended. Pour over the cake mix. Bake in a preheated 325 deg oven about 45 minutes. Cool in pan, and cut into squares.

Jean Millis gave me this recipe. Don't let her kid you about exercising, eating right, blood sugar, and all that stuff. She gives me recipes for Hershey Bar Cakes and Chess Squares. So keep your eye on her. I mean this one has everything we are told to avoid--fat, sugar,--everything. I just love it!

Now let me tell you a secret. When Jean gave me this recipe, I was anxious to try it. We didn't have a yellow cake mix, but did have a devil's food cake mix. Could I wait? NO! It was wonderful. I'm going to try spice cake next.

Now, we discussed earlier why Chess Pie is called Chess Pie. I still don't know, but you can see that these squares have the same basic ingredients. You don't have a good chess pie recipe? Well, you do now. Straight out of _**Kinfolks and Custard Pie**_, and if your bookstore doesn't have that little wonder, ask them why!

CHESS PIE

1 cup sugar
3 eggs
6 TBSP butter, melted
1 cup milk
2 TBSP each, flour and cornmeal
1 tsp vanilla
½ tsp lemon extract

Mix sugar, flour, and cornmeal. Beat in eggs, one at a time. Stir in melted butter. Add the milk slowly until fully blended, then add vanilla and lemon. Pour into an unbaked 9" pastry shell, and bake in a preheated 350 deg oven for about 40 minutes or until a knife inserted in the center comes out clean. Allow to cool before cutting.

Walter N. Lambert, Noonday Chef

CORNBREAD SALAD (TV 228)

1 8½ oz pkg Jiffy or White Lily corn muffin mix
½ cup sweet pickle cubes with 2 TBSP juice
½ cup each, onion and green pepper, chopped
2 tomatoes, peeled, seeded and chopped
1 lb mild sausage
½ cup mayonnaise

Prepare cornbread according to package directions, and bake in an 8x8 pan. Allow to cool, then crumble. Cook the sausage, crumbling it as it cooks; drain very well. Add all remaining ingredients to the crumbled bread and mix thoroughly. Chill and serve.

This is one of those highly improbable dishes which are very good. I first had it at a family gathering a couple of years ago. Then at a recent picnic, a co-worker brought it along and everyone really enjoyed it. I thought you might also.

Now let me give you a couple of tips passed along from the picnic. If you really want to get all the fat off the sausage, when you have just about finished frying and crumbling it, pour about a cup of water over the sausage and allow to come to a boil. Then drain off the water and turn sausage out onto paper towels to finish draining. Further, you can use low fat mayonnaise nicely in this dish. In fairness, as fat as the corn bread is, it probably doesn't make much difference.

Now a tip from me. Don't bother with the *Jiffy* mix unless you are just so inclined. Simply make some cornbread with corn meal mix. For this much salad, use about 1½ cup of corn meal mix, 1 egg, and about ½ cup milk. Pour into a well greased 8x8" pan and bake in a hot (400 deg) oven until brown. Turn out, allow to cool, crumble and proceed.

I must tell you that I absolutely love corn bread. I like it best made in the traditional East Tennessee way To do this, use ½ cup flour to 1½ cups course ground corn meal, 1 TBSP baking powder, ½ tsp soda and 1 cup buttermilk. Turn it into a very well greased pan and bake hot until it is done. If you just have to, add an egg and about 4 TBSP of melted butter. The next best alternative is simply to use *White Lily Buttermilk Corn Meal MIX* according to the package directions.

I personally bake my corn bread in an iron skillet which has been used for nothing else for the last 20 years. Using an iron skillet gives a wonderful bottom crust, which is the best part. If you are not lucky enough to have such a skillet, I'm sorry.

Walter N. Lambert, Noonday Chef

BLACK AND WHITE BEAN SALAD (TV 229)

1 can each, navy beans, and black beans
1 cucumber peeled, seeded and chopped
½ cup each, red onion slices and green pepper strips
3 TBSP chopped cilantro (or parsley)
½ cup mayonnaise
Sprinkle of black pepper (optional)

Rinse and drain beans. Mix thoroughly with all other ingredients and chill.

This is so easy that I feel guilty about giving it to you. But it is so good and so simple and versatile that I would feel more guilty if I did not.

Now let's talk about that versatility. First, you can use any kind of white beans. Navy looks best. I think great northern beans taste best, and that is what I used on the show. I use red onion only because it looks good with the green pepper. The same amount of white onion or even sliced green onions will work just as well. I have noted already my preference for cilantro. This is one of the most fragrant and tastiest of the herbs around. It is a little hard to find, and when I cannot, I use curly parsley.

It you want this to be a main dish salad, it is as easy as pie. Well, actually, it is as easy as ham. Simply cube up a couple of cups of cooked ham and toss with the other ingredients. Be sure you use nice, lean ham for this. One of the nice things about beans is that they give you lots of good, complex carbohydrates and lots of fiber and little fat. Oh, and I forgot to tell you. Low (or no) fat mayonnaise works great in this. The flavors are bright enough and the texture is good enough that you don't need real mayonnaise.

Do you like black beans as much as I do? Then let me give you a quick, easy way to have black beans and rice. Serve this for supper with a nice green salad with a light dressing and you have a meal:

In a heavy skillet cook 1 cup of chopped onion in 1 TBSP olive oil until the onion is soft. Stir in 2 cloves of chopped garlic. Cut about ½ lb smoked sausage into thin slices and stir with the onion and garlic until hot through. Add 2 cans of black beans, ¼ tsp Tabasco sauce (or other hot sauce) and heat to boiling. Serve over boiled rice with a little sliced green onion, chopped cilantro (or parsley), and sour cream to put on top. If you try this, you may never have red beans again.

Walter N. Lambert, Noonday Chef

POTATO CASSEROLE (TV 230)

1 32 oz pkg frozen hashed brown potatoes, thawed
½ cup butter or margarine, melted
1 can cream of chicken soup
2 cups each, sour cream, grated cheddar cheese and
 crushed cornflakes
2 tsp each, dried onion and parsley flakes
1 tsp each, salt and black pepper

Combine potatoes, butter, soup, sour cream and seasonings and blend well. Turn into a greased 9x13" pan. Sprinkle with cheese, then the cornflake crumbs. Cover and bake in a 350 deg oven for about 30 minutes. Uncover and bake an additional 15 minutes or until browned.

This is one of those casseroles which makes the rounds at church suppers and everybody likes. I agree. This one came to me by way of my secretary from a friend of hers. This makes a great side dish for almost any plain meat. However, it can easily be turned into a main dish by tossing in about two or three cups of cubed cooked chicken or a pound of good sausage, which has been cooked and drained. Add either of these to the potato mixture and you are ready to go.

Walter N. Lambert, Noonday Chef

APPLE CHEESE BISCUITS (TV 231)

    2 cups White Lily self-rising flour
    ½ cup grated sharp cheese
    ¾ cup cooked apples, chopped fine
    2 TBSP sugar
    ¼ cup cooking oil
    ½ cup milk

Toss together flour, cheese, apples, and sugar. Mix together milk and oil and pour into flour mixture. Stir just to mix completely. Drop onto a lightly greased cookie sheet by ample teaspoons, and bake 12 to 14 minutes in a 425 deg oven. Serve hot.

I love biscuits. Plain or fancy, flavored or not. I think these are naturals for Fall. Try them with a little ham, roast pork, or smoked turkey. Now, let me give you a couple of tips: I use canned apples. I buy sliced apples and chop them in a food processor (don't make them into applesauce, chop them). You can cook your own. Just use an apple like the Granny Smith which does not cook up too easily, and boil them lightly without sugar. A couple of times when I have been slightly desperate, I have used apple pie filling. When I do this, I cut the sugar back to one TBSP because of the sugar already in the apples.

If you want sweet biscuits to serve at a luncheon, let me suggest a simple alternative to these. Leave out the cheese and increase the apples to one cup. Increase the sugar to ¼ cup, and add 1 TBSP good cinnamon with the flour and sugar. You can add half a cup of raisins if you like. This makes a sweeter biscuit which is very nice.

Now on the matter of these being drop biscuits, I do it that way simply because it is easier. If you want nice round biscuits, increase flour by ¼ cup which will make a firmer dough. Pat the biscuits out on a piece of waxed paper, and cut to the desired size. Bake as directed above. If you want to get really decadent about it, make a glaze of ¾ cup powdered sugar which is mixed with about ¼ tsp vanilla and enough milk (about a TBSP) to make a light glaze. Spread over the hot biscuits and serve.

With all this talk, I probably need to remind you about secret biscuits. Mix 2 cups **White Lily Self-rising** flour with ⅓ cup cooking oil and ⅔ cups milk to make a soft dough. Knead two or three times in the mixing bowl and press out on waxed paper. Cut and bake. Remember, you did not hear this here.

20

Walter N. Lambert, Noonday Chef

HAMPLE CASSEROLE (TV 232)

3 cups ham, cubed
3 cups sour dough bread, cubed
2 cups apples, chopped
1 cup each, onion and celery, chopped
16 oz ginger ale (or beer)

Mix together all ingredients except ginger ale. Place in a 2 quart casserole which is coated with a cooking spray. Pour ginger ale (or beer) over. Bake uncovered in a 350 deg oven about one hour or until browned and the juices are thick. Serve hot.

This is a modification of a casserole which I did on the program a long time ago. I called it "Tipsy casserole" and it used rye bread with leftover roast pork. If you want to give that a try, use the same amount of bread and pork. Increase the onion and celery to 1½ cups and leave out the apple. Use a 16 oz can of beer. I still like it a lot. Now about the issue of the beer versus ginger ale. Many of you don't want anything to do with alcohol at all. I respect that. Therefore I give you the option. With this one, I have to admit that I prefer the ginger ale. With the rye bread and roast pork, I like the beer. It really is a matter of taste.

Walter N. Lambert, Noonday Chef

DATE NUT JUMBLES (TV 233)

    ½ cup butter
    1½ cup sugar
    3 eggs
    1 TBSP each, vanilla and grated lemon peel
    3 cups flour
    1 tsp each, baking soda and salt
    1 cup chopped nuts, walnuts or pecans
    1 pound chopped dates

Cream sugar and butter, add eggs, vanilla, and lemon peel. Blend thoroughly. Mix flour, soda, and salt; add to creamed mixture. Blend. Stir in the nuts and dates. Drop by generous teaspoonfuls onto a lightly greased cookie sheet. Bake in a 375 deg oven about 10 minutes. Makes about three dozen.

Cookies. Everyone loves them. This is a variation on a recipe from cookbooks that date back to the Revolutionary War. They are called jumbles because you just "jumble" everything up and bake it. I personally prefer walnuts in this recipe, but others prefer pecans. You may choose. In case some among you might not like dates, raisins work nicely.

CINNAMON JUMBLES

    ½ cup shortening (I use half butter and half Crisco)
    1 cup sugar
    2 cups flour
    1 egg
    ½ tsp salt
    ¾ cup buttermilk
    ½ tsp baking soda
    1 tsp vanilla
    ¼ cup sugar
    1 tsp cinnamon

Cream sugar with the shortening. Beat in egg, then buttermilk and vanilla. Mix flour, salt, and soda and blend into mixture. Chill dough for at least one hour. Mix ¼ cup sugar with cinnamon. Drop generous tsp of dough onto a greased cookie sheets. Sprinkle with cinnamon sugar mixture. Bake in a preheated 400 deg oven about 8 to 10 minutes. Allow to cool a little before removing to a rack to cool completely. They are very soft when they come from the oven.

Walter N. Lambert, Noonday Chef

CHILI CASSEROLE (TV 234)

    4 cups **Fritos**, crushed lightly
    1 cup onions, chopped
    2 cups cheddar (or American) cheese, grated
    1 30 oz can chili with beans

Spray an 8x8" dish with cooking spray. Place half the **Fritos** in the bottom of the pan. Pour on half of the chili and sprinkle with onions. Spread the remaining chili over the onions, and sprinkle the cheese and the remaining Fritos over the top. Bake in a 350 deg oven about 50 minutes until brown and bubbly. Serve hot.

I started to call this "Petros Casserole", but I couldn't reach either of the **Vidmar** brothers to get their permission. I love those things and get by East Town or West Town to have one whenever possible. If that is not possible, make this casserole. If you want the full **Petros** effect, sprinkle the casserole with shredded lettuce, chopped tomato and add a dollop of sour cream.

Now the real reason for doing this is so I can give you **Anne's** cousin, **Hope McPherson's**, Tamale Pie recipe. If you love old fashioned tamales like I do, this is an easy way to have them. This does not imply that Hope is old fashioned. After all, she is only a little past ninety one and is as up to date as they come.

HOPE MCPHERSON'S TAMALE PIE

    2 lbs lean ground beef
    ½ lb pork sausage
    4 large onions, chopped
    2 TBSP chili powder
    4 large cloves, garlic, chopped
    1 quart hot water

Mix all together in a large kettle, and cook on medium heat for 45 minutes. Add ground hot pepper to taste (I used about 1 tsp but you may want more). Place a colander over a large bowl and drain, saving the liquid.
Add sufficient water to the cooking liquid to make 1 quart. Add 2 (more) TBSP chili powder and more ground hot pepper to taste and bring to a full boil. While boiling slowly, stir in 2 cups corn meal stirring constantly until the mixture is very thick and pulls away from the sides of the pan. Line a casserole dish with the corn meal mush and pour in meat mixture. Cover with the rest of mush and sprinkle lightly with black pepper and dot with butter. Bake 20 minutes in a preheated 400 deg oven.

Walter N. Lambert, Noonday Chef

PUMPKIN APPLE PIE (TV 235)

1 9" deep dish pie shell, unbaked
2 cups coarsely chopped apples, uncooked
¾ cup sugar (divided)
2 TBSP flour
½ tsp each cinnamon and ginger
pinch of salt
1 16 oz can of pumpkin (or 1½ to 2 cups cooked pumpkin)
⅔ cup evaporated milk
1 egg, slightly beaten

Mix ¼ cup sugar, flour, and cinnamon. Toss with apples and distribute evenly in the pie shell. Mix all remaining ingredients; pour over the apples. Bake in a 425 deg oven for 15 minutes. Reduce heat to 350 deg, and cook an additional 35 to 40 minutes. Cool and chill before serving.

This pie mixes two of my favorite ingredients of fall-- apples and pumpkin. In fact, it can also be done with two cups of cooked and mashed sweet potato for a sweet potato apple pie. If you decide to do this, substitute ½ tsp nutmeg for the ginger. By the way, some folks like cloves in pumpkin pie. I do not. If you happen to like it, simply add ¼ tsp ground cloves to the pumpkin part of the recipe above.

Now let me tell you about the strangest pumpkin dish I have run into in a while. Our friend **Layla Mishu** gave it to us, and since Layla is never wrong, I knew it would be at least interesting. It is fried pumpkin served as a vegetable. Use about 1 to 1½ lbs of raw pumpkin which has had the center junk removed, peeled, and cut into slices about ½" thick. I make each one into sections about 2 to 3 inches long. On a heavy griddle on medium heat, add a little oil and fry the pumpkin in a single layer, turning to brown on both sides. It should cook about 15 to 20 minutes or until it is tender. Remove from pan, and cook a couple of thinly sliced onions which have been separated into rings in the same pan. Salt pumpkin lightly, and pour the onions over the top. Sprinkle it with freshly cut parsley, and squeeze lemon juice over the whole thing. I use one lemon. Try it!

Walter N. Lambert, Noonday Chef

TRADITIONAL FRIED CHICKEN (TV 236)

1 frying chicken (3 to 4 lbs), cut up
½ cup flour
1 tsp salt
1 tsp black pepper
grease for frying

Mix salt and pepper with the flour. Place in a heavy plastic bag (gallon size is about right). Place several pieces of chicken in the bag, seal and shake gently to coat completely. In a heavy skillet, heat oil or solid shortening about ¼ inch deep. When hot, add the chicken in a single layer. Keep the grease hot. Cover and cook about 10 to 15 minutes or until brown on the bottom. Turn and cook until brown on the other side. Drain on paper towels.

Welcome to chicken week! Now what I have given you is the way chicken was cooked when I was growing up. There are as many variations as there are cooks to make them. One popular way is to coat the chicken in flour as above. Then dip each piece in a mixture of an egg in a cup of milk, then roll in the flour mixture again. If you want a real crust, roll in the flour, then dip into buttermilk, then roll in the flour again. Fry either of these as above. If you do not cover the skillet, the crust will be crisper, but the chicken will brown more quickly and you have to be careful to get it cooked through before it gets too brown.

Now I am of the opinion that you should not have fried chicken without milk gravy. That is how I stay thin.

MILK GRAVY

6 TBSP grease in which chicken was fried
6 TBSP flour
4 cups milk
salt and pepper to taste

Drain and reserve grease from the pan in which chicken has been fried and return 6 TBSP of it to the skillet. Heat the grease until fairly hot; stir in the flour. Stir constantly while allowing flour to cook and start to brown. Stir in all the milk. Continue to cook over medium-high heat, stirring constantly. Be sure to stir along the bottom of the pan to loosen any brown bits from frying the chicken which may be clinging. Continue to boil and stir until the gravy boils and starts to form both large and small bubbles. Serve hot with biscuits. Both the chicken and gravy instructions are from ***Kinfolks and Custard Pie***.

25

Walter N. Lambert, Noonday Chef

SUGAR COOKIES (TV 237)

> 1 pkg White Lily Biscuit Mix
> ⅔ cup sugar
> 1 egg
> 1 TBSP each, oil and water
> ¼ tsp lemon extract

Combine biscuit mix and sugar. Mix in egg, oil, water and flavoring. Drop teaspoons of dough into a small bowl of sugar. Roll in sugar to coat. Place on a lightly greased baking sheet. Flatten slightly with the bottom of a glass. Leave plenty of room for cookies to spread. Bake in a preheated 350 deg oven about 10 minutes until slightly brown. Remove to a rack to cool. Makes about 2 dozen.

Welcome to Cookie Swap. Today's winner is **Helen Williford** of Knoxville. She says these are so simple a child could make them. Right on Helen. Helen says these cookies are the hit of the party at the Tennessee School for the Deaf where she works. I can see why. By the way, this is really two recipes in one. Because if you use vanilla extract instead of lemon and then roll the cookies in sugar which has cinnamon mixed in (about 1 TBSP for each 1 cup of sugar), you have a whole new taste. By the way when Helen says leave room for the cookies to spread, she means it. So there.

Here is another cookie recipe that is very different, but equally good. It is from **Pamela McGrew** of Somerset, KY.

FRUIT CAKE COOKIES

> 1 cup brown sugar
> 1 cup white sugar
> 1 cup butter
> 3 eggs
> 3 cups self-rising flour
> 1 tsp cinnamon
> 1 tsp soda
> 1 pkg white raisins
> 1 8 oz pkg chopped dates
> ½ lb candied cherries, chopped
> ½ lb candied pineapple,
> 5 cups pecans, chopped

Cream sugars and butter. Add eggs, flour, cinnamon and soda. Stir in fruits and nuts. Drop by teaspoonfuls onto greased cookie sheet. Bake at 300 deg for 15 to 20 minutes.

Walter N. Lambert, Noonday Chef

FOREVER AMBER (OR BIG ORANGE) COOKIES (TV 238)

    1 lb orange slice candies, chopped fine
    2 3½ oz cans flaked coconut
    1 tsp each orange and vanilla flavoring
    2 cans sweetened condensed milk
    1 cup pecans, finely chopped
    sifted confectioners sugar (about ¾ cup), sifted

Combine all ingredients except sugar; mix well. Spread mixture in a lightly oiled 10x15" baking pan (jelly roll pan), and bake at 275 deg for 30 minutes. Remove from oven and while still hot, spoon mixture into bowl of sifted powdered sugar. Roll into balls the size of small walnuts and cool. Makes about 72 cookies.

In week two of the cookie swap, what **Pay Gary** has sent us may not be a cookie. It may be a candy. It sure is good. Now let me tell you a couple of things we tried which worked nicely. Proceed exactly as above, except roll in some more coconut. We like coconut. We also tried crushing vanilla wafers into very fine crumbs and rolling the hot mixture in them. This may have been our favorite, though the original is mighty good.

Now we get to the second recipe of this week. It comes from **Eulah Warwick** who live somewhere between Fountain City and Inskip which is a pretty good place to live. Again, this cookie is as good as any winner, it just is a little complicated to fit into our time slot.

SUGAR DIP RAISIN COOKIES

    1½ cup raisins
    1 cup water
    1 cup shortening
    1½ cup sugar
    3 eggs
    1 tsp vanilla
    3½ cups flour
    1 tsp each, baking powder and soda.

Boil raisins in the water until water is absorbed. Set aside to cool. Cream together shortening and sugar and add the eggs one at a time. Beat well. Add vanilla. Sift together the flour, baking powder, and soda; stir into the creamed mixture. Fold in the raisins. Chill the dough. Shape into 1" balls and place on a greased cookie sheet about 2" apart. Flatten with fork. Bake at 375 deg about 10 to 12 minutes. Change from lower to higher rack about half way through. Makes 5 dozen.

Walter N. Lambert, Noonday Chef

GUSTINE COOKIES (TV 239)

> 1½ sticks butter
> ¾ cup sugar
> 1 egg, separated
> 2 cups plain flour
> brown sugar (about ¾ to 1 cup)
> chopped pecans (about ¾ to 1 cup)

Cream sugar and butter. Add egg yolk and blend. Add flour and mix thoroughly. Press into ungreased and unfloured 10½ x 15½" jelly roll pan. Smear unbeaten egg white over the dough. Sprinkle evenly with brown sugar and then the nuts. Bake at 375 deg about 15 minutes. Cut immediately into squares, and remove from pan to cool on a rack.

Mrs. Fred (Jean) Millis sent us these good cookies which are named for her grandmother who first made them. It is no surprise that Jean would send us good cookies. She has sent me a couple of recipes which we have used, and she can be depended on to do good work. I think these are extraordinary. Jean says they freeze very well. They have never lasted long enough at our house for us to find out. The bottom crust of these cookies is a good, plain, butter cookie. It is good with almost any flavor added and baked without the brown sugar and nut topping. It can also be chilled and rolled. Try it with lemon flavoring and a little grated lemon pee. Roll into balls, and then roll in powdered sugar while warm.

Now our second place cookie for this week is similar to a cookie I have done before, but I think this one from a viewer named **Penny Lee** is better. It requires precision in timing which we could never have done on the show. So here you are:

PEANUT BUTTER KISSES

> 1 cup peanut butter
> ½ cup each, butter, brown sugar and white sugar
> 1 egg
> 1½ cup all purpose flour
> 1 bag Hershey kisses (unwrapped)

Cream butter and peanut butter. Cream in the sugars. Add the egg and blend. Blend in the flour. Form into round balls, about 1" across. Place on a cookie sheet, and bake at 350 deg about 7 minutes. Pull from the oven and press a Hershey kiss into the top of each cookie. Return to the oven and bake an additional 7 minutes. Remove to a rack to cool. Then, give everyone a kiss.

28

Walter N. Lambert, Noonday Chef

THE BEST PEANUT BUTTER COOKIES (TV 240)

    1 cup each, shortening, and peanut butter
    1 cup each, sugar, and brown sugar
    2 eggs
    1 tsp vanilla
    3 cups White Lily self-rising flour

Cream together the shortening, peanut butter, and sugars. Add eggs and vanilla. Blend. Add flour gradually and mix well. Shape into balls (about 1 tsp in each) and drop on ungreased cookie sheets. Flatten balls with a fork to form a criss-cross. Bake about 10 minutes at 350 deg. Makes about 5 dozen.

When **Linda Nichols** of Maryville sent us this recipe, I knew immediately that I had to make them. I did right then. I was not disappointed. They are like cookies I ate in Corryton Elementary School when **Mrs. Troutt** ran the lunch room there. I have recaptured my childhood. And the Child within me loves it. By the way, if you like chunks of peanut in your cookies, simply use chunky peanut butter. Could anything be simpler. Linda, I thank you for great cookies and great memories. This week's second cookie is also a winner. It is from **Mrs. Johnnie R. Gourley** in Sweetwater who writes us regularly. It is far too long to get on the air, but is it ever good.

OATMEAL-PUMPKIN COOKIES

    ½ cup margarine, softened
    ½ cup sugar
    1 egg
    1 cup canned pumpkin
    ½ tsp, each, lemon and vanilla extract
    1½ cups all purpose flour
    1½ cups quick oats (uncooked)
    1 tsp cinnamon
    ½ tsp baking soda
    ⅓ cup walnuts, chopped

Cream margarine in a bowl. Add sugar and beat together until light and fluffy (about 5 minutes). Add egg. Beat well. Add pumpkin and blended flavorings. Beat until well blended. Mix flour, cinnamon, soda and blend. Stir in oats. Gradually add the dry ingredients to the creamed mixture. Stir in walnuts. Cover and chill for 30 minutes. Drop by TBSP onto cookie sheet coated with a cooking spray. Bake at 375 deg for 15 minutes or until lightly browned. Transfer to a wire rack to cool. Makes about 4 dozen.

Walter N. Lambert, Noonday Chef

SANTA'S THUMB PRINTS (TV 241)

 1½ cup butter flavor **Crisco**
 1 cup brown sugar, firmly packed
 1 egg
 1 TBSP vanilla
 2½ cups rolled oats (quick or old fashioned)
 2 cups all purpose flour
 ½ tsp salt
 1¾ cups nuts, finely chopped
 ⅔ cup strawberry preserves (or jam)

Cream **Crisco** and sugar until fluffy. Beat in the egg and vanilla. Mix flour, oats, and salt, and beat into creamed mixture. Form 1" balls and roll in nuts. Place 2" apart on ungreased cookie sheet. Press center with thumb, fill with preserves (jam). Bake 12 to 15 minutes or until lightly brown. Remove to wire rack to cool.

When **Mrs. Susan Harris** sent us this recipe. She said her family liked these cookies still warm, with <u>hot cider</u>. She says they do cider by heating a bag of "red hot" candies with a large can of apple juice. We have tried this and recommend it. Our second recipe today comes from **Nancy Linn-Emig**, who is a regular viewer and a nice lady whom we met at a book signing at **Proffitts**. They are called:

STARLIGHT MINT SURPRISE COOKIES

 1 cup sugar
 ½ cup brown sugar, firmly packed
 ¾ cup margarine or butter, softened
 2 TBSP water
 1 tsp each, vanilla and baking soda
 2 eggs
 3 cups all purpose flour
 ½ tsp salt
 2 (6 oz) pkg Andes mint candy wafers (unwrapped)
 60 walnut halves or pieces

In a large bowl, combine sugars, margarine, water, vanilla, and eggs. Blend well. Lightly spoon flour into measuring cup; level off. In another bowl, combine flour, baking soda and salt; mix well. Add to sugar mixture and mix at low speed until well blended. Cover with plastic wrap; chill for at least 2 hours for easier handling. Using about 1 TBSP dough, press dough around each candy wafer to cover. Place 2" apart on ungreased cookie sheet. Top each with walnut half or pieces. Bake 7 to 9 minutes or until light brown. Cool on wire rack. **CRUNCHY CHEESE**

30

Walter N. Lambert, Noonday Chef

CRACKERS (TV 242)

    1 stick butter (or margarine) at room temperature
    1 cup finely shredded sharp cheddar cheese
    1 cup all purpose flour
    1 tsp tabasco sauce
    2 cups Rice Krispies

Cream the margarine, cheese, and tabasco sauce until well blended. Beat in flour. Stir in rice krispies. Shape into small balls (about ¾" across), and flatten onto an ungreased cookie sheet. Bake in a preheated 350 deg oven about 12 to 15 minutes or until lightly browned. Cool on a wire rack.

We have done these little wonders for years at Christmas time, and it just wouldn't be Christmas without them. Sometimes, we make them with ½ cup cheddar cheese and ½ cup crumbled blue cheese. They were included in **_Cooking with the Noonday Chef_**, and we now do them here for your benefit.

A similar cheese cracker which we like follows. These also make a nice base for canapes with cheese or pate. Personally, I like to just eat them. Be sure to roll them thin and bake until crisp.

SESAME CHEESE SQUARES

    1 cup all purpose flour
    ¼ cup sesame seed, toasted
    1 tsp ground ginger
    1 egg white, beaten
    ½ tsp salt
    ⅓ cup butter, melted
    1 cup sharp cheese, grated
    1 tsp sugar
    1 TBSP Worcestershire sauce
    1 TBSP water

Sift the flour, salt, ginger, and sugar. Stir in cheese; mix well. Stir in sesame seeds. Combine melted butter, water, egg white, and Worcestershire sauce. Add to cheese mixture. Stir to form a ball. Roll out on a lightly floured board to ⅛ inch thickness. Cut into squares about 1½ " on each side. Or cut into circles about 1½" across. Place on ungreased baking sheet and bake in a preheated 360 deg about 12 to 15 minutes or until lightly brown. Remove to a wire rack to cool. Store in a tightly closed container.

Walter N. Lambert, Noonday Chef

CRANBERRY SURPRISE PIE (TV 243)

   1 lb fresh cranberries
   1½ cup sugar, divided
   ¾ cup walnuts, chopped
   2 eggs
   1 cup self-rising flour
   ½ cup butter or margarine, melted

Wash cranberries and place in a 9" square pan, uncooked. Sprinkle with ½ cup sugar and nuts. Mix together all remaining ingredients. Pour evenly over the berries. Bake in a preheated 325 deg oven about 1 hour or until browned. Serve warm.

I am sure that you have everything organized at Christmas, and you do not need any short cuts or time savers. Therefore, you have no interest in this wonderful tart-sweet pie which comes from the now out of print, *Bearden Cooks* which **Anne** edited for Bearden Elementary School about 25 years ago. But if you should need a good dessert in a hurry, here you are. By the way, my favorite way to have this dessert is warm with some vanilla ice cream. They were made for each other.

Cranberries also mix nicely with apples and the two can work together in this pie. Simply peel, core, and chop about 1 cup of good sour apples (Granny Smith, Winesap, etc.), mix with the cranberries, and proceed as above.

Now while we are revisiting *Bearden Cooks*, let me give you another cranberry recipe from the same master work.

CRANBERRY SALAD

   2 cups fresh cranberries
   1 cup water
   1 cup sugar
   1 pkg red **Jell-O** (cherry or raspberry)
   1 cup crushed pineapple
   1 cup celery, cut in small pieces
   ½ cup nuts

Cook cranberries, water, and sugar until cranberries are tender. Pour over **Jell-O**, stir to mix. Allow to cool. Stir in the pineapple, celery, and nuts. Chill before serving.

Walter N. Lambert, Noonday Chef

BISCUIT POCKETS (TV 244)

    2 cans flaky, refrigerated, biscuits (10 per can)
    5 slices salami, quartered
    5 slices cooked ham, quartered
    5 slices cooked turkey, quartered
    5 slices American (or Swiss) cheese, quartered
    brown mustard

Roll or stretch each biscuit into a 4" round. Place 2 pieces of each meat and cheese and a dab of mustard on 10 of the biscuits. Cover with other biscuits and press edges together and fold over to seal completely. Place on an ungreased cookie sheet, and bake in a preheated 400 deg oven 12 to 15 minutes or until brown. Allow to cool for three or four minutes before cutting into quarters to serve as appetizers.

These little wonders are quick, easy, and good. Any time we make them, they disappear immediately. We sometimes fix them for kids, leaving them whole to serve as little sandwiches. We halve them to serve with a salad, and cut them into quarters for appetizers. They go well however they are served. Now you can see that there is nothing perfect about this mixture of bread and cheese. You could make them with cheese alone or with your favorite combination of meat and cheese. The important thing is to leave sufficient space around the edges to seal them. Otherwise, you have an oven full of melted cheese and a general mess.

Canned biscuits don't show me a whole lot as biscuits, but they can be handy for all sorts of casseroles. Try the following, and I think you will agree:

LEMON CHICKEN PIE

    1 can flaky, refrigerated biscuits (10 per pkg)
    2 whole chicken breast, skinned, boned and cubed
    1 TBSP oil
    ¼ cup each, chopped onion, celery, and carrots
    1 TBSP flour
    ¼ tsp each, garlic powder and ground ginger
    2 TBSP lemon juice
    1 cup water

In an ovenproof skillet, saute the chicken in the oil until it is white (about 2 minutes). Add vegetables, and stir fry a couple of minutes more. Stir in the garlic powder, ginger, flour and blend. Stir in the lemon juice and water. Cook stirring until it comes to a full boil. Arrange the biscuits on the top, and place into a preheated 400 deg oven about 20 minutes until biscuits are brown. Serve hot.

Walter N. Lambert, Noonday Chef

ANN'S BLACK-EYED PEA DIP (TV 245)

    2 cans (15.8 oz) black-eyed peas
    ¼ lb cooked ham, chopped
    1 can (10 oz) Kroger tomatoes with green chilies
    1 medium onion, chopped
    ¼ tsp garlic powder
    ¾ lb Velveeta cheese
    Tabasco sauce to taste

Mix the black-eyed peas, ham, tomatoes, onion, and garlic powder in a heavy sauce pan. Simmer about 10 minutes. Drain and reserve liquid. Place the cubed Velveeta cheese and pea mixture in a food processor with the metal blade and blend. Add enough (3 or 4 TBSP) of the cooking liquid to get the desired consistency. Add tabasco to taste if desired. Serve hot.

It has become a challenge to find some new way to eat black-eyed peas on **New Year's day**. **Ann Kemmer**, Home Economist for Proffitt's Department Store, does a more complicated version of this which is the inspiration for mine. By the way, keep an eye out for classes which Ann teaches in the housewares departments of Proffitt's store. They are great, and so is she.

Now you may have noticed that these do not have hog jowl as a part of them. I can carry tradition only so far. But if you insist, fry out the hog jowl and substitute cubes of it for the ham. Or simply fry it and serve on the side. Or...

Now maybe just a word about the traditional way to fix black-eyed peas would be appropriate.

BLACK-EYED PEAS

    1 lb dried black-eyed peas
    4 or 5 thick slices hog jowl bacon
    1 large onion, coarsely chopped
    1 large pod dry red pepper (or ½ tsp pepper flakes)
    water

Place the peas in a large bowl and cover with hot water. Allow to soak several hours or overnight. Drain the peas, cover with fresh water and wash. In a heavy pan with a tight fitting lid, fry the bacon until crisp. Remove and fry the onion in the bacon grease. Add the washed peas, bacon, pepper, and water to cover. Bring to a full boil; reduce heat to a simmer and allow to cook, covered about 1 ½ to 2 hours until peas are tender. Add more water if necessary. Serve hot with thick chunks of cornbread and maybe a side dish of good turnip greens. Happy New Year!

Walter N. Lambert, Noonday Chef

QUICK SWISS STEAK (TV 246)

    2 lbs round steak, cubed
    2 or 3 TBSP cooking oil
    1 cup flour
    2 tsp salt
    1 tsp each, black pepper, oregano, and basil
    1 large onion, chopped
    1 28 oz can crushed tomatoes
    ½ tomato can water

Mix the flour, salt, and pepper in a flat container. Work as much as possible into the meat. Heat oil in a deep skillet with a tight fitting lid. Brown the meat in a single layer until browned. Remove to a plate. Saute onion in oil until soft and it starts to brown. Return the steak to the skillet; add oregano, basil, tomatoes and water. Stir to blend. Bring to a full boil and reduce heat to a simmer. Cook covered, stirring occasionally, about two hours until meat is very tender and sauce is thick.

I thought you might need to get back down to earth after all the holiday hoopla. And what is more down to earth on a cold winter night than Swiss steak, mashed potatoes, and green beans. With maybe a piece of cornbread or even hot rolls.

While this dish requires some time to do right, it could not be simpler. It may be that you like green peppers in your Swiss steak. Fine. Just add a cup of chopped green peppers when you add the onion, and proceed exactly as above. Also, some folks like more salt and pepper. I suggest waiting until the dish is finished, then salt and pepper to taste.

Perhaps I should say just a word about the meat in this dish. I buy top round steak and ask the butcher to cube it for me. To do this, he runs it through a machine which cuts into the tough connectors in this meat and tenderizes it. My mother and grandmother did the same thing by putting the pieces of meat on a cutting board and whacking it with the back of a heavy knife until it had broken down sufficiently. During this process, the flour and salt and pepper were worked into the meat. Thus the admonition to work the flour into the meat not just coat it.

Now this dish is the first cousin to one of my absolute favorites of all times--country style steak. To do country style steak, follow the instructions above in every detail except use all water instead of tomatoes. When you have returned the browned meat to the skillet, add enough water to cover, then proceed. I guarantee you will love it.

Walter N. Lambert, Noonday Chef

QUICK BLACK BEANS AND SAUSAGE (TV 247)

    ½ lb country sausage, hot
    1 onion, chopped
    2 15 oz cans black beans
    cooked rice
    salsa and sour cream (optional)

In a heavy pan, fry the sausage, breaking it up as it fries. Drain any excess fat. Add chopped onion and fry, stirring constantly, until the onion is transparent and starts to brown. Add beans, undrained, and bring to a full boil. Reduce heat, cover, and allow to simmer about 20 minutes to blend flavors. Serve over hot cooked rice, topped with salsa and sour cream if desired.

We just spent some time in Key West and everywhere you went, you found black beans and rice in Cuban restaurants. I love Cuban roast pork or fried pork cubes with black beans and rice. I have also found that if you add a little meat, you have a complete winter evening meal. That is what this dish does.

Now, you have lots of options with this dish. First, you need not use hot sausage if you like mild better. In fact, you may want to use mild sausage and add a little Tabasco sauce for added flavor. Alternatively, you may like smoked sausage better than country sausage. If you can find a good, spicy chorizo or andouille sausage, slices of it would be great. Prepare the dish as above, except that you would start by cooking the onion in a little oil. Then add the slices of sausage and proceed.

Now I have abbreviated the process considerably by using canned black beans. That is just a matter of convenience. If you want to use dry black beans, this same recipe will work just fine. Simply follow the instructions on the package for cooking the beans and then proceed with the beans when they are fully cooked. I would suggest that to get a really rich creamy texture to the beans, use ½ canned chicken broth and ½ water for cooking the beans. A pound of dry beans will make about twice as much as the two cans, so use a pound of sausage and a couple of onions. And invite the neighbors, you are going to have a lot of beans.

Now a word about black bean soup. If you like it, prepare the black beans and meat just as we did above and add a can of chicken broth and ½ broth can of water with the beans. Again, allow the mixture to come to a full boil, reduce the heat, and allow to simmer, covered, about ½ hour. I like to serve the soup surrounded with rice, chopped onion, green onion, salsa, cheese, and sour cream. Let everyone dress their own.

36

Walter N. Lambert, Noonday Chef

LOW FAT "CREAMED" SOUP (TV 248)

> 2 cups (approx), each carrot, onion, turnip, parsnip, cabbage, and butternut squash
> 2 cans chicken stock with an equal amount of water
> 1 cup instant potato flakes
> salt to taste

Prepare the vegetables and chop coarsely. Place in a large pot with a tight fitting lid with the chicken stock and water. Cover and bring to a boil. Reduce heat, and simmer about 30 minutes or until vegetables are very tender. Remove from heat and mash vegetables to break them up. Return to a boil. Remove from heat and stir in the potato flakes. Salt to taste. Serve hot or cold.

I like this soup for a number of reasons. First, it tastes good. Second, it is easy. Finally, because it has almost no fat. In fact, if you are a strict vegan, you can simply leave out the chicken stock, use all water or substitute a good vegetable stock, and you are in business. Now I can already hear you saying, why not just eat it without the mashing, the potatoes, and all that business. Be my guest. If you want that, why not throw in potatoes to equal the other vegetables and cook away. What the mashing and adding the potatoes does is give a nice creamy consistency, which we usually get from adding butter, cream, and fat and calories. Did I mention that I sometimes use the little hand blender and make the soup relatively smooth before I add the potatoes?

By the way, because of the carrots and butternut squash, this has a pretty color and just a trace of sweetness. I like that. If however, you do not, substitute more of the other vegetables to replace them. When we serve this soup hot, we sometimes sprinkle the top with chopped green onion. We sometimes put a dollop of low fat sour cream on top and then add onions. **Anne** likes it with a little sour cream and a sprinkle of nutmeg.

Let me say a word here in behalf of **parsnips**. You may have wondered what in the world people did with those white carrot looking things. My grandmother cooked them like carrots, drizzled butter over them, and thought they were good. That was a little much for me. But I love to add them to soups and stews for the tangy flavor they give.

Finally, a word about that cold business. Because this soup has no fat, it can be prepared as above, allowed to cool, and then served cold. It maintains its texture and taste and is great for lunch with a grilled cheese sandwich.

Walter N. Lambert, Noonday Chef

CORNBREAD-CHICKEN CASSEROLE (TV 249)

1 lb cooked chicken (about 2 cups), cut into chunks
1 pkg frozen chopped broccoli
1 medium onion, chopped
1 can cream of mushroom soup
1 tsp salt
1 cup self-rising cornmeal mix
¼ cup grated Parmesan cheese
1 cup chicken stock (or water)

Mix first five ingredients; turn into an 8" square pan which has been sprayed with a cooking spray. Smooth the top of the chicken mixture in the pan. Mix together the cornmeal, cheese, and stock; pour evenly over the top. Bake at 350 deg about 45 minutes until hot through and brown on top. Serve hot.

Please note that this casserole has no added butter, milk, cream or any of those other fat things we think we need to make a good casserole. Instead, it depends on good ingredients and simple preparation.

Now I will remind you again how I cook chicken for this kind of recipe. I put the chicken (I use skinless, boneless chicken breasts) in a pot with a good lid, and cover it with cold water. I place the covered pot on the stove and bring it to a full boil. I turn it off and allow the chicken to cool in the water. Then cut it into whatever kind of pieces needed. In this recipe, I use the poaching water to make the cornbread topping.

There are a great many ways to do this basic idea which changes the flavor considerably. First, you can change the flavor of the soup. I also like the new cheddar cheese soup very much. With it, I still use the Parmesan in the cornbread. Oh, by the way, in this recipe, the plain old Parmesan in the can works even better than the good, fresh, real stuff. I also do the recipe with cream of celery soup. When I do this, I add about ½ tsp of rubbed sage to the cornbread instead of the Parmesan cheese.

This recipe can also be done with ground beef instead of the chicken. If you do so, be sure to drain off all (that is A L L) of the fat. When I do this with beef, I add about ½ of a soup can of water to make it a little juicier. I sometimes add a small can of tomato sauce and about ½ tsp of oregano instead of the water to give an Italian sort of flavor to the dish. Now one last variation. Using either the chicken or the beef, leaving out the broccoli, add a can of chili flavored beans and a couple of tsps of chili powder along with a small can of tomato sauce to the meat. Put it in the pan as above and top with the cornbread.

38

Walter N. Lambert, Noonday Chef

FUDGE CAKE (TV 250)

½ cup butter, melted
2 cups sugar
4 eggs
¼ lb semi-sweet chocolate, grated
½ cup flour
1 tsp baking powder
2 cups pecans, chopped

Blend sugar with the melted butter. Beat in eggs. Stir together chocolate, flour, and baking powder, and stir into the egg mixture. Stir in the pecans. Turn into a greased and floured 9" square pan and bake for 30 minutes at 350 degrees. Allow to cool and cut into squares.
This recipe comes from a cookbook which was edited by **Mrs. Cary F. Spence** for the Women's Association of the Second Presbyterian Church in Knoxville in 1932. This recipe was submitted by Mrs. W. A. Shelton. I assume that it could be considered the mother of brownies.

This book was one of several that my lifelong friend **Betty Castellaw** gave me for Christmas. They had belonged to her mother, **Nell Thompson**, and had been stored away in the basement since Aunt Nell's death. All the books, except the one from which this recipe was taken, were give-away books from baking powder companies, or Jewel Tea Company, and may well be the source of future recipes. It is a delight to read them anyway.

Now one more recipe from those days which proves that we did not discover getting rid of fat and cholesterol in our generation. By the way, the candied fruit called for in this was originally <u>citron</u>. I hate having even a little citron in anything. Therefore, I always use either pineapple or cherries.

EGGLESS, MILKLESS, BUTTERLESS CAKE

1 cup brown sugar
1 tsp cinnamon
1 ¼ cup water
½ tsp salt
1 cup raisins
2 cups flour
2 oz candied fruit, cut fine
5 tsp baking powder
⅓ cup shortening
1 tsp nutmeg

Boil sugar, water, fruit, shortening, salt, and spices together in a sauce pan for 3 minutes. Allow to cool. When cool, mix flour and baking powder and add to boiled mixture. Mix well. Bake in a loaf pan in moderate oven about 45 minutes.

Walter N. Lambert, Noonday Chef

LOVERS TORTE (TV 251)

    1 4 oz pkg sweet baking chocolate, broken into pieces
    2 TBSP butter
    1 8 oz pkg regular or chocolate whipped topping
    1 9" chocolate cake layer, split into two layers

Microwave chocolate and butter at 30 second intervals (about 1½ to 2 minutes) until the chocolate is melted. Stir to blend and allow to cool about 5 minutes. Stir in 2 cups of the whipped topping. Spread between the cake layers. Frost cake with the remaining whipped topping. Allow to stand in the refrigerator at least 2 hours before serving.

This is one of those incredibly easy dishes that it is almost an exaggeration to call a recipe. But given its ingredients, it contains all those things we love, especially chocolate.

As far as the cake in this is concerned, I usually just make a cake mix cake. I have used both devil's food and German chocolate; both work very well. In fact, when I make cakes, I will often make a couple of extra layers and wrap and freeze them. They are then easy to slice and are ready on a moments notice. In fact, cakes will slice better frozen than not. Always be sure to use a serrated knife, using a sawing motion to cut so you do not tear the cake.

I often do not frost the whole cake with the whipped topping. If the cake edges are smooth, I pile the chocolate mixture in the center, then apply the remaining whipped topping thickly on the top and not on the sides. I really think it looks prettier. If you like, you can decorate the top with nut halves, maraschino cherries, or even shaved chocolate. Here is a related recipe:

CHOCOLATE TRUFFLE LOAF

    12 oz sweet baking chocolate
    ⅓ cup water
    1 8 oz pkg cream cheese
    ¼ cup sugar
    1 tsp vanilla
    ½ tsp almond extract
    1 8 oz tub whipped topping

Grease a loaf pan and line the bottom and sides with waxed paper. Microwave the chocolate and the water until the chocolate is almost melted (about 1½ to 2 minutes). Stir until smooth. Beat cream cheese and sugar until smooth. Beat in the extracts and chocolate mixture. Fold in whipped topping. Turn into loaf pan and refrigerate until firm (about 4 hours). Turn out and decorate with additional chocolate or berries.

Walter N. Lambert, Noonday Chef

GIRL SCOUT DIRT CAKE (TV 252)

    1 pkg Girl Scout mint cookies, crumbled fine
    1 5.1 oz pkg instant pudding mix (vanilla or chocolate)
    1½ cup each milk and sour cream

Line a new flower pot with aluminum foil which does not come quite to the top. Sprinkle about ½ cup crumbs in the bottom of the pot. Layer the pudding and the crumbs ending with a heavy layer of crumbs, filling the pot full. Chill and serve.

If you have not bought **Girl Scout** cookies yet, now is the time. Each year, we have prepared some dish which used these fine cookies. This is so you could buy some extras and still use them in a timely fashion. After all, that is better than sitting in front of the TV set and eating a whole box on your own.

This year, we have chosen to do the ever popular dirt cake. Now if you really want to make this fancy, use cake icing to glue several additional cookies to skewers and insert them into the pot for flowers growing out of the dirt. I also always add a couple of gummy worms from the specialty foods section at **Kroger** to give a little added touch. Kids (of all ages) love it. Please note that I use half milk and half sour cream when making instant pudding. It relieves the cloyingness a little and gives a nice additional taste.

Now, if your are the sort that doesn't believe in mixes, I advise making your own pudding with this recipe from ***Kinfolks and Custard Pie.***

VANILLA (OR CHOCOLATE) PUDDING

    3 eggs
    4 cups milk
    1 ½ cups sugar
    4 TBSP flour
    1 TBSP vanilla

In a heavy saucepan, blend together the sugar and flour. Beat in eggs. Stir in milk, and place the mixture over medium heat. Stir constantly until the pudding comes to a boil and is thick. Remove from heat, stir in the vanilla. Serve cold.

To make a good rich chocolate pudding, stir ½ cup good cocoa into the sugar and flour mixture and proceed as above. Oh, by the way, for a passable butterscotch pudding just use brown sugar.

Walter N. Lambert, Noonday Chef

DIANE'S TAMALE CASSEROLE (TV 253)

    1 lb ground beef
    2 TBSP oil
    1 cup onion, chopped
    1 16 oz can tomatoes, chopped
    1 12-15 oz can whole kernel corn
    ½ cup plain corn meal
    1 tsp salt
    2 TBSP chili powder
    ½ cup ripe olives
    ¾ to 1 cup grated cheese

Brown meat and onions. Drain thoroughly. Add tomatoes, corn liquid, and corn meal. Stir to blend and cook on low heat until very thick (about 10 minutes). Add corn, salt, chili powder, and olives. Turn into a 9" square pan, and bake in a preheated 350 deg oven about 25 minutes. Sprinkle cheese evenly over the top. Bake an addition 15 minutes. Serve hot.

This recipe comes from the lady, **Diane Cooper**, who strives (against the odds) to keep my hair and beard looking reasonably neat. It came from our discussion of the ways we like to use corn meal. There may be some use of it that I do not like, but I haven't found it yet. That caused Diane to remember this recipe which she has been making for years.

Now I should tell you that Diane uses only 1 TBSP of chili powder when she makes it. If I had my way, I would use ¼ cup. The two TBSP represents a compromise. Use as much as tastes good to you. And if you happen to be interested in hot in a big way, substitute an equal amount of **Kroger** chopped tomatoes with green chilies for the regular tomatoes. I guarantee you it will be lively.

One other word about variations. Some folks love green peppers in a dish of this sort. If you do, simply add about ½ cup chopped green peppers when you add the onions. Again, this is a matter of taste. And speaking of taste, you can make one great big casserole of this by leaving out the corn meal and adding macaroni or noodles. To do this, cook about 8 oz of macaroni or broad egg noodles according to package directions. Once you have prepared the meat and onions and drained off the grease, stir in the remaining ingredients including the macaroni or noodles. Turn into a casserole dish and bake for about 25 minutes before sprinkling with the cup of cheese and baking another 15 minutes. I like to blend about ½ cup of grated dry Parmesan cheese with the grated cheddar cheese for the topping. It adds both a little extra texture and a little more taste.

Walter N. Lambert, Noonday Chef

BLARNEY ONION TART (TV 254)

pastry for a 10" pie
¼ cup butter
1 ¾ lb onion, sliced very thin
1 cup half and half
2 eggs
½ tsp each salt, pepper and nutmeg
1 cup grated blarney cheese

Roll pastry thin and line a 10 or 11" tart pan with a removable bottom and bake until lightly brown. Melt butter in a heavy skillet and add onions. Cook on medium heat, stirring frequently, until the onions are very soft and golden (about 45 minutes). Stir in salt and pepper and allow to cool. Spread onions in the crust. Beat together the milk, eggs, and nutmeg. Spread the cheese over the onions and pour milk mixture over. Bake in a 325 deg oven about 50 minutes or until puffed. Allow to cool. Serve warm.

I know, I know. This recipe is longer and more complicated than usual. But it is for **St. Patrick's** day, and is therefore worth it. I mean we need to celebrate, and the food does not have to be green to be good. This is a modern version of an old peasant Irish dish. If you can't find blarney cheese, use fontina, and if you can't find fontina, use Swiss. They are best in that order. The blarney cheese is getting to be very hard to find, but it has a wonderful buttery taste that I love. **Kroger's Cheese Shop** has the fontina or can get it for you.

Now about that pastry. I generally use Pillsbury ready to use pastry from the dairy case. However, if you like to make your own, you will love this one which adds a little sour cream for both texture and flavor.

RICH PASTRY

1 ½ cup plain flour
¼ tsp salt
½ cup (1 stick) butter
¼ cup sour cream
1 egg yolk

Blend flour and salt. Add butter, and cut in until mixture resembles coarse meal. Beat egg yolk into sour cream; add to flour mixture. Mix just until the mixture will form a ball. Gather the dough into a ball and flatten it. Wrap and refrigerate about 30 minutes. Roll thin and proceed with recipe. This makes a great crust for cream pies as well as for cheese tarts.

Walter N. Lambert, Noonday Chef

TREACLE TART (TV 255)

> ½ cup each, sorghum molasses and white corn syrup
> zest of one lemon
> 3 TBSP lemon juice (juice of one lemon)
> 1½ cup fine, fresh bread crumbs
> 2 eggs
> pastry for a one crust pie

Line a 9" pie pan with pastry and freeze. (I use a pre-frozen 9" pie shell.) Mix all remaining ingredients. Beat well. Pour into pie shell and place into a preheated 425 deg oven for 10 minutes. Reduce heat to 350, and cook for an additional 30 minutes until pie is set in the center. Allow to cool before cutting into thin wedges. Serve with whipped cream.

This is a modern adaptation of an old Irish treat. If you will remember, in "Pop goes the weasel", it was"a penny for a loaf of bread, a penny for some treacle". Well here that penny's worth of treacle (a golden colored syrup much like molasses) is baked into a tart. I guess it could be looked on as an Irish version of a rich bread pudding in a crust.

For the bread crumbs in this dish, do not use the dry crumbs which you get in a box. Use good white bread and crumble it to make the tart. I personally have found that nothing beats a good homemade sour dough bread for this purpose, but I often settle for store bought.

Now let's finish off this **St. Patrick's Day** with a very modern adaptation of an Irish meat pie. One way to make this pie is to put the cooled filling off center on a circle of dough, and fold the rest over and seal the edges and bake. If you do this one that way, it will make two good pies. I have suggested a pie pan, but that is up to you.

MRS. O'LAMBERT'S MEAT PIE

> 1 lb very lean ground beef
> 2 cups finely shredded cabbage
> 1 cup grated carrots
> ½ tsp each, salt and black pepper
> 1 envelope dry mushroom onion soup mix
> 1 cup hot water
> 1 pastry for double crust

Brown the meat in a heavy skillet, add cabbage and carrots and cook slowly for ten minutes, covered. Uncover, add soup mix, salt, pepper, and hot water. Cook 5 minutes, uncovered. Remove from heat and allow to cool. Line a 9" pie tin with half the pastry. Add the cooled filling. Cover with remaining crust and seal. Bake 30 minutes at 350 deg, or until brown.

Walter N. Lambert, Noonday Chef

BAKED CHICKEN REUBEN (TV 256)

1½ to 2 cups rye bread cubes
4 boneless, skinless chicken breast (about 1 to 1 ½ lb.)
1 16 oz can shredded kraut
4 slices Swiss cheese
1 cup thousand island dressing

Spray a 9" pan with cooking spray. Scatter bread cubes in bottom of pan. Cut chicken into bite-sized chunks, and scatter evenly over bread. Squeeze kraut dry and distribute evenly over chicken. Cover with slices of cheese and spread dressing evenly over the top. Cover with foil, and bake at 350 deg one hour. Remove cover and bake an additional 15 minutes. Serve hot.

I first got this idea from a regular viewer, **Nancy Emig**. I subsequently saw a similar recipe in the **News-Sentinel**. Of course, I had to fiddle with it a little. Neither of the recipes used the bread cubes, but I think they add a little. If you prefer, leave out the bread and proceed exactly as above. When finished, carefully lift the finished chicken out onto slices of toasted rye bread.

Now, I know you are accustomed to Reubens made with corned beef. Fine, this recipe works great with sliced corned beef, used instead of the chicken. It also is excellent with cubes of pork instead of the chicken. If you use pork, cook at 325 deg for 1½ hours, and then uncover and cook.

However, I must remind you that the chicken has much less fat. In the interest of fat reduction, I have tried this recipe with low fat Swiss cheese and with fat free thousand island dressing. It works just fine. It will look different, but it will taste essentially the same.

Now a little bonus out of the past.

TIPSY PORK CASSEROLE

3 cups roast pork, cubed
3 cups rye bread, cubed
1 ½ cup each, onions and celery, chopped
1 tsp salt
1 16 oz can beer

Mix all together in an ovenproof casserole. Bake in a preheated 375 deg oven about 35 to 40 minutes until very brown and most of the liquid has cooked out. It is important not to undercook if you are to get the full flavor. Serve hot.

Walter N. Lambert, Noonday Chef

QUICK WHOLE WHEAT ROLLS (TV 257)

1⅓ cup warm water
¼ cup each, vegetable oil and honey
2 pkgs yeast
1 tsp salt
1 egg
2½ cups whole wheat flour
1¾ cup bread flour, divided

Mix warm water, oil, honey and yeast. Allow to stand, covered, 15 minutes. Add salt and egg and mix. Add all whole wheat flour and 1 ¼ cup bread flour. Blend. Put remaining ½ cup bread flour on table and turn dough out and knead about 5 minutes or until smooth. Shape into rolls, place on a baking pan which has been sprayed with a cooking spray. Allow to rise in a warm place about 10 minutes. Bake in preheated 425 deg. oven about 15 minutes or until brown on top.

I love these rolls. They are quick and easy and go with almost anything. Now, a couple of words about them. First, do not stint on the kneading. It is critical if your rolls are to hold air and be light. Second, you will note that there is no milk in these rolls. That give you a firmer crust. Third, note that I do not butter the top of the rolls. The crust again. If you like a soft top crust, simple brush on melted butter when the rolls are fresh out of the oven.

Now a word about shaping. If you want cloverleaf, shape three small balls for each roll and drop them into a regular muffin tins (remember the cooking spray). I usually just cut them into about 1 inch circles and place them in a pie pan with the edges touching. This forces them to rise up and not out. This gives nice pull apart rolls. I first had them rolled about ½" thick and cut into about 2" circles which were placed touching on an oiled biscuit sheet. Others like to roll the dough fairly thin, cut with a biscuit cutter and fold over into **Parker House** rolls. These rolls do not rise much in the first period but puff up nicely during baking.

Now, If you do not like whole wheat, you can do these as white rolls. I recommend using bread flour for them. It holds air a little better and gives a slightly better bite. It may require just a little less white than whole wheat flour.

Finally, these rolls freeze very well. To reheat in a microwave, roll in a paper towel and heat about a minute if the rolls are frozen. Be careful about overheating. Microwave does bad things to bread if overused.

Walter N. Lambert, Noonday Chef

LEFTOVER HAM AND EGG CASSEROLE (TV 258)

    4 cups (approx.) cold mashed potatoes
    1 cup sour cream
    2 eggs
    ½ lb (approx.) cooked ham, chopped fine
    4 to 6 hard cooked eggs, peeled and chopped
    1 cup green onions, cut fine
    dry Parmesan cheese

Spray an 8" square pan with cooking spray and dust lightly with Parmesan cheese. Mix together potatoes, cream, and eggs. Toss the ham, eggs and onion together. Put half of potatoes into the pan. Spread the ham mixture over them. Cover top with remaining potatoes and dust the top generously with Parmesan cheese. Bake in a 350 deg oven about 45 minutes or until hot through and brown on the top. Serve hot.

This is one of many ways to use all the leftover ham and eggs on the day after Easter (or any time you want a good hearty treat). The original recipe was a lot fatter, and you might still want to do it that way. To do that, melt a stick of butter into a two quart glass casserole. Tilt the dish to coat with the butter. Layer potatoes and ham as above. Sprinkle top with Parmesan cheese. Bake until the bottom is brown. Use a spatula to loosen the casserole and turn out onto a plate.

You can make a couple of nice variations on this dish. One is to simply sprinkle a layer of American or cheddar cheese (or a mix of the two over ham mixture. I use about one cup which is half Velveeta and half cheddar. The other is to mix the ham and egg mixture with a can of cream of mushroom soup to make a softer center in the casserole.

There is one final, and very good way, to do this casserole. Forget that it is a casserole. Simple mix everything together in one big mess. Wet your hands, and scoop up about ½ cup of the mixture and shape into a patty about ½ inch thick. Coat both sides with flour. Heat a griddle to medium heat and coat lightly with butter. Arrange the patties in a single layer and cook until brown on the bottom. Turn and cook until brown on the other side. Be sure not to cook too fast or the outside will be brown and the patty will not be cooked through. Serve hot. Enjoy.

Now you say that you do not have leftover mashed potatoes. Don't tell anyone that I told you, but instant potatoes work fine for this. I especially like a brand called **"Real" by Idahoan**. Remember don't tell.

Walter N. Lambert, Noonday Chef

SPRINGTIME CHICKEN SALAD (TV 259)

> 3-4 cups cooked cubed chicken breast
> 3-4 cups lightly cooked asparagus, cut into 1" pieces
> 1 cup celery, chopped
> ½ cup green onions, chopped
> ½ cup each, fat free mayonnaise and thousand island dressing

Toss together chicken, asparagus, celery, and onion. Stir together mayonnaise and thousand island dressing. Pour over chicken mixture and toss to mix. Cover and refrigerate overnight or for several hours. Serve cold.

I love spring. Things in bloom. Warm, sunny days. Asparagus. This recipe includes several of them. Now you remember how to cook chicken for this recipe. Place the chicken breasts in cold water, bring to a full boil, turn off and allow to cool. Cut into cubes.

To poach the asparagus, you will need a slightly different procedure. I first get rid of the tough part of the asparagus by bending it until it breaks. Throw away the tough part and cut the remaining part into about 1" lengths. Bring a pot of water to a full boil. Dump in asparagus and bring back to a full boil. Immediately pour into a colander and pour cold water over it until it is cool. Allow to drain.

It is vital not to overcook asparagus. I like to barely poach it the way I describe above. If I need full spears, I put the water into a skillet and proceed as above. This keeps nice long straight stalks. I simply pour it out into an empty sink to cool it.

One of my very favorite ways to have asparagus is to poach it, place it in a flat container with a tight lid, and pour a good French or Italian dressing over it. Cover and chill overnight. These spears make a great side dish or a wonderful addition to a salad. Or you can just eat them like potato chips.

Another great way to do fresh asparagus is one that I found at the fancy **Tiberio's** restaurant in Washington, D.C.. These good folks poach asparagus spears lightly. They then sprinkle them with a good olive oil and a little balsamic vinegar. Then they sprinkle several spears with a good Parmesan cheese and broil it lightly just to melt the cheese. Serve immediately.

By the way, I can hear you saying, "What if fresh asparagus is not available?" Well, just forget these recipes--they need fresh.

Walter N. Lambert, Noonday Chef

FRESH APPLE TORTE (TV 260)

    1½ cup fresh chopped apples
    ¾ cup sugar
    ⅔ cup plain flour
    1 tsp baking powder
    ¼ tsp salt
    1 tsp each, vanilla and cinnamon
    ⅔ cup chopped pecans
    2 eggs

Place apples, pecans, and all dry ingredients in a bowl. Toss to mix. Beat eggs with vanilla. Pour over apple mixture, and stir to mix. Turn into a 9" greased pie pan, and bake about 40 minutes in a 350 deg oven. Serve warm with whipped cream or ice cream.

This is one of those really neat, really easy dishes which requires one dish and one mixing. It is best served warm but is still passable cold. Now let me tell you a little secret. Done the way I describe above this looks much like a pie. If we are in a hurry for a coffee cake, we mix this just like it is described above. We then sprinkle the top with about ⅓ cup more pecans and a little cinnamon mixed with 3 or 4 TBSP of sugar. Sprinkle over the top. Bake as above. Serve hot. It will be the high point of breakfast, I promise.

While we are at it, let's look at another great use for fresh apples.

APPLE POUND CAKE

    2 ½ cups plain flour
    1 TBSP baking powder
    ¼ tsp baking soda
    1 cup sugar
    ½ cup butter or margarine, softened
    ¼ cup buttermilk
    4 eggs
    2 cups peeled, cored and chopped apples
    2 tsp vanilla

In a large mixing bowl, cream butter and sugar until fluffy. Add the eggs, one at a time. Beat in the buttermilk. Mix flour with baking powder and soda. Beat into the creamed mixture. Fold in the apples and vanilla. Turn into a 10-cup tube pan, which has been greased and floured. Place into a preheated 350 deg oven and bake for one hour. Allow to cool about 5 minutes in the pan before turning out onto a rack to cool completely.

49

Walter N. Lambert, Noonday Chef

MORE THAN CHOCOLATE CAKE (TV 261)

> 3 cups self rising flour
> ½ cup cocoa
> 3 eggs
> 1½ cup sugar
> 1 16 oz can beets, drained and grated fine
> ¾ cup corn oil
> grated zest of one orange
> juice of one orange (about ½ cup)
> 2 tsp vanilla
> 2 cups semisweet chocolate chips

Combine flour and cocoa; set aside. In large mixing bowl, combine eggs, sugar, beets, oil, orange juice, and zest. Beat well. Stir in flour mixture. Stir in vanilla and chocolate chips. Pour into a greased and floured 9x13" sheet pan, and bake in a preheated 350 deg oven about 40 minutes. Allow to cool about 5 minutes in the pan. Turn out and ice if desired.

This is once again one of those strange recipes which makes the rounds sometimes for some reason that I do not fully understand. Now if you are curious about the beets, they perform two functions. First, they deepen the color of the cake. Second, they make it more moist. They serve the same purpose for this cake that carrots serve for a carrot cake. Except you can't taste them as much.

Now I usually bake this cake as a sheet cake. It will also make two good 9" layers or even three 8" layers. Given the texture of this cake, it frosts very well. You can do a fancy cooked frosting if you have a mind to. I don't know why you would.

I make a simple chocolate icing by mixing one pound of powdered sugar with ½ cup cocoa. I blend in a stick of softened butter, a tsp of vanilla, and enough milk to give the proper consistency to spread. I spread this thickly over the cake, let it stand a few minutes and away we go. Now, let me give you a snack chocolate cake so rich, you won't need icing.

MAYONNAISE CAKE

> 2 cups flour
> 1 cup each, sugar, water and mayonnaise
> 4 TBSP cocoa
> 2 tsp soda

Mix the sugar, water, and mayonnaise. Stir soda, cocoa, and flour together; blend into other mixture. Bake in 9"square pan at 350 deg for 35 to 40 minutes.

Walter N. Lambert, Noonday Chef

OVEN BAKED CHICKEN (TV 262)

    8 chicken breast halves, boneless and skinless
    ⅛ tsp pepper
    2 TBSP mustard
    1 egg
    ½ cup Parmesan cheese
    ½ cup fine cracker crumbs
    cooking spray

Sprinkle chicken breasts with pepper. Add mustard to egg, and beat until well blended. Stir cheese and bread crumbs together. Dip chicken in egg mixture, and roll in crumb mixture to coat. Let stand on wax paper 10 minutes to set coating. Place on rack in pan sprayed with cooking spray. Bake at 400 deg for 40 minutes or until coating is browned.

This is one of those super simple recipes which gives you good taste and less fat at the same time. The secret is in having a coating on the chicken which will allow it to cook without drying out. The egg mixture accomplishes that. By the way, you remember that if you have a problem with eggs, simply use two egg whites instead of the whole egg. **Egg beaters** also works nicely for this.

Now just how healthy is all this. Well, a three ounce breast half cooked this way has 22 grams of protein, 126 calories, and only 3 grams of fat. Chicken thighs also work nicely this way, but have a slightly higher fat content. These days, I find breast tenders on sale often. They also work well. Just cook a little shorter time (about 20 minutes) and all is well.

Now let me give you another way to cook chicken which gives you flavor with very low fat. In fact, this is two ways in the same recipe.

LEMON CHICKEN

    ⅓ cup lemon juice
    ¼ cup soy sauce
    1 clove garlic, minced
    ½ tsp each, salt, ground ginger, and black pepper
    2 pounds chicken breasts, skinned and boned

Combine first 6 ingredients in a shallow container, and stir to mix completely. Add chicken; cover and refrigerate at least 2 to 3 hours. Overnight is good. Turn occasionally. Drain and discard marinate. Now you may either grill the chicken or place it into a pan sprayed with a cooking spray and bake at 325 deg about 1 hour.

51

Walter N. Lambert, Noonday Chef

LOW SUGAR STRAWBERRY PIE (TV 263)

    1 quart strawberries, capped and sliced
    3 TBSP cornstarch
    1 3 oz sugar free strawberry **Jell-o**
    2 cups water
    2 pkg **Sweet and Low**
    1 deep dish pie shell, baked and cooled

Combine water and cornstarch. Bring to a boil. Remove from heat, and stir in jell-o and **Sweet and Low**. Stir until **Jell-o** is completely dissolved. Allow to cool to room temperature. Stir in berries and turn into crust. Chill until firm.

A young lady named **Mary Helsley** who works with me at The University of Tennessee made this pie and brought it to the office. I liked it a lot, and then found that it was low sugar. Quite a bonus. If you cut this pie into 8 pieces, each piece will have 66 calories. If you just must add some topping at least use light whipped cream or light cool whip. And besides, just a little of either of these will be just as good as a lot.

Now, I want to give you a fat strawberry recipe so you can go either way. This is a cake which my **mother** has made for years, and just loves. It is a little sweet for my taste, but **Anne** says that just shows that there is something wrong with me.

STRAWBERRY CAKE

    1 pkg white cake mix
    1 3 oz pkg strawberry **Jell-O**
    ½ cup each water and oil
    3 eggs
    1 10 oz pkg frozen strawberries, thawed

Stir **Jell-O** into cake mix. Add oil and water, and beat 2 minutes with a good mixer using the flat blade. Add eggs and beat 5 minutes more (this beating is important) at medium speed. Drain strawberries and retain juice. Add drained berries to cake and stir. Pour into 2 greased and floured 9" pans and bake in a 350 deg oven for about 25 minutes. Or turn into a floured and greased tube pan and bake about 1 hour. Allow to cool in the pan before turning out.

STRAWBERRY ICING

Soften ⅔ stick margarine (or butter) and mix with 1 lb sifted powdered sugar. Add about 4 TBSP of the reserved strawberry juice until you have the right consistency. Ice cake.

Walter N. Lambert, Noonday Chef

STRAWBERRY MOUSSE (TV 264)

        1 quart strawberries
        ½ cup sugar
        4 envelopes un-flavored gelatin
        ½ cup cold water
        1 cup boiling water
        2 cups whipping cream, whipped with ½ cup powdered sugar

Puree strawberries with sugar in a blender or food processor. Soften gelatin in cold water. Add boiling water; stir until dissolved. Cool. Stir in strawberries. Allow to cool until it starts to thicken. Fold in whipped cream and spoon into a mold and chill until set.

I love strawberries. I love whipped cream. I love a mousse. Here you are. This dish needs fresh strawberries to achieve its full flavor. Now if you are in a hurry, use a 3 oz pkg of Jell-o (either with or without sugar) instead of the un-flavored gelatin.

This also makes a very nice pie filling. Just spoon into a graham cracker crust and away you go. If you use it this way, place strawberry halves around the edge of the pie for a great look.

Now here is a real bonus for you. It is sweet and pretty and altogether good.

LEMON-STRAWBERRY PIE

        1 cup sugar
        3 TBSP cornstarch
        1 cup water
        2 egg yolks, beaten
        ¼ cup butter
        ¼ cup plus 2 TBSP lemon juice
        1 baked 9" pie shell
        2 cups fresh strawberries
        2 3 oz pkg cream cheese, softened
        ¼ cup powdered sugar
        ¾ cup whipping cream, whipped

Combine sugar and cornstarch in a heavy saucepan, and gradually stir in water, egg yolks, and butter. Cook over medium heat until the mixture comes to a boil. Cook 1 minute stirring constantly. Remove from heat and stir in lemon juice. Pour into pastry shell and cool. Arrange strawberries on top of filling. Combine cream cheese and powdered sugar. Fold into whipped cream and spread over the strawberries. Cover and chill. Serve cold.

Walter N. Lambert, Noonday Chef

FAIRY CAKE (TV 265)

1½ cup sugar, divided
¼ cup each, melted butter and milk
¼ tsp each, salt and cream of tartar
2 tsp vanilla, divided
1 cup cake flour
2 tsp baking powder
4 eggs, separated

In a large mixing bowl, beat the egg yolks until light and lemon colored (about 10 minutes). Beat in ½ cup sugar, butter, milk, salt, cake flour, baking powder, and 1 tsp vanilla. Turn into 2 greased and floured 9" pans. In another large bowl, beat 4 egg whites with the cream of tartar until frothy. Slowly add the remaining cup of sugar and beat until stiff peaks form. Stir in remaining vanilla. Spread on cake batter in pans. Bake at 350 deg for 30 minutes. Cool before removing from pans.

Stack the cake with the meringue on the bottom layer down and on the top layer up. Stack with whipped cream, cool whip, or ice cream. Serve with fresh fruit. If you wish, you may include a layer of fresh fruit (my preference is strawberries) in the center with the filling.

This cake comes from a very old cook book which was given to us by **Mrs. Jessie Stout**. Ms. Jessie gave us a whole collection of books and recipes, and it was a sweet thing for her to do. She insists that at 89 and nearly blind she doesn't use her recipes much any more. But she assures me that she can still do those simple things that everyone likes. I don't doubt her for a minute.

Here's another cake from the same book. But I have to tell you, it made us more glad than sad. The name, by the way, comes from the moist, heavy texture of the cake.

SAD CAKE

1 box light brown sugar
4 eggs
2 cups **Bisquick**
2 tsp vanilla
1 cup chopped nuts

Mix the ingredients in the order given. Bake in a greased and floured bundt pan 45 minutes at 350 deg. Allow to cool in the pan before turning out. Serve warm.

Walter N. Lambert, Noonday Chef

FEEDING FATHER FAST (TV 266)

1 to 1½ lb lean ground beef
1 3½ oz pkg sliced pepperoni
1 jar spaghetti sauce
8 oz uncooked macaroni
3 cups hot water
1 cup mozzarella cheese, grated

In a heavy oven-proof pan, brown beef and drain completely. Add pepperoni and stir in. Add spaghetti sauce and allow to come back to a full boil. Stir in macaroni and hot water. Cover and bake at 350 deg for 20 minutes. Remove cover, stir, smooth down and sprinkle with cheese. Bake uncovered an additional 15 minutes. Serve hot.

This recipe is an adaptation from one sent to me by **Shannon Laws Hawk** of Strawberry Plains. Shannon suggests doing this as a spaghetti sauce and that works fine. I have made the changes above to make the recipe simpler for a young cook to be able to prepare it almost unaided. In fact, the only part of this that would require more than adult supervision is the draining of the ground beef. Serve this with a tossed salad, and you have a meal. If you want to do this as spaghetti sauce, proceed exactly as above up through the adding of the spaghetti sauce. At that point, allow the mixture to simmer about 10 minutes. Put cooked spaghetti on a plate and sprinkle a good pinch of cheese over it. Spoon on the sauce and serve immediately. Shannon says it tastes like pizza and who am I to argue. If you want to finish the meal off with a quick and easy dessert try:

CRAZY CAKE

In an UNGREASED 9x13" oblong pan, mix

3 cups plain flour
2 cups sugar
½ cup cocoa
1 tsp each, soda and salt

Make three holes in the above mixture. In one pour 1 TBSP vinegar, in next put 2 tsp vanilla and in the third put ¾ cup cooking oil. Pour 2 cups water over all and mix well with a fork. Bake 45 minutes at 350 deg.

For **ICING CRAZY CAKE**, mix 1 stick margarine, ½ cup milk and ¼ cup cocoa. Bring to a boil and simmer for 5 minutes. Beat in one box of confectioners sugar. If icing is too thick, add a little hot coffee to thin. Spread on cool cake. Enjoy!

Walter N. Lambert, Noonday Chef

CRUNCHY PEACH PIE (TV 267)

    1 9" deep dish pie shell, unbaked
    3 cups peaches, coarsely chopped
    4 TBSP flour
    1 cup brown sugar, divided
    ½ cup each, flour, orange juice and sour cream
    4 TBSP butter, room temperature
    1 cup oatmeal, uncooked

Blend peaches, flour, ½ cup brown sugar, orange juice, and sour cream. Set aside. In a separate bowl, mix butter, flour, remaining brown sugar, and oatmeal until fully blended and crumbs form. Pour peach mixture into pie shell. Sprinkle crumb mixture evenly over peaches. Bake in preheated 350 deg oven about 45 minutes or until brown.

I love peaches. In fact, the way I like them best is to slice nice, ripe peaches, place them in a bowl and put a little sour cream and brown sugar on them and eat away. But I am willing to cook with them. And this is a tasty, fancy version of almost the same dessert. I think it makes a nice finish to a spring meal. Now let me give you a couple of other quick peach recipes which are designed to make the most of the taste of the peaches.

PEACH BROWN BETTY

    4 cups bread cubes (I like sourdough bread best)
    4 cups peaches, chopped
    1 cup brown sugar
    3 TBSP grated orange rind
    ½ cup orange juice
    ½ cup butter, melted

In a well greased 1 ½ quart casserole, put about ⅓ of the bread cubes. Sprinkle half of peaches over bread crumbs. Sprinkle half of sugar and orange rind over peaches. Top with ⅓ of the bread cubes. Sprinkle on remaining peaches, orange rind, and sugar. Sprinkle on remaining bread cubes, and pour orange juice and melted butter over top, being careful to have all the bread moist. Place uncovered in a 350 deg oven, and bake about 1 hour or until the top is brown and the Betty is bubbly. Serve warm with ice cream.

Now one last go at it. Quick peach cobbler can be made by melting ½ stick of butter in an 8x8" pan. Mix together ½ cup each, self-rising flour, milk, and sugar. Pour into the melted butter. Pour 4 cups chopped peaches evenly over the top. Do not stir. Bake in a 350 deg oven about 45 minutes or until brown.

56

Walter N. Lambert, Noonday Chef

FRESH VEGETABLE DELIGHT (TV 268)

>1½ cup each, green beans, broken and cauliflower florets
>¾ cup carrots, sliced
>8 oz rotini pasta, cooked
>¼ cup each, low fat sour cream and mayonnaise
>1 TBSP each white wine vinegar and Dijon mustard
>2 TBSP fresh dill, chopped
>tomatoes for garnish

Bring about 4 cups water to a full boil. Pour in all vegetables and bring back to a full boil. Boil about 3 minutes. Drain and put into ice water to chill. Drain thoroughly. Blend all dressing ingredients, and toss with drained vegetables and the cooked pasta. Put in a covered container in the refrigerator several hours before serving. Serve garnished with tomato wedges or cherry tomatoes.

This is one of those special delights of summer. This salad will work with frozen vegetables, but it is wonderful with fresh ones. This by the way is proof that green beans do not have to be cooked to within an inch of their life to be good. We have used this salad both as a side dish and as a salad.

Now let me tell you that this will work with almost any combination of vegetables that you like. Broccoli is great mixed with cauliflower and carrots. If you do this, cook the broccoli separately from the other vegetables to preserve the color.

Now let me tell you a secret about the pasta. Use any shape which you like. Bow ties are fun. I just like the looks of the rotini. Now let me tell you something else. If you want to make this salad even lower in calories, just leave it out and you will have a pure vegetable treat.

While we are talking about vegetables, let me give you a couple of tips for fine summer side dishes. If, like a lot of us, you have been ordered to reduce the fat in your life, but would like to maintain at least a trace of flavor, try this:

MEXICAN GREEN BEANS

>1 lb fresh green beans, strings removed and broken
>¾ cup salsa
>1 TBSP fresh cilantro, chopped (optional)

Drop green beans into boiling water and cook until tender crisp. Drain beans and stir salsa into beans; bring back to a boil. Add salt if necessary. Sprinkle with cilantro and serve.

Walter N. Lambert, Noonday Chef

PEACHES AND CREAM PIE (TV 269)

    2 cups peaches, chopped, divided
    8 oz cream cheese
    ½ cup half/half
    2 eggs
    1 cup sugar
    2 TBSP flour
    2 tsp each, vanilla and lemon extract
    1 9" deep dish pie shell, unbaked

Sprinkle 1 cup of peaches into pie shell. Stir together sugar and flour. In a mixer beat cream cheese with the cream and eggs until completely mixed. Beat in the sugar/flour mixture, extracts, and remaining peaches. Pour over peaches. Bake in a preheated 350 deg oven about one hour or until puffed and brown. Allow to cool before serving.

This was inspired by a nice man who wrote asking me if I knew how to do a peach pie in an egg custard. I did not. I started working on how you might do one. I came up with two. I am sure neither of these are what **Mr. Owen** remembers, but they are pretty darned good. Now in truth, I like the second one better, but it would be impossible to do in the time we have. So on the air you get the simpler one, and if you write, you get:

PEACH MERINGUE PIE

    3 cups peaches, chopped
    2 cups sugar, divided
    4 TBSP flour
    3 eggs, separated
    1½ cup half and half
    2 tsp vanilla
    ⅛ tsp cream of tartar
    1 9" deep dish pie shell, baked

Place peaches and half cup sugar in a heavy saucepan with a tight fitting lid. Place on medium heat, and stirring occasionally, cook until just tender. In a food processor or blender, place 1 cup sugar, flour, egg yolks, half and half and blend. Add about 2 cups of the peaches and blend again. Pour cream mixture into the saucepan with peaches and cook over medium heat, stirring constantly, until the mixture boils and thickens. Cool completely. Pour cream mixture into pie shell. Place egg whites with cream of tartar into a heavy mixer, and using whip beater, beat until fluffy. Beat in ½ cup sugar gradually and beat until stiff peaks form. Spread meringue over the cream mixture, being sure to seal to the edges. Bake in a 400 deg oven until brown. Chill before serving.

Walter N. Lambert, Noonday Chef

ORIENTAL CHICKEN SALAD (TV 270)

    1 lb chicken, cooked and cubed
    1 cup green onion, sliced
    2 cups each, bean sprouts and other vegetables, chopped
    ¼ cup each, chopped mint, basil, and cilantro
    ½ cup each, soy sauce, white wine vinegar, and salad oil
    2 TBSP hot pepper sauce (Thai chili sauce preferred)
    lime slices

In a large bowl, mix chicken, onions, sprouts, chopped vegetables, mint and basil. Toss lightly. In a separate container, blend together soy sauce, vinegar, oil, and pepper sauce. Pour over chicken mixture; toss to mix. Cover tightly and refrigerate several hours or overnight. Drain and arrange on lettuce leaves on a platter and sprinkle on the chopped cilantro. Pass the lime slices to squeeze on just before eating.

I started to call this a Thai chicken salad, but it is not really hot enough. And then I started to call it Chinese, but the herbs are distinctly Thai, and then I thought about Vietnamese, but I don't know much about Vietnamese, except that they love basil. Therefore, I decided to call the salad Oriental. That way we can't go wrong.

Now once again, I am giving you this recipe as a starting point rather than a finishing point. I strongly suggest that you experiment a little. If you like a little bit of a sweet taste, add a couple of TBSP of light brown sugar to the sauce. If you like it hotter, increase the hot sauce. If you are going for really low fat, simply leave out the oil. If you want a little oil and a lot of flavor, add about two TBSP of good sesame seed oil instead of the ½ cup salad oil. If you want to go for really hot, remove the seeds from some fresh green chilies and chop them into the salad. Oh, did I tell you, the chopped vegetables above can be celery, jicama, zucchini or a mix. It is once again a matter of taste.

If you want this to appear really exotic, buy some fine Rice Noodles at an oriental food store. Unwrap the package of noodles and cut through the twisted bundle of them with sharp scissors. It will not be easy, but keep trying. When you have finished, drop the noodles into very hot oil, Allow them to cook about 30 seconds until they puff up and turn white. Scoop the noodles out with a slotted spoon and allow to drain on paper towels. When you are ready to serve the salad, spread the lettuce leaves as above. Spread the fried noodles on the lettuce leaves and chicken salad on the noodles. It is lovely and good.

Walter N. Lambert, Noonday Chef

PICKLED BEANS (TV 271)

    2 lb fresh green beans (Blue Lake preferred)
    2 cups water
    2 medium onions, sliced and separated into rings
    1 cup white vinegar
    ¾ cup sugar
    ¼ cup salt
    ¼ cup salad oil (olive oil is nice)

Break ends from the beans and string, if necessary. Break into large pieces. Place in a heavy pan with water. Cover and bring to a full boil. Cook about 5 minutes or until just tender. Drain, reserving 1 cup of water from the beans. Place beans and onion rings into a refrigerator container with a tight lid. Mix water with all other ingredients. Bring to a boil and pour over beans and onions. Allow to cool, and refrigerate for at least 48 hours before serving cold.

This is another recipe from the inimitable **Ruth DeFriese**. Some time back, I said on the show one day that Ruth had taught at Young High School for 100 years. That was an exaggeration-- several of you told me so. I have now checked, and she did not teach that long. It turns out that it was only 95. And she was wonderful every one of those years. She gave me this recipe, and frankly it didn't sound that good to me. But I tried it and she was right. (There Ruth, I said it.) Now let me let you in on a secret. If you get "a hongering" for these beans in the dead of winter, you can make them from canned beans. Use two cans of blue lake beans. Heat them to just a boil. Drain a cup of water, drain off the rest, and follow the instructions above. Are they as good. No! Are they good. Yes, indeed! Now, one more pickle recipe. I made these on the show on July 10, 1989, and people still ask me about them.

FRESH DILL PICKLES

    small pickling cucumbers to fill a gallon jar
    4 or 5 fresh dill blossoms
    2 cloves garlic, peeled
    2 cups white vinegar
    5 cups water
    ½ cup pickling salt

Pack cucumbers into washed, sterilized jar with the dill blossoms. Place garlic cloves on top. Bring all remaining ingredients to a boil; pour over the cucumbers. Allow to cool and refrigerate for two or three days before eating. Keep refrigerated. This will keep for several weeks in refrigerator.

Walter N. Lambert, Noonday Chef

ORIGINAL MILLION $ PIE (TV 272)

    2 graham cracker crusts (chilled)
    1 12 oz whipped topping (lite or regular)
    1 8 to 10 oz can crushed pineapple (drained)
    1 8 to 10 oz can mandarin oranges (drained)
    1 8 oz cream cheese (lite or regular) softened
    ¾ cup pecans
    ⅔ cup lemon juice

Stir cream cheese until smooth. Beat in fruit and pecans. Stir in whipped topping until well mixed. Stir in lemon juice until mixture begins to thicken slightly. Turn into pie shells, and refrigerate several hours or overnight. Serve cold.

You will remember that some weeks back, we had **Eva Ogle of Eva's for Lunch** on the program. She made her version of million dollar pie. Recently when going through the mail, I found a nice letter from **Mrs. Tami Jordan** who told me how her family had been making Million dollar pie for years, and pointing out the differences. It called to mind something I have known for a long time, but keep forgetting. There are few original recipes in the world. And we all keep improvising on them. I thought putting this in contrast with Eva's would be a good way to show that.

Let me give you a couple of pointers which Mrs. Jordan included with her recipe. First, always put the lemon juice in last. Always! It causes the mixture to set up, and if you put it in earlier, you will have trouble mixing and not get a good, smooth mixture. Second, if yon don't like these fruits, substitute something you do like in similar proportions.

 Now in case you did not get Eva's recipe when we did it before, I am repeating it below. This allows direct comparison.

MILLION DOLLAR PIE

    1 can sweetened condensed milk
    ¼ cup lemon juice
    1 cup crushed pineapple drained
    1 ½ cup strawberries, sliced
    1 cup chopped pecans
    1 12 (or 16)oz carton of Whipped topping

Mix milk and lemon juice. Fold in all remaining ingredients. Turn into two 9" baked pie shells. Chill before serving.

Walter N. Lambert, Noonday Chef

WANDA'S ZUCCHINI (TV 273)

    4 or 5 small zucchini squash
    ⅔ cup mayonnaise
    ⅓ cup blue cheese, crumbled
    ¼ cup Parmesan, grated
    ¼ tsp each, garlic salt and oregano

Snip the ends off the zucchini; boil until just tender. Slice thinly. Spread in even layer in 8x8 dish which has been sprayed with a cooking spray. Mix together all other ingredients and spread over the zucchini. Place in a preheated 350 deg oven, and bake about 25 minutes or until brown. Serve hot.

This is one of those too quick and too easy dishes which can be so good. We got this recipe from **Anne's cousin Wanda Kalthoff**. Wanda is a fine cook and a great herb grower. She does her herbs up in little bouquets and lets them look pretty before using them to make really good dishes. This is a really good dish.

Now, you may have noticed that this is a little heavy on the fat. I'm sorry about that. I have tried it with low fat mayonnaise and with low fat sour cream, and it did not work. Scrimp on something else this week, and go ahead with the recipe as we have prescribed.

This dish works best with small, fresh squash. However, if the squash is a little on the big side, you can still do ok. If you are using zucchini, slice the squash in half lengthwise. Cook until just barely tender. Using a spoon, scoop out the seeds. Mix the ingredients as above except that you should add ⅔ cup dry bread crumbs. Use the mixture to lightly fill the cavity in the squash and bake until the center is fully melted and nicely browned. This will make enough filling for 2 large squash. Each half will make a generous serving.

A word in passing about the Parmesan cheese is appropriate. I like the flavor that plain old dry Parmesan gives this dish. In fact, I sometimes sprinkle a little extra cheese onto the dish after I spread the cheese mixture around. However, if you are not put off by the oil involved, you can use fresh Parmesan. Substitute fresh, finely grated cheese in the same amount.

Also, the shape you cut the squash into does not matter. I have suggested slicing it because that is the easiest way I have found. If you like the looks of halves with the cheese evenly divided, go for it. Chunks also work nicely. Oh, I almost forgot. Yellow squash or a mixture of yellow and zucchini will work as well. Just remember. Do not overcook the squash.

Walter N. Lambert, Noonday Chef

LUSCIOUS CHICKEN LOAF (TV 274)

4 cups cooked chicken, chopped fine
1 cup bread crumbs
4 eggs, beaten
2 cans condensed cream of chicken soup
2 TBSP onion, chopped fine
¼ tsp garlic, chopped fine
½ tsp each, salt and pepper

Combine all ingredients, and pack into a well greased (or cooking spray coated) loaf pan. Bake one hour at 350 deg. Allow to cool for a few minutes. Turn out onto a warm platter to serve. If you wish, you may top the loaf with a sauce which is made by heating an undiluted can of cream of chicken soup mixed with about ¼ cup of pimento.

This recipe comes from a fine lady here in Knoxville, **Mrs. H. A. Bernhardt**. Her friends call her "**Sparky**", and believe me, she brings plenty of spark to whatever she does. She is also the mother of one of my favorite sisters-in-law, and we are glad we know her. She has been kind enough to let us wander through her fine recipe collection and make some copies.

Sparky tells us that she usually pours the sauce over the whole chicken loaf. I do not recommend that. Keep it on the side and pour a little onto each slice on the plate. This way, you keep the left over loaf sauce free. The reason you want to do that is that cold, sliced chicken loaf makes great chicken sandwiches. Oh, and by the way, the original recipe did not have the garlic. But this recipe is perfect for it so I put it in. Here is another of Mrs. Bernhardt's good recipes.

CHICKEN SCALLOP

⅓ cup rice
2 cups chicken broth
2 ½ cups cooked chicken, diced
⅓ cup celery, chopped
¼ cup pimentos, chopped
2 eggs, beaten
¾ tsp salt
pinch of poultry seasoning (or rubbed sage)

Cook rice in chicken broth until almost tender (about 20 minutes). Combine with remaining ingredients. Pour into casserole sprayed with a cooking spray. Bake in a slow oven (300 to 325 deg) about 45 to 50 minutes. Serve hot.

Walter N. Lambert, Noonday Chef

BUTTERMILK SALAD (TV 275)

1 large can crushed pineapple
1 large (or 2 small) pkg strawberry **Jell-O**
2 cups buttermilk
1 12 oz pkg whipped topping
1 cup strawberries
1 cup nuts

Heat the pineapple to boiling. Stir in the Jell-o until it is dissolved. Cool completely. Add buttermilk, whipped topping, fruit, and nuts. Turn into a 2 quart mold and chill until set.

What you see above is a coincidence. Actually, it is an example of several great minds working together. First, when I was at the **Knox County Farmers' Market** recently, I ran into **Mr. and Mrs. H. W. Brabson** from up toward Gibbs way. We were talking about the wonderful buttermilk that **Mrs. Cheri Cruze** has for sale there. **Margarete Brabson** asked if I knew about buttermilk salad. I allowed as how I thought I used to, but had forgotten. She kindly sent me a recipe.

On the same day it arrived, the nice lady at the front desk here at **WKXT** gave me a recipe which her friend **Frances** had given her for buttermilk salad. What you see above is a combination of Margarete's and Frances' buttermilk salad.

Now let me tell you a couple of things about low-calorie Buttermilk Salad. First, you can use sugar free Jell-O and lite whipped topping, which will cut down dramatically on the sugar and calorie content of this dish. Second, use no-sugar-added pineapple and cut down even further. Third, do not limit yourself to strawberry Jell-O and strawberries. I tried it with lemon Jell-O and added no additional fruit, and it was excellent. Fourth, if you are cutting back on fats and calories, leave out the nuts altogether. Or even better, as Margarete Brabson suggests, use them as a garnish rather than including them. Fifth, you can make this with commercial buttermilk and it is good. If you go to the **Farmers' Market** and get buttermilk from Mrs. Cruze, it will be much better. (You may want to get some ice cream while you are there. She makes the best in the whole wide world.)

Now let me make a confession to you. I really don't like gelatin salads very much. My mother loves them, and she periodically questions my judgment on this score. But what can I tell you. Is that her favorite is to make lime Jell-O, making sure to use sugar free, and folding into it a generous portion of small curd cottage cheese and some sugar free crushed pineapple. And that is my last tip. Use lime Jell-O and this is delightful.

64

Walter N. Lambert, Noonday Chef

SPICY BEAN SALAD (TV 277)

    1 lb pinto beans
    1 each, medium green pepper, red sweet pepper and onion, chopped fine
    1 can whole kernel corn, drained
    ¼ cup each, catsup and olive oil
    ½ cup vinegar
    2 TBSP each, Worcestershire sauce, chili powder, and Dijon mustard
    2 tsp each ground cumin and salt
    ½ tsp pepper

Cook the beans according to package directions until just tender. **DO NOT OVERCOOK.** Drain and cool. Toss beans with peppers, onion, and corn. In a saucepan, combine all remaining ingredients. Bring to a boil and pour over beans. Toss to mix. Cover and refrigerate overnight before serving.

When I was growing up, a varied diet meant beans and potatoes one day and potatoes and beans the next. And then beans went out of style. They were high calorie and high carbohydrate and...they had that... other problem. And they went out of style.

Then, we discovered that if we were going to cut down on meat, it was imperative that we get the right kinds of vegetable protein in the right combinations, and we re-discovered beans. All kinds of beans. In a visit recently to the **Fetzer Winery Gardens** in beautiful downtown Hopland, California, we were shown almost fifty kinds of beans they now grow. For this salad, we used pinto beans. Plain old pinto beans.

By the way, take any recipe which calls for kidney beans or red beans and try substituting pintos for them. I think it helps the flavor and these beans have a nice texture.

Oh, did I mention that this works nicely with canned beans? Simply open about 3 cans of pintos, wash them off in a colander, then proceed as above. And while we are at it, it also works nicely with white beans, either great northern or navy beans.

You have made baked beans with limas? Nothing to it. Cook either dry green or white limas according to package direction until barely tender. Drain, reserving one cup of liquid. Blend one cup liquid with 1 cup catsup (or chili sauce), ¼ cup brown sugar or molasses, 2 TBSP salad mustard, and ½ cup dry onion flakes (or I medium onion chopped). Mix with beans. Turn into a 2 quart casserole and bake uncovered until thick and brown on top. Serve hot or at room temperature.

Walter N. Lambert, Noonday Chef

A TASTE OF TENNESSEE (TV 278)

1 lb country sausage (**Tennessee Pride or Jimmy Dean** brand)
1 medium onion, chopped
3 cups tomato, peeled, seeded and chopped
¼ cup fresh basil, chopped
2 cups grated sharp cheese (**Tennessee Valley** brand)
1 cup **White Lily** Self-rising flour
2 TBSP oil with milk to make ½ cup

Cook sausage in a heavy, ovenproof skillet until brown. Stir in onion, and cook until soft. Drain any excess grease. Stir in tomatoes. Bring back to a full boil. Stir in basil and remove from heat. Spread cheese over top. Mix flour with oil and milk. Pat out to fit the top of the skillet. Lay on hot sausage mixture, and bake 20 minutes in a 375 deg oven. Serve hot.

This dish is based on the idea that it is possible to put together a dish with almost any taste which is made entirely from products grown in **Tennessee**. You notice that I suggested **Tennessee Pride or Jimmy Dean** sausage. Both are made in Tennessee. By the way, use mild, hot, or sage to suit your own tastes. Onions are grown commercially in West Tennessee. **Grainger County, in East Tennessee** (along with a number of other counties in this area) have become famous for their tomatoes, which are grown both to be sold fresh and to can. If, perchance, you should not want to peel, seed, and chop tomatoes, use a 28 oz can of **Kroger** brand crushed tomatoes.

The cheese in this recipe is the only ingredient which is not readily available at your favorite **Kroge**r store. I have used cheese made at the **Tennessee Valley Cheese Co.** in Morriston, TN., which is near McMinnville. You can write for their catalog at P.O. Box 8, Highway 55, Morriston, TN, 37357. Or you could just call them at 1-800-4-CHEESE, and they will send a catalog with several wonderful choices. We have eaten the sharp cheddar and the hot pepper cheese. Both are outstanding.

This program came about because a nice young man who works for the **Tennessee Department of Agriculture** came on the show and talked about the range of foods available in Tennessee. His name is **Stanley Trout**, and we enjoyed talking to him. He subsequently sent me a list more than 4 pages long of food products made in Tennessee.

Like **White Lily Flour**, of course, which has always been one of my favorites. Next week, we are going to use a new White Lily product, bread flour, and it is as good as everything else they make. And then there is **JFG**, **Martha White**, **Goo Goo clusters**, and,.... well, you get the idea.

66

Walter N. Lambert, Noonday Chef

HERB BATTER BREAD (TV 279)

   3 cups bread flour
   1 cup non-fat cottage cheese
   2 TBSP each, dry onion flakes, sugar, and dill weed
   1 tsp salt
   1 cup milk
   1 pkg yeast dissolved in ¼ cup warm water

In a food processor, using the plastic blade, combine flour, onion, sugar, and dill. Pulse to blend. Add all remaining ingredients, and run about 2 minutes or until completely blended. Turn into a 2 quart casserole, and smooth the top with wet fingers. Cover with a dish towel and allow to rise at room temperature one hour, or until doubled in bulk. Bake in a 350 deg oven about 45 to 50 minutes or until brown. Serve hot.

Variations: batter breads are a good quick, easy way to have the good flavor of yeast breads without all the kneading, rising, shaping and stuff which goes with most loaf bread. This is one which exemplifies that kind of bread. If fresh dill is available, you may substitute ¼ cup chopped fresh dill for the dry. You can even substitute fresh onion for the dry. However, if you use both fresh onion and dill, cut the milk back to about ¾ cup or the batter will be too soft. If you are fortunate enough to not have to worry about the fat, let me give you a couple of great variations. Instead of the cottage cheese, use one cup of grated cheddar cheese. Or use 1 cup grated hot pepper cheese and leave out the dill altogether.

This also makes a really good and easy cinnamon bread for breakfast.

CINNAMON BATTER BREAD

   3 cups bread flour
   1 cup non fat cottage cheese
   ½ cup brown sugar
   1 TBSP cinnamon
   1 cup milk
   1 pkg yeast dissolved in warm water

Using the plastic blade, place all ingredients in the food processor and run until fully blended. Turn into a 2 quart casserole which has been sprayed with a cooking spray. Allow to rise and bake at 350 for 45 minutes. If you like, you may work in ½ cup raisins at the end of mixing.

As an added bonus, both of these recipes work nicely in a bread machine.

Walter N. Lambert, Noonday Chef

SOUR CREAM RAISIN PIE (TV 280)

½ cup sugar
2 TBSP flour
1 cup sour cream (divided)
2 cups raisins
2 eggs
1 tsp vanilla
½ tsp nutmeg
1 9" pie shell, pre-baked

In a heavy saucepan, mix together sugar and flour. Beat in eggs. Stir in ¾ cup sour cream and 2 cups raisins. Place over medium heat. Stir constantly until mixture comes to a boil and thickens. Stir in vanilla and nutmeg. Allow to cool, turn into pie shell, spreading evenly. Smooth remaining sour cream over the top. Chill before serving.

My **mother** always loved raisin pies. She made them whenever possible. My **father** always made fun of them. He ate them, but he made fun of them. I don't want to go into how he made fun of them, but trust me he did. He was wrong. Now I must admit that raisins generally become an add-on rather than the main event. After all, what would bran muffins be without raisins. Or oatmeal cookies. Or bread pudding. Or cinnamon rolls. They are great added to stuffing for roast pork or for baked chicken. But generally, we do not put them center stage. Raisin pie does that. In case you don't have one, here is a more traditional raisin pie.

RAISIN PIE

2½ cups raisins
2¾ cups water
½ cup molasses
½ tsp salt
¼ tsp cloves
1 tsp cinnamon
3 TBSP each, cornstarch and water
1 tsp grated lemon rind
1 TBSP lemon juice
pastry for a two crust 9" pie

Combine cornstarch and 3 TBSP water; stir to blend. Mix raisins, water, molasses, salt, and spices. Stir in cornstarch mixture. Cook, stirring until thickened. Stir in lemon juice and rind. Turn into a 9" pie plate which has been lined with pastry. Roll remaining pastry very thin and use to cover filling. Seal edges, and cut vents into the top of the pie in an attractive pattern. Bake in a 400 deg oven about 40 minutes or until brown. Cool before serving.

Walter N. Lambert, Noonday Chef

SUGAR FREE APPLE BUTTER (TV 281)

1 lb. dried un-sulphured apples (approximately 5 - 6 cups)
1 12 oz. can unsweetened apple juice concentrate
½ juice can water
2 tsp ground cinnamon

Place all ingredients in heavy sauce pan. Bring to a boil. Reduce heat to a simmer. Several times during simmering process stir apples down into the juice. Allow to simmer about 20 minutes or until apples are very tender. Add additional water if necessary, but apples should be very thick. Blend in food processor or blender until smooth. Store in refrigerator.

I love apples. I love apple butter. But they usually have lots of added sugar. In fact, most apple butter has about half apples and half sugar. These are an exception. A version of this recipe came to me from our good friend **Margarete Brabston**. She tends to have good recipes. Now in her version, there is 1 tsp cinnamon, ½ tsp allspice and ½ tsp cloves. Try it. I personally prefer just the taste of cinnamon, but you may not agree.

Be warned. If you are diabetic, or for any other reason are greatly restricting your sugar intake, you must still use this apple butter in moderation. It is made sweet by concentrating the natural sugar of the apples. This happens both because of dried apples and concentrating the juice. But I think you will find that just a little of this goes a long way to give a good apple taste with relatively low sugar.

Let me give you a version of this that I have sometimes for breakfast when I am being a good boy. Toast a slice of good white bread. While still hot, spread thinly with this apple butter. Over that, spread a thin layer of non fat cottage cheese. Sprinkle a little extra cinnamon over the top and run under the broiler for just a minute. Good stuff. Healthy too. Don't you just hate it.

Now let me say a word about fruit sugar which is called fructose. It is now available in dry, crystal form which can be substituted for regular sugar. Generally, you can substitute about ½ to ⅔'s as much fructose as regular sugar in any recipe.

Good baked apples can be made by peeling and slicing apples and placing them in a Pyrex dish, which has been sprayed with a cooking spray. Sprinkle with cinnamon, then with crystal fructose. Cover with foil, and bake in a 350 deg oven about 30 minutes. Uncover and allow to brown slightly. Serve hot.

Walter N. Lambert, Noonday Chef

POTATO-COLLARD CHOWDER (TV 282)

2 TBSP butter or margarine
1 large onion, chopped
4 medium sized potatoes, peeled and cubed (about 4 cups)
2 14½ cans chicken stock
1 12 oz can beer
1 lb (approximately 8 cups) collard greens, chopped
1½ cup milk
¼ cup flour
1 TBSP cumin
salt and pepper to taste

Heat butter in large heavy soup pot. Add onion, and saute until tender and starting to brown. Add potatoes, chicken stock and beer. Bring to a boil and stir in greens. Cover and simmer about I hour or until the potatoes are very soft. Add the cumin, increase the heat to bring mixture to a full boil. Mix the four thoroughly with the milk, and stir into boiling mixture. Stir until thick. You may puree the soup if you wish.

It's fall. It's time for soup. I grew up loving soup. **Anne** grew up thinking it was what you ate when you were sick. I have had to educate her. I think I am making some headway. This soup has helped in her education. It has potatoes, which everybody swears by in soup but then treats collards in a way I haven't seen them treated before.

Now I need to tell you one thing about this soup. This version is one I developed which is relatively low fat. In the original version of this, it was made with butter, white wine, and cream. It was truly fat city. I found it a little too much. However, I liked the basic taste of it.
By the way, if you are a dedicated collard hater, use kale. You need change nothing else. Just substitute the same amount of curly kale and have at it. Turnip greens would work as well. Don't use spinach. It is too soft.

The **Chinese** do a version of a greens soup which I like very much. It basically is a good stock with some flavor added. I use about 8 cups of good, defatted stock. Bring this to a boil; stir in about ¼ cup soy sauce, 2 TBSP sugar, and about 1 TBSP shredded fresh ginger. You may add water chestnuts (chopped), bamboo shoots (shredded) or shiitake mushrooms cut into slices. Bring to a full boil and add about 3 cups of shredded spinach. Allow just to come back to a boil and serve very hot. Sprinkle the top with thinly sliced green onions, if you wish. The flavor will be light and fresh and just the thing at the start of a big meal.

Walter N. Lambert, Noonday Chef

SPICY MOLASSES CAKE (TV 283)

¾ cup butter or margarine, softened
½ cup sugar
1 cup molasses
2 eggs
2½ cup self rising flour
1 tsp each, allspice, cinnamon and cloves
1 cup hot water

Cream butter and sugar. Beat in eggs and molasses. Mix spices with flour and beat into molasses mixture. Beat in hot water. Turn into a greased and floured tube or bundt pan, and bake about 45 minutes in a preheated 350 deg oven. Allow to cool in the pan 5 minutes before turning out.

This is a wonderful old fashioned spice cake which is enhanced with molasses. As far as I am concerned, that is an unbeatable combination. While I have you bake it in a bundt pan, it works nicely as layers. Simply turn into two 8" pans and bake for about 35 minutes. If you want to turn this cake into something fancy for a dinner party, bake it in layers and ice it with a good caramel icing. Alternatively, you might want to ice it instead with whipped cream frosting to which you have added about a half cup of powdered sugar and a couple of tablespoons of **Jack Daniels** whiskey. Spread a thick layer of the whipped cream on the bottom layer of cake. Place on the top layer, and top it all with another layer of the whipped cream. Call it something clever like **Sin on a Plate** and listen for the compliments.

Here is a very old molasses recipe given to us by our neighbor **Dr. Nell Logan**. It is from a cookbook published before I was born. Now that's old. It has an unusual taste which grows on you.

MOLASSES PIE

½ cup cracker crumbs
1 cup sugar
¾ cup molasses
¼ cup cider vinegar (or lemon juice)
¼ cup melted butter
2 eggs, beaten
1 tsp cinnamon or nutmeg
1 9" deep dish pie shell, unbaked

Mix ingredients in order given. Turn into pie shell, and bake 30 minutes in a preheated 350 deg oven. Serve cold.

Walter N. Lambert, Noonday Chef

PUMPKIN BREAD PUDDING (TV 284)

      3 cups soft bread crumbs
      1 cup pumpkin, cooked and mashed
      1 cup sugar
      2 eggs
      2 cups milk
      ½ tsp each cinnamon, nutmeg and allspice
      2 tsp vanilla

In a 2 quart casserole dish, sprayed with a cooking spray, sprinkle bread crumbs. Beat together the sugar and eggs. Beat in all remaining ingredients. Pour over bread crumbs, and allow to stand at least 30 minutes. Place in a preheated 350 deg oven and bake about one hour. Serve warm.

Bread pudding is one of those desserts that people pretend they never eat, but that almost everyone finds comforting. It is also something which gives itself to an almost endless range of variations. What you see above is one of those variations. Now do not allow yourself to be limited by this. If you like coconut in your bread pudding, by all means add some to this one. About ¾ cup should be about right. The same goes for raisins. If you like them, add them. Now it is only fair to tell you that I have used this set of spices because it is the combination I like best with pumpkin. If you like, simply use pumpkin pie spice. It is a little strong on cloves for my tastes. But, about ¼ tsp of cloves added to the combination above is not bad.

This bread pudding would not be bad with whiskey sauce. The classic **New Orleans Whiskey Sauce** is made by blending 1½ cups powdered sugar into 1 stick of melted butter, stirring over medium heat until the butter is completely absorbed. Remove from heat and beat in two egg yolks. Beat in about ½ cup (or to taste) good bourbon whiskey. The sauce will thicken as it cools. Serve warm.

Walter N. Lambert, Noonday Chef

SPECIAL MEAT LOAF WITH VARIATIONS (TV 285)

 ¾ lb each, ground beef, ground pork and ground ham
 ½ cup each, onion and green pepper, chopped fine
 ½ cup bread crumbs
 1 tsp each salt and black pepper
 2 TBSP soy sauce and Worcestershire sauce
 2 eggs

Mix the meat thoroughly. Mix all remaining ingredients, and blend with the meat using a wooden spoon (or your hands). Pack firmly into a loaf pan which has been sprayed with a cooking spray. Bake in a preheated 350 deg oven about 1 hour or until brown and firm. Drain off fat and allow to cool in the pan about 10 minutes before turning out onto a warm plate.

Meat loaf is still the ultimate comfort food. There is just something plain and good about it. This is kind of a fancy one, but it is still good. I like it hot with some mashed potatoes or cold on sandwiches. It makes me feel good.

Now a couple of words about variations on this theme. It is not necessary to mix these meats to get a good meat loaf. You can do that with just ground beef. I admit that this one is better, but 2 lbs of beef will work. As will 1 lb of ground beef and 1 lb of bulk pork sausage. As will 1 lb of beef and 1 lb of turkey sausage. As will...do I need to go on?!

Now I should tell you that some folks like to jazz up the seasonings a little. Be my guest. Try some chopped dry oregano, parsley, and sweet basil. Use about 1 tsp of each. Or a TBSP of fresh basil and parsley. Or leave out the green peppers and add about 1 tsp of finely chopped garlic.

Let me now say a word about gravy. If you must get involved in this ritual to fat, I will tell you an easy way. Drain the grease and cooking liquid off the meat loaf into a measuring cup. Add water, or some combination of catsup and water, to make two cups. Pour into a saucepan. Beat two TBSP flour into another ¼ cup of cold water. Stir into the pan drippings and bring to a boil, stirring. Continue to stir until thick. Serve hot.

I suppose by now you have noticed that I have not put much in the way of tomatoes into this meat loaf. Again, that is a matter of taste. If you like a tomato flavor, add ¼ cup catsup with the other ingredients in the basic meat loaf recipe. When the meat loaf has been baking about 45 minutes, spread another ¼ cup of catsup over the top and allow to brown as the meat loaf finishes cooking. Is that simple enough?

Walter N. Lambert, Noonday Chef

CURRIED PORK CHOPS (TV 286)

    4 pork chops
    1 medium onion, chopped
    1 medium apple, peeled, cored and chopped
    2 TBSP cooking oil
    3 TBSP curry powder
    ¾ cup Uncle Ben's converted rice
    1¼ cup water

Brown pork chops in the oil in a heavy ovenproof skillet with a tight fitting lid. Remove from skillet and cook the onion in the oil until lightly brown. Stir in apples and curry powder and cook two or three minutes, stirring constantly. Add rice and return pork chops to the pan; pour water over the mixture. Cover and place in a preheated 350 deg oven for about 45 minutes. Serve hot.

Here we go again. This is another of those meals in a skillet I am so fond of. But this mixture with a green salad makes a perfect light supper.

Oh, wait, you say, I don't eat pork. Fine, I say, substitute four skinless, boneless, chicken breast halves and follow the instructions above exactly. So there!

Now a word about those apples and onions. They make a great combination. They are nice, off-setting flavors which are very complimentary. The fruit also adds greatly to the taste of the curry. In fact, I have been known to add a handful of raisins along with the rice and water. Or even, when the pork and rice have been placed on the plate, sprinkle with a few toasted slivered almonds. All these flavors work nicely together.

Now let me give you a couple of other alternatives to this dish. Let's just suppose that you are cutting down on carbohydrates in your diet, and you want better control than you can get with the rice cooked this way. Then try this. Drop the rice and water from the recipe. Instead, use two cups of shredded cabbage. When you add the apples, stir in cabbage and cook stirring about 5 minutes, or until the cabbage begins to wilt. Place pork chops (or chicken) back into the skillet, cover and bake as above. You will find you will have a delicious vegetable blend which makes a nice side dish for the meat. When you do it this way, you may find you have some excess liquid. I suggest removing the vegetables with a slotted spoon. Then cook the liquid down on top of the stove until it starts to thicken naturally. Then pour it over the meat and vegetables. This will depend on unknowns, like how tight the lid on your pot fits.

74

Walter N. Lambert, Noonday Chef

APPLE CRANBERRY CHUTNEY (TV 287)

    3 cups apples, peeled and chopped
    1½ cups cranberries
    ½ cup golden raisins
    3 TBSP each, brown sugar and cider vinegar
    2 TBSP orange peel
    ½ tsp each cloves, nutmeg, cinnamon

Combine all ingredients in a non aluminum saucepan. Place over high heat, and bring to a boil, stirring constantly. Reduce heat and simmer, uncovered, 15 minutes or until apples are tender. Remove from heat and allow to cool. Cover and chill.

This is a good substitute for traditional cranberry sauce to serve with turkey. I personally think it is very nice. Of course, I like the strange cranberry sauce with sour cream and horseradish which I made a couple of years ago. That will give you some idea of how strange I can be.

Now let me tell you that this version can be spiced up a little by adding 3 TBSP of **Cointreau** (or other orange liqueur) with the other ingredients. This is not necessary, but is good. You may also want to experiment a little with the spices as well to find the mixture that appeals to you most.

This recipe originally called for the mixture to run in a food processor until it was smooth after it had been cooked. I have conferred with a number of experts, and we all agree that we like it better chunky. Do whichever you like. Did I mention that I love this on turkey sandwiches? I love this on turkey sandwiches.

Now a little bonus:

CRANBERRY SALSA

    2 cans whole berry cranberry sauce
    ½ cup green onions, sliced thin
    1 TBSP chopped jalapeno peppers
    1 TBSP chopped cilantro
    1 TBSP lime juice

Combine all ingredients in a large bowl. Cover and allow to stand for at least an hour before serving at room temperature with nacho chips. This also makes a fine topping for baked chicken breasts. Bake the breast about 45 minutes. Top with salsa and return to oven about 15 minutes or until brown.

Walter N. Lambert, Noonday Chef

EASY NUT BARS (TV 288)

1 roll ready to bake chocolate chip cookie dough
1½ cup chopped nuts (walnuts or pecans)
½ cup each, chocolate chips and butterscotch chips

Coat a 9x13" pan with a cooking spray. Cut the cookie dough into small pieces and spread over bottom of pan, pressing to coat the bottom of the pan evenly. Sprinkle the nuts over cookie dough and press in lightly. Bake in a preheated 350 deg oven about 15 minutes or until lightly brown. Remove from the oven and sprinkle chocolate and butterscotch chips over the tops of the cookies. Return to the oven for a couple of minutes until the chips melt. Spread over the top of the cookies. Allow to cool completely in the pan. Cut into bars or triangles.

This is designed to make a very simple task look much more complex than it really is. The **Christmas** holiday is enough trouble without having to worry about whether you have cookies when you need them. Besides, I will not tell that they are from a mix if you won't.

Now let me give you another little tip. You can make a great looking gift from half a roll of sugar cookie dough. Here is how to make a quick Christmas wreath.

CHRISTMAS COOKIE WREATH

Cover a large cookie sheet with aluminum foil. Slice half a roll of very cold sugar cookie dough into eighteen slices about ¼" thick. Arrange the slices with one edge slightly overlapping to form a circle on the foil. Sprinkle with green sugar. Bake about 15 minutes or until just starting to brown. Remove from oven and allow to cool on the foil. Remove carefully from the foil and decorate with small candies to look like a wreath. Add a little bow and you have a great gift. Use that other half to make another wreath or the following treat.

Spray small muffin tins with a cooking spray. Press a small piece of commercial sugar cookie dough (one whole roll should make 48 cookies) into each cup. Press a small (unwrapped) **Reece's Peanut Butter Cup** into the center of each piece of dough. Bake at 350 deg for about 15 minutes or until browned. Allow to cool in the pan at least 10 minutes before removing.

Now I'll bet with a little work, you could think of any number of other ingenious ways to get the most from this good dough. Good luck and good cooking.

Walter N. Lambert, Noonday Chef

HOLIDAY STUFFED TURKEY (TV 289)

1 turkey breast (approx. 3 lb., boned)
1½ cup mushrooms, sliced
½ cup each, carrots, celery, onion (minced)
1 tsp thyme
¼ tsp tarragon
¼ loaf bread (cubed)
¼ cup brown gravy
1 TBSP butter
salt and pepper to taste

After boning turkey, butterfly breast to flatten using a meat mallet. Saute mushrooms until half cooked. Mix with the rest of the ingredients. Spread mushroom mixture evenly over turkey. Roll up turkey tightly in a double layer of **Saran Wrap** and tie the ends. Bake at 350 deg until internal temperature of 160 degrees is reached. Remove from oven and let rest for 10 to 15 minutes. Slice into 12 slices. Serve with cornbread dressing, turkey gravy and cranberry relish.

Our guest chef today is **David Colburn** who is executive chef at **Dollywood**. Perhaps his cooking is what keeps **Miss Dolly** so healthy looking. This is a great variation on an old standard. David and the good folks at Dollywood are a major contribution to this community and many a charity has benefitted from their good works. It is a privilege for us to have him on the show. Here is the classic recipe for cornbread dressing which we used on the show on November 13, 1989. To date, we have had more requests for this recipe than any we have ever done.

DRESSING WITH TURKEY OR CHICKEN

4 cups each, cornbread and biscuit crumbs
2 medium onions, minced
4 stalks celery, cut small
2 tsp each, black pepper and salt
1 tsp ground cayenne pepper
1 to 2 TBSP rubbed sage
2 cups water
4 cups hot chicken or turkey broth (approximately)

Place chopped onion, celery, and water in saucepan. Bring to a boil. Place crumbs and rest of ingredients, except broth, in large mixing bowl; mix thoroughly and pour the onion-celery mixture over. Add broth and stir until mixture is soft but still holds its shape. Taste and adjust seasonings if necessary. Place in a greased, large, flat baking dish and bake in a 350 deg oven until browned and firm. May be served hot, cold, or warm.

Walter N. Lambert, Noonday Chef

MEAL IN A LOAF (TV 291)

> 1 loaf **Kroger's in house baked California Sour Dough Bread**
> 1 pound stew beef, cut in 1" cubes, dredged in flour
> 2 TBSP cooking oil
> 1 cup each: Diced onions, potatoes, carrots, mushrooms
> 1 8 oz. can tomato sauce
> 1 can chicken broth
> ¼ tsp garlic powder
> salt and pepper to taste

Brown well-coated beef cubes, sprinkled with salt, pepper, and garlic powder in hot oil in a heavy skillet or roaster. Add tomato sauce, chicken broth, diced carrots, onions, and potatoes. Simmer over low heat for 2 hours. Slice top off of sour dough bread. Scoop out inside, leaving about one inch of bread around the sides and bottom. (Save stuffing for bread pudding). Fill empty loaf with this delicious stew, replace "lid" and bake about 25 minutes in a 350 deg oven.

I love this meal. I love the look and smell of it. I especially love the fact that the stew can be made the day ahead and placed in the refrigerator. About a half hour before you plan to serve it, place it into the loaf of bread, put it in the oven to get hot, and you are ready to go. Perfect for a busy night when you have shopped til you are ready to drop.

You simply scoop out the stew, tear off a piece of the bowl and eat up. A green salad turns this into a meal.

Now a word about this bread. It is fairly new at **Kroger** and comes in a number of shapes. If you want this to be really fancy, choose small loaves and make individual servings. That is a lot of trouble but is worth it. For this recipe, you need the square loaf. Be sure that it is not pre-sliced.

Now this bread is great for a lot of other things. As noted above, it makes a great bread pudding. You will have about three or four cups of crumbs from one of the square loaves. Tear them up coarsely and place in a 1½ to 2 quart casserole. Toss in a handful of coconut or raisins. Mix together 2 cups sugar, 2 eggs, 2 cups milk, and 2 tsp vanilla; pour over the bread mixture. Allow to stand about an hour at room temperature. Bake at 350 deg for about 45 minutes and serve warm with a little ice cream or even whipped cream for a real treat.

I personally prefer this bread sliced fairly thick, toasted, spread with pimento cheese, or peanut butter, or even just cream cheese. It will stick to your ribs (and your hips probably.)

Walter N. Lambert, Noonday Chef

MODERN SUGARPLUMS (TV 292)

1½ cups sugar, divided
8 oz almonds (toasted)
zest of one medium orange
8 oz pitted dates
8 oz Sunsweet assorted dried fruit
one orange, peeled and seeds removed

In a heavy duty food processor, place 1 cup sugar, almonds, and orange zest. Run about 30 seconds or until nuts are coarsely ground. Add dates; run until chopped. Repeat with the dried fruit. Add the orange and run until it is completely chopped. Stir to mix completely. Shape into balls using a scant teaspoon of mixture for each. Roll in remaining sugar. Place on waxed paper on a cookie sheet and allow to air dry over night. Store in a tight container.

All your life, you have talked about those children with "visions of sugar plums" dancing in their heads. Did you ever eat a sugar plum? Of course not! This is a modern version of the ancient candy which was made by mixing sugar with ground nuts and dried fruits. Almost everything was used at one time or another to bind it together. I decided that I like orange best. If you do not want to bother with the whole orange and getting the seeds out and all that, simply use enough orange juice (about ¼ to ½ cup) to hold the mixture together. I personally like the orange better. Do not leave out the zest. Remember, that you want only the orange part of the peel. Use a peeler or a good zester to remove it without the pith under it.

Now the assortment of dried fruits which I have used is completely arbitrary. If you do not like dates, use all pitted prunes. If you like a tarter flavor, use 8 oz of dried apricots instead of the mixed fruit. If you like walnuts better than almonds, use them. It will not be a bit traditional, but why should that stop you. Simply experiment until you get a flavor you like. How about lemon zest instead of orange? Sure!

Now let me tell you about a first cousin to this which we used to make. It is in one of the earlier cookbooks, but it bears repeating. Grind one whole orange with only the seeds removed with about ¾ lb dried apricots and 1 cup sugar. Shape into balls and roll in additional sugar. Allow to air dry at least over night and store in a tight tin.

Now, a reasonable question is whether you could do this without a food processor. You could. I wouldn't. If you want to try it, grind the nuts, zest, and dried fruits with a food mill, then mix with sugar and orange juice, and proceed.

Walter N. Lambert, Noonday Chef

BAKED BLACK EYED PEAS (TV 293)

    1 lb dried black eyed peas
    1 8 oz can tomato sauce
    1 10 oz can chopped tomatoes with green chilies
    ½ cup molasses (or honey)
    2 cups hot water (approx)
    ¼ lb hog jowl bacon, chopped (optional)

Wash peas, cover with hot water, and allow to soak for several hours or overnight. Drain. Stir in the tomato sauce, tomatoes, bacon (if you are using it), and molasses. Turn into an ovenproof casserole with a tight fitting lid. Pour water over peas. Cover and bake in a 325 deg oven about 1½ hours. Remove cover and bake an addition ½ hour. Serve hot.

As anyone who has been properly raised knows, it is downright dangerous to not have black eyed peas cooked with hog jowl on **New Years Day**. Most folks are of the opinion that you do this out of necessity rather than because you like black eyed peas. I have to admit that I like them, but then who can account for taste.

Over the past several years, we have made them into salad, jambalaya, dip, and all sorts of ways to disguise them. This year, I decided to give them a little flavor and go right at the tradition head on.

Now a word about the hog jowl. Purists will tell you that this is vital to maintain the lucky nature of this dish. Who am I to argue? But I will tell you that these baked peas are quite good without the bacon. In fact, that produces a high fiber, fat free dish which is good and good for you. Can you make this dish with canned peas? Yes, if you just must. I do not recommend it. The peas simply cook up too much, and you get black eyed mush instead of peas. However, in the interest of being broad minded about things, I will tell you that you can drain a couple of cans of peas, mix them with tomato sauce and tomatoes, ¼ cup of the sweetener, and heat the mixture to boiling on top of the stove. Allow to simmer about 10 minutes and serve. It is not as good as the baked version, but not too bad.

One last word about New Years and luck. In addition to black eyed peas and hog jowl, custom calls for having greens on New Years day. The peas bring luck, the greens bring money. If you want good fresh greens, wash about 3 or 4 bunches of greens (any kind) and chop coarsely. Place in a kettle with a tight fitting lid with a little bacon and a couple of cups of water and bring to a boil. Reduce heat, and simmer about 2 hours or until tender. If you want, you can cook an additional few minutes to boil out any excess water. Don't forget the cornbread.

Walter N. Lambert, Noonday Chef

CHOCOLATE CAKE (TV 294)

    2 cups flour
    1 cup sugar
    ½ cup cocoa
    2 tsp soda
    1 cup each *JFG* **Mayonnaise** and water
    1 tsp vanilla

Stir together all dry ingredients. Add all remaining ingredients and beat to mix thoroughly. Turn into 2 greased and floured 8" or 9" cake pans, and bake at 350 deg for 30 to 35 minutes or until it tests done. Allow to cool in pan about 15 minutes before turning out. Can also be baked in a bundt pan at 325 deg for about 45 to 50 minutes.

This fine little chocolate cake comes to us from **Mrs. Richard Phillips** who lives up toward Jacksboro. She read in ***Cooking With the Noonday Chef Volume 2*** that I remembered an old cake recipe which called for mayonnaise and she sent me one. I tried it in layers as she suggested, and I tried it in a bundt pan as I suggested--it worked just fine both ways. One word of caution. When this cake comes out of the oven, it is very fragile. Allow it to cool before turning it out or it will break up. Don't say I didn't warn you. But this very moist, tender nature is what makes it such a good cake.

Now I love chocolate with coconut, so I stacked the layers of this cake with a coconut filling. It really is very simple to make.

COCONUT FILLING

    ½ cup each sugar and evaporated milk
    1 3½ oz can flake coconut
    1 egg white
    1 tsp vanilla

Mix the sugar, milk, coconut, and egg white. Place over medium heat, and stir constantly until the mixture boils and is thick. Stir in vanilla. Allow to cool and spread on bottom layer of cake. Top with other layer and frost with your favorite chocolate frosting. When I do the bundt version of this cake, I like to top it with a pure, white glaze. The cake is almost black and really shows up the glaze. To make a simple glaze, combine 1 cup powdered sugar, ¼ tsp white vanilla, and 1 TBSP water. Stir thoroughly. Add water (a drop at a time) until it will just pour from a spoon. Drizzle over the cool cake.

Walter N. Lambert, Noonday Chef

CORNBREAD NUGGETS (TV 295)

    2 cups self-rising corn meal mix
    1 10 oz can **Kroger** chopped tomatoes with green chilies
    1 cup grated cheddar cheese
    ¼ - ½ lb lean ham, chopped (about 1 cup)
    ½ cup milk (Approx)

Mix all ingredients except the milk. Add milk to form a stiff batter. Turn into miniature muffin tins which have been sprayed with a cooking spray. Makes about 4 dozen. Bake in a 400 deg oven about 20 minutes or until brown. Serve hot.

These little goodies are excellent as nibbles at a cocktail party or to serve with chili or any good hot winter soup. They also freeze very well. Just place frozen nuggets on a cookie sheet and warm in a 350 deg oven about 15 minutes. Serve immediately. Sometimes, we make them the day ahead and allow to cool and put them into a plastic bag in the refrigerator. We then warm about a dozen of them at a time so they are hot through a party. Out of the refrigerator, they will heat in about 10 minutes.

I like things of this sort which have a little body to them. I hate to tell you that I actually use canned biscuits sometimes, but I do. I make a good, simple chicken salad and put it into canned flaky biscuits to serve at parties. Of course, if you insist, you can make your own little biscuits.

QUICK CURRIED CHICKEN SALAD

    1 lb cooked chicken, chopped fine
    ½ cup mayonnaise
    1 cup toasted, slivered almonds
    2 TBSP mild Indian curry powder
    1 cup celery, chopped fine
    ½ cup mango chutney (optional)

Toss the chicken, almonds and celery together. Mix the mayonnaise and curry powder. Mix in the chutney (if you are using it). Mix with the chicken mixture. Place in a covered container and refrigerate overnight before serving. This will make enough filling for about 20 to 30 biscuits if you use canned biscuits.

Oh! If you wonder why we are continuing to do all this fat stuff just after **Christmas**, just stick with us. This week and next are given to recipes which you could use to entertain when the boys come over to watch the **Superbowl**. Then we will celebrate a couple of things like **Valentine's Day** and a special anniversary here on **Noonday**. Then, watch for low calorie specials.

Walter N. Lambert, Noonday Chef

RED CHICKEN CHILI (TV 296)

2 TBSP oil
1 cup chopped onion
¼ cup chili powder
4 15½ oz cans beans (pinto, great northern or mixed)
2 cups medium salsa
2 lb chicken, cooked and cubed
2 cups (approx) chicken stock or water

Heat the oil in a large, heavy saucepan and saute the onion until tender and starting to brown. Add chili powder and cook, stirring, about 30 seconds. Add all remaining ingredients, adding water last and using as much as needed for desired consistency. Bring to a full boil, reduce heat, cover and allow to simmer for about 30 minutes before serving. Stir and serve hot.

Some time back (yes, it is included in *Cooking With the Noonday Chef Volume 2*) I made white chili. It was an extremely popular recipe. But some folks are never satisfied. They wanted a low fat chili but still wanted red. Well, for those folks (and just in time for the **Superbowl**) is a real red. Now truth demands that I tell you that true red chili is red from the chili powder and does not have tomatoes. Nobody ever accused me of being hide-bound.

Let me say a word about the beans in this recipe. I usually use pintos. However, I have done it with great northerns and with a mix of these two. I have done it with a mix of canned black beans and great northerns. In other words, suit yourself. I must tell you that I am not crazy about kidney beans in chili. Have we ever done red beans and rice? We'll have to do that. I don't use the big kidney beans in that either, but that is another story altogether.

I like to serve this chili with a number of add ons. I serve a little extra salsa, sour cream, grated cheddar cheese, and sliced green onions (or even chopped onions). I also like to include some oyster crackers on the tray for those who are so inclined. Now if you do this for a crowd on **Superbowl** day, be real California about it and just serve a salad along with your chili and a nice light dessert and you will have it made. Oh, and if the crowd is real big, just double the recipe, it works fine. Just allow a little more time for it to get hot through.

For dessert, I would suggest something simple. Maybe the **Five Flavor Pound** cake on page 18 of the aforementioned cook book would be nice. It can be made a day ahead and will be ready when you are.

Walter N. Lambert, Noonday Chef

CHINESE PORK CHOPS (TV 297)

    8 pork chops (about 2 - 3 lbs)
    2 TBSP cooking oil
    2 TBSP chopped fresh ginger
    1 tsp chopped garlic
    1 cup chopped onion
    8 cups shredded celery cabbage
    ½ cup soy sauce

In a heavy skillet, heat oil and brown pork chops on both sides. Place in a 9x13" casserole. In an oiled skillet, brown the onion, garlic, and ginger stirring constantly. Stir in cabbage and the soy sauce. Bring to a full boil. Distribute the cabbage over pork chops and pour sauce over. Cover tightly and bake in a 350 deg oven about one hour.

If you wish, you may thicken the sauce. To do this, remove the pork chops to a platter, lift out the cabbage with a slotted spoon, and place over pork chops. Pour the juices into a heavy saucepan. Blend 3 TBSP cornstarch with ¼ cup water. Stir into pan juices and bring to a full boil, stirring. Cook until thick. Pour over cabbage and pork chops and serve hot.

Are you ready for the **Year of the Pig**. Most of the Orient operates on a calendar based on the moon rather than the sun. This produces four approximately equal weeks in thirteen approximately equal months. From January 31 to February 6 we will celebrate the beginning of the new year in that calendar. This is the biggest holiday of the year in China, Japan, Thailand, and all across Southeast Asia. Now add to that knowledge the fact that the Chinese zodiac is divided into twelve years, each one named for an animal. Like dog, rat, snake, and pig. One of the twelve is named for a mythical animal, the dragon. Being born in the year of the dragon is the luckiest. I couldn't do that. So I did the next best thing. I married someone born in the year of the dragon. I was born in the year of the pig. If you have been listening, you will know that since we are entering my birth year, it means that my age is divisible by twelve. For your information, I will not be 48 this year.

Now back to the dish. This is not an authentic dish. It is an authentic Chinese flavor which I have adapted to an American entree. Now we serve this with rice and call it a meal. If you don't like Chinese cabbage, use regular cabbage. Red cabbage also works nicely. I personally prefer the flavor of the Chinese cabbage and they almost always have it at **Kroger**. So enjoy the year of the pig and "**Gung Hsi Fa Tsai**" (that is Happy New Year)!

Walter N. Lambert, Noonday Chef

SWEETHEART PINK COOKIES (TV 298)

    3 egg whites
    ¼ tsp salt
    ¾ cup sugar
    3½ TBSP raspberry gelatin (not sugar free)
    1 TBSP vinegar
    1½ cups chocolate chips

Beat salt and egg whites until foamy. Mix the gelatin and sugar together, and gradually add to the egg whites while beating. Beat until stiff. Fold in vinegar and chocolate chips. Drop by teaspoons onto lightly oiled cookie sheet. Bake at 325 deg for about 25 minutes. Remove to a wire rack to cool.

As **Valentine's Day** approaches, I try to be as nice to my bride of 34 years as possible. After all, if I am not going to give her a gift, I should at least be nice. These cookies are part of that. She absolutely loves meringues. I do not know why, but she does. So when our friend **Dawn Thompson** gave us this recipe, I knew it was for **Anne**.

Now meringues are basically sugar held together with egg white and baked. These are made pretty and pink by adding raspberry gelatin. If you were making these for **St. Patrick's Day**, you could use lime gelatin and get green ones. Of course, you could make white ones: Follow this recipe except use just under one cup of sugar and 1 TBSP of vanilla, leaving out the gelatin.

Now on the matter of the chocolate chips. If you like them, leave them in. If not take them out. Add chopped pecans or walnuts if you prefer, or even add half chocolate chips and half nuts. I would not expect this amount of meringue to hold much more in nuts or chocolate than 1 ½ cups total. If you prefer, you can leave them out altogether. By the way, the traditional way to bake meringues was on parchment or brown paper. I personally just spray the pan with a cooking spray, then wipe it off. Don't leave much oil or it will affect the texture of the cookies.

CHOCOLATE MERINGUES

    3 egg whites
    1 cup sugar
    6 oz unsweetened chocolate, melted and cooled
    ½ tsp vanilla and 1 TBSP vinegar

Beat the egg whites until frothy. Beat in sugar gradually. Fold in remaining ingredients and drop by teaspoons onto lightly oiled cookie sheets. Bake at 325 deg for 25 minutes.

Walter N. Lambert, Noonday Chef

BLACK FOREST UPSIDE DOWN CAKE (TV 299)

    1 can cherry pie filling
    2 cups flour
    1 cup sugar
    1 TBSP baking powder
    ½ cup cocoa
    2 eggs
    ¼ cup oil
    ¾ cup milk
    1 TBSP vanilla

In a 9" square pan sprayed with a cooking spray, spread the cherry pie filling. Blend together all dry ingredients. Beat in the oil, eggs, milk and vanilla. Pour evenly over the cherries. Bake in a 350 deg oven 45 minutes. Remove from oven, and carefully turn out onto a plate while still warm.

This is a quick version of an old time favorite. The taste of chocolate and cherries blends perfectly. This way, it blends easily. I should note that this cake is good warm or cold. A little ice cream or some whipped cream does not hurt it.

I personally cook this cake in a #8 skillet (about 12" across) just as I would any other upside down cake. It makes it a little thinner, and I like it better. This same cake batter works wonderfully well with pears. It requires a little more work, but is worth it.

CHOCOLATE PEAR UPSIDE DOWN CAKE

    1 stick butter
    ½ cup sugar
    2 pears
    2 cups flour
    1 cup sugar
    ½ cup cocoa
    1 TBSP baking powder
    2 eggs
    ¼ cup oil
    ¾ cup milk
    1 TBSP vanilla

Peel and core pears and slice thin. Melt the butter in a heavy pan, spread the sugar over it, and allow the sugar to melt. Arrange pear slices in the pan. Mix the cake as above and pour over pears. Bake about 40 minutes at 350 deg. Turn out and allow to cool.

Walter N. Lambert, Noonday Chef

CHOCOLATE CHERRY CHEESECAKE SQUARES (TV 300)

3 cups Oreo Cookie crumbs (about 25 to 30 cookies)
4 TBSP butter melted (½ stick)
8 oz cream cheese (at room temperature)
1 cup sugar
2 eggs
2 tsp vanilla
1 20 oz can cherry pie filling

Mix cookie crumbs and butter and press evenly on bottom of a 9x13" dish. Bake in a 325 deg oven about 10 minutes; allow to cool. With a heavy mixer (or a food processor) beat the cheese, sugar, eggs, and vanilla together thoroughly. Pour evenly over cookie crust. Spoon cherry pie filling evenly over top. Bake in a 325 deg oven about 35 minutes or until top is lightly browned. Allow to cool before cutting into squares.

Can you believe that we have done 300 shows? I expected this to last about a month and here we are almost six years later still at it. I think the reason is that all of you have been so wonderful. You write for recipes (don't forget that self- addressed-stamped envelope), you talk to us at **Kroger Knox Plaza** and other places, and you invite us to come to your churches and garden clubs. **Anne** and I have a wonderful time doing all of that.

Both Anne and I want to thank all of you for your support. We also want to thank all the folks at **Channel 8**, at **Proffitt's** for equipping the kitchen, **Kroger Knox Plaza** for their continued support, and everyone else that I should think of and probably have forgotten.

Now a word about this recipe. I love it. It has three of my favorite flavors and I thought of it after we had done the chocolate cherry upside down cake last week. I will tell you that you can also do this as a cheesecake instead of the squares if you wish. To do that, use only about 2 cups of the Oreo crumbs. Mix them with the butter and press into the bottom of a spring form pan. Bake as above and allow to cool. Pour the cheesecake mixture over and spoon cherries over the top. Bake for about one hour. Turn off and allow to stand in the oven about an hour. Then remove, remove the sides of the pan and chill before serving. Other pie fillings will work as well. I like apple, but everyone tells me I am crazy. I do it just exactly the same way, and then sprinkle the top with a little cinnamon. When done this way, the fruit cooks down in the cheesecake rather than on top of it. I like it better that way. If you do not, bake the cake about 45 minutes and then pour the fruit onto the top and bake an additional 10 to 15 minutes.

Walter N. Lambert, Noonday Chef

BROCCOLI SALAD (TV 302)

> 6 cups broccoli, chopped
> 1½ cup each raisins and dry-roasted salted peanuts
> 2 or 3 TBSP onion, grated fine
> 1 cup mayonnaise
> ⅓ cup red wine vinegar
> ¼ cup sugar

Place the broccoli, raisins and peanuts in a mixing bowl. Mix together the remaining ingredients and pour over the broccoli mixture. Toss to mix completely. Place in a covered bowl and refrigerate several hours or overnight before serving.

This recipe comes from the beautiful **Scarecrow Inn** in Cookeville, Tennessee. If you have not had lunch or dinner with these good folks, I recommend it to you most heartily. Located in a strange, rambling building put together out of old log cabins, it is a treat from beginning to end. **The Fitzpatricks** who operate it were kind enough to share this recipe.

When I do this right, I cut the florets off the broccoli, peel any tough outside off the stalks and then cut them up fine. Sometimes, I just buy the florets already cut and prepared in the produce section of **Kroger**. Have you tried the broccoli cole slaw which they now have. It is the inside portion of the broccoli stalks which has been cut up with carrots. Use your favorite cole slaw dressing (or the dressing above) and you have an interesting dish.

Broccoli makes a wonderful stir-fry. Just be careful not to overcook it.

BROCCOLI STIR-FRY

> 3 cups broccoli, chopped
> 1 cup carrot, cut into chunks
> ½ cup onion, chopped
> 2 TBSP oil
> ¼ cup soy sauce
> 2 TBSP sugar (optional)
> salt to taste

In a heavy skillet or wok, heat the oil until very hot. Add onion and stir until soft and starting to brown. Add carrots and cook, stirring constantly for about 2 minutes. Add the broccoli and continue to cook, stirring, until the broccoli becomes a bright green. Sprinkle on sugar and pour the soy sauce over. Continue to stir about 1 minute and serve hot. Salt to taste.

Walter N. Lambert, Noonday Chef

SUGAR-FREE FUDGE (TV 303)

¼ cup diet margarine
2 oz unsweetened chocolate
24 packets equal sweetener
1 tsp vanilla
1 8 oz pkg reduced fat cream cheese
½ cup chopped nuts (optional)

In a small saucepan, melt margarine over low heat (or in microwave). Add chocolate and stir just until melted. Remove from heat and stir in sweetener and vanilla. Beat chocolate mixture into cream cheese until smooth. Stir in nuts and spread mixture into an 8" square pan which has been sprayed with a cooking spray. Refrigerate until firm. Cut into 1" squares. Each square has about 22 calories and under 2 grams of fat.

It is really your fault that I am doing another low fat, sugar- free recipe. If you had not written so much for the last set, I could have done brownies or some such. But we will get back to that. I do appreciate your overwhelming amount of mail about "Doing the Unthinkable".

Anne found this recipe somewhere and to my great surprise, it is not bad. Remember that it is sugar-free, but it is not calorie free. A 1" square is not much so you will need to eat sparingly. It will give you something when you are having a real "sweet attack".

Now here is a little bonus for one of your low fat days. Note that it is not sugar free and sugar substitute will not work.

CINNAMON POPCORN

10 cups popped popcorn, popped without fat or salt
2 egg whites
1 cup granulated sugar
1 tsp ground cinnamon
1 tsp salt

Place popcorn in a large bowl. In a small bowl, beat egg whites until stiff. Fold in the sugar, cinnamon, and salt. Spoon the egg white mixture over the popcorn, and stir lightly to coat the corn. Spread evenly on a baking sheet which has been sprayed with a cooking spray. Bake 1 hour, stirring every 15 minutes. Cool completely on the pan. Store in an airtight container. 1 cup is 126 calories and 0 grams fat. It does have more than 30 grams of carbohydrate so be careful.

Walter N. Lambert, Noonday Chef

DUBLIN/SCOTCH EGGS (TV 304)

> 5 eggs
> 1 lb country sausage
> ½ cup dry breadcrumbs
> oil for deep frying

Boil 4 of the eggs until hard; peel. Beat the other egg. Place dry bread crumbs onto a plate. Dip each boiled egg in the beaten egg and roll in bread crumbs. Cover with sausage. Dip again into the beaten egg and roll in the bread crumbs. Fry in deep fat about 10 minutes or until completely brown. Serve hot or cold.

I first ate these little beauties in an **Irish pub** where they were called Scotch eggs. I later had them in an Irish restaurant where they were called Dublin eggs. I don't care what you call them, they are good.

I have spent considerable time trying to bake these instead of frying them. In fact, it works very well as far as flavor is concerned. Unfortunately, they don't look as good. They crack open and the egg shows through. They still taste good! In fact, I have tried mixing self-rising flour and grated cheese (about ¾ cup of each with a pound of sausage) with the sausage just the way you do for sausage balls. I then proceeded as above. They tasted great, but they looked awful. Try for yourself.

I love this with an old Irish dish called Colcannon which I did a couple of years ago. Here for your pleasure is that recipe.

COLCANNON

> 6 to 8 potatoes, peeled and cut into pieces
> 4 cups uncooked cabbage, chopped
> 4 TBSP butter
> ¼ cup cream (approx)
> 1 tsp salt (approx)

Place the potatoes in a heavy saucepan with water to cover. Cook until tender. Meanwhile, melt 2 TBSP butter in a heavy skillet with a tight fitting lid. Stir in the cabbage and about half the salt. Cook over medium heat, stirring often until soft. When the potatoes are tender, drain the water and add remaining butter. Mash potatoes, adding enough cream to soften them. Add salt to taste. Stir in the cabbage, and serve hot with additional butter to pour on top.

Walter N. Lambert, Noonday Chef

SAVORY POT ROAST (TV 305)

    2 tsp salt
    1 4 to 5 lb bottom round roast
    ¼ cup soy sauce
    ¼ cup red wine vinegar
    1 cup approx. onion, chopped
    ½ cup water

In a heavy Dutch oven (preferably oven proof), sprinkle the salt and over high heat, allow to become very hot. Place the roast into the hot pan, and allow to brown, turning so that it browns on all sides. Pour soy sauce and wine vinegar over the roast. Add onion and stir together around the roast. Add the water. Cover tightly and bake in a 325 deg oven about three hours. Remove roast and slice to serve. May serve hot or cold.

This somewhat abbreviated version of how to prepare a wonderful pot roast is really just the start. It will make a roast which is tender and flavorful and produce a gravy which is heavenly-- whether you thicken it or not. Oh, if your Dutch oven is not oven proof, you can cook the roast at very low heat on top of the stove instead of the oven.

On the air today, I am doing one of many variations. In this one, I have added:

    1 cup each, apricots, mushrooms and water
    1 tsp fresh ginger, grated

Soak the apricots in water and stir in along with the mushrooms and ginger --at the point I had you add the onions above. By the way, keep the onions in, but drop in the extra half cup of water. Just add the apricots and the water they soaked in.

Now let me say a word or two about the gravy. If I do it with the mushrooms and apricots as I described above, after you have removed the roast, just mash the vegetables and fruits in the gravy until they are broken up. Serve the gravy hot to pour over the meat and mashed potatoes. If you must thicken the gravy, make a roux of 4 TBSP butter which you cook with 4 TBSP of flour until it is thick and lightly browned. Stir this into the gravy and cook, stirring constantly until the mixture thickens. If you absolutely insist, you can do this by thoroughly mixing 4 TBSP flour with ¼ cup water and pouring it into the boiling gravy. It will thicken nicely, but will not taste as good as if you make the roux. Personally, I serve it natural --and nobody has complained yet. Be sure that you cool the beef without gravy so you can make roast beef sandwiches.

91

Walter N. Lambert, Noonday Chef

SAUSAGE AND APPLE QUICHE (TV 306)

8 oz mild sausage
1 unbaked 9" deep-dish pie shell
1 large apple, thinly sliced
1 large onion, chopped
1½ cup cheddar cheese
3 eggs, beaten
1 cup milk
3 TBSP flour
⅛ tsp celery seeds and dry mustard (optional)
2 TBSP parsley, chopped

Brown sausage in a skillet until crumbly. Spoon into pie shell. Saute onions and apples in the same skillet until brown (3 to 5 minutes). Spoon over sausage. Sprinkle cheese over apples and onions. Combine eggs, milk, flour, parsley, celery seeds, and dry mustard. Pour over cheese until the pie shell is full. Bake at 375 deg about 40 minutes or until puffed and brown.

This recipe is from a new book from the **Tennessee Arthritis Foundation** called _**Help Yourself**_. Not a bad idea. And a very good cookbook it is. The book can be ordered through the local Arthritis Foundation office or through the state office at 1719 West End Avenue, Nashville, Tn.. 37203. The book is $14.95 plus $1.23 tax and $3.00 shipping and handling. It can also be bought at your area Kroger Stores. I prefer the latter.

Now a word about this quiche. It is very good. It makes a delightful late breakfast or Sunday night supper. It is also very easy to adapt to your own tastes. For example, if you do not like sausage, this will work nicely with <u>ham</u>. Use 8 oz of cooked ham which you have slivered or cut into small cubes. In a heavy skillet put about 2 tsp oil. Saute the onions and apples in the oil until lightly browned. At the last minute, stir in the ham until it is just hot. Spoon into the quiche shell, sprinkle on the cheese, pour the milk and egg mixture over and away you go.

By the way, the mustard, celery seed, and parsley are all optional. Use them or leave them out. If you happen not to have dry mustard, you can stir about 1 tsp of salad mustard into the egg mixture. If you want this to look fancy, you might consider cutting the parsley off like little bushes and laying it into a nice pattern on the top. Further, by the way, if you like your crust a little crisper, you can prebake it about 10 minutes before putting in the quiche mixture. To do this, put a piece of waxed paper into it, fill it about half full of rice and bake. Remove the rice and the paper before filling.

Walter N. Lambert, Noonday Chef

PEANUT BUTTER POUND CAKE (TV 307)

¾ cup butter
1 cup sugar
3 large eggs
½ cup peanut butter
1 cup plain flour
2 TBSP chopped peanuts

With a heavy mixer, cream butter and sugar until light and fluffy. Add eggs, one at a time, and beat until thoroughly mixed. Beat in peanut butter. Stir in flour. Turn batter into a greased loaf pan and sprinkle with the chopped nuts. Bake in a preheated 325 deg oven about 1 hour or until lightly brown and tests done.

If you promise not to tell anyone, I will let you know that I absolutely love peanut butter. I love it on toast for breakfast. I love it on crackers as a bed time snack, and anytime in between. I am always looking for some new way to enjoy it. Here is one for you:

This is a snack size cake which I prefer cold with a glass of milk. But I should also tell you that the cake bakes fine if you double the recipe and use a tube pan. Because the top of the cake is prettiest, I wouldn't use a bundt pan, but just a regular tube pan. You will need to bake a tube cake using a doubled recipe about 1 ½ hours and be sure to test for doneness. This cake is also nice with a cup of miniature chocolate chips stirred into the batter. If you want to do a really fancy dessert out of it, slice a good slice of the cake, top it with vanilla or chocolate ice cream and then sprinkle that with a few more chopped peanuts. It is elegant and easy.

I would remind you that peanut butter is not limited to desserts. All over the Orient, peanut butter is added to sauces to give body and flavor. One of the favorites is a dressing which combines ¼ cup soy sauce, ¼ cup vinegar (preferably rice wine vinegar), ½ cup peanut butter, 2 TBSP sesame oil and ½ tsp ground cayenne pepper to make a sauce which can be used over bean sprouts, noodles, or as a dip for grilled pork. My personal favorite is over noodles. Cook eight ounces of fettuccine, drain, wash with cold water and allow to cool. Add ½ cup each, finely chopped onion, carrot, and cucumber. Pour 1 recipe of the sauce described above over the noodles and toss to mix thoroughly. Place in a covered dish and refrigerate overnight. Toss again before serving. This makes a great side dish to serve with grilled chicken or pork chops. It is also nice that it must be made the day before.

Walter N. Lambert, Noonday Chef

QUICK CORN PUDDING (TV 308)

 3 eggs
 1 cup self-rising meal
 1 cup milk
 1 each, 15 oz can cream corn and drained whole kernel corn
 1 10 oz can tomatoes and green chilies
 2 cups cheddar cheese, shredded

Beat eggs and mix in corn meal, then the milk. Add corns, tomatoes, and cheese; stir to mix. Turn into a 9x13" dish which has been sprayed with a cooking spray. Bake in a 350 deg oven about 45 minutes or until puffed and brown. Serve hot, warm, or cold.

Corn pudding probably dates back to the **Indians** who greeted the folks at **Plymouth Rock**. We seem to love corn also--any way it can be served. Baked into a pudding is certainly one of the most popular. This version has the tomatoes and green chilies added to give it just a little more snap. I love it hot served with cold sliced ham, and that is why I thought of it just before **Easter**.

Now about that canned corn. Sorry. If you are offended by that, do not use it. Simply substitute 3 cups of freshly cut corn for the canned, and proceed as above. By the way, these proportions make a fairly soft pudding. If you like it firmer, simply add a little more corn meal. If you like it spicier, use half cheddar and half hot pepper cheese.

Now one more good corn dish, just for a bonus. It is also a corn pudding, but very different from the one above.

CORN PUDDING WITH BACON

 ½ lb bacon
 ¾ cup diced onion
 ½ cup diced green pepper
 1 15 oz can whole kernel corn, drained
 2 eggs
 2 cups milk
 ½ cup cornmeal
 pepper to taste

Cook, drain, and crumble the bacon, reserving 3 TBSP bacon drippings. Saute onion and green pepper in the bacon grease. Drain. Mix all ingredients together and pour into a 2 quart baking dish, which has been sprayed with a cooking spray. Bake in a preheated 350 deg oven about 45 minutes. Serve hot.

94

Walter N. Lambert, Noonday Chef

PASTA, HAM AND EGG SALAD (TV 309)

    1 8 oz pkg pasta (shells, rotini, or macaroni)
    1 cup each, chopped onion and celery
    ½ cup each, sweet relish and dill relish
    4 to 6 hard cooked eggs, chopped
    2 to 3 cups cooked ham, cubed
    ½ cup mayonnaise
    ¼ cup salad mustard

Cook pasta according to package directions. Drain, wash, and cool. Add all other ingredients and toss to mix. Place in a covered dish, and allow to chill several hours or overnight before serving. Toss again just before serving.

Well, here it is. Monday after **Easter** again. I look upon it as my mission to help you get rid of leftover Easter eggs and ham on the Monday after Easter. You will remember that in the past we have done ham loaf with hard boiled eggs in it. And we have done yellow eggs and ham. Now we have pasta salad with ham and eggs.

You know that with this recipe, as so many we do, I give you a very basic recipe. You are then free to do variations as you please. Let me suggest such a variation. You can chop the ham, as much as you may have, very fine and mix it with the chopped eggs and add chopped onion and celery, pickle relishes and mayonnaise and have a very good ham and egg salad to use as a sandwich spread. It is especially good on fresh whole wheat bread. I use the pasta because it stretches the ham so. Just a little ham will go a long way in a salad like this.
Now let me give you a quick casserole using leftover ham and eggs with is also very nice.

HAM AND EGG CASSEROLE

    8 oz macaroni, uncooked
    ½ cup each, onion and celery, chopped
    4 to 6 hard cooked eggs, chopped
    2 to 3 cups ham, cubed
    1 can cream of celery soup
    1 soup can milk
    2 cups grated cheddar cheese, divided

Cook macaroni according to the package instructions, adding the onion and celery to the cooking water. Drain and mix in all remaining ingredients except 1 cup of cheese. Turn into a 1½ quart casserole dish which has been sprayed with a cooking spray. Sprinkle the remaining cup of cheese on top. Bake in a 350 deg oven about 35 minutes or until brown. Serve hot.

Walter N. Lambert, Noonday Chef

FRESH APPLE COOKIES (TV 310)

> ½ cup margarine or butter
> 1⅓ cup brown sugar, packed
> 2 eggs
> 2 cups flour
> 1 tsp each, baking soda and cinnamon
> ¼ cup apple juice
> 1 cup each, chopped nuts, raisins, chopped fresh apple

Cream the margarine and sugar. Add eggs one at a time, beating after each. Mix flour, soda, and cinnamon. Add to creamed mixture alternately with apple juice. Fold in nuts, raisins, and apples. Drop by teaspoonfuls onto a lightly greased cookie sheet. Bake about 15 minutes in a preheated 350 deg oven.

These are good cookies. They are tender and remain so, You will need to be careful in handling them or you will have cookie crumbs and not cookies. If you store them, be sure to place a sheet of waxed paper between each layer of cookies in the storage container. These cookies are also nice to glaze if you want to make them fancy. Mix together 1 TBSP softened margarine with 1½ cup confectioners sugar. Cream together completely. Stir in 2½ TBSP apple juice and ¼ tsp vanilla. Mix completely and spread on hot cookies. Allow to cool completely before stacking.

SPICY APPLE COOKIES

> 2 cups sifted flour
> 1 cup chopped nuts
> 1 tsp baking soda
> 1 cup raisins
> ½ tsp salt
> 1 6 oz pkg butterscotch
> 1½ tsp nutmeg
> ½ tsp cloves
> 1 ¼ cup brown sugar
> 1½ cup chopped apples
> ½ cup margarine
> 2 eggs
> ¼ cup apple juice

Mix together all dry ingredients. Cream margarine with the brown sugar and beat in the eggs. Add dry ingredients alternately to the creamed mixture with the apple juice. Fold in all remaining ingredients and drop by teaspoonfuls onto a greased cookie sheet. Bake in a 400 deg oven for 8 to 10 minutes or until brown.

Walter N. Lambert, Noonday Chef

SMOKEY'S REBEL-LIOUS CORN BREAD (TV 311)

1 lb ground beef, fried and drained
¼ cup vegetable oil
1 recipe thin corn bread batter
(4 cups corn meal mix with 3 cups milk)
1 large onion, chopped
1 16 oz can creamed corn
8 slices Velveeta Mexican cheese

Heat oil in a 13x9" baking pan. Stir hot oil into corn bread batter. Layer half the batter in the pan with ground beef, onion, corn, and cheese. Pour remaining batter over the top. Bake at 400 deg for 1 hour. Serve hot.

Welcome to cowboy cooking! The recipe above is from the new cookbook to benefit the **Lady Vols** called **_A Slice of Orange_**. It is a fine cookbook, and I am glad it came along just when we were ready to do cowboy cooking. Because nothing could be more cowboy (or country) than beans and corn bread. And this corn bread with some good dry beans makes a great meal. Later, we will be doing more recipes from this good cookbook and you should look for it. You will want a copy, and want to help the Lady Vols. Now let's get to some real "cowboy food." Dry pinto beans were a staple throughout the frontier in America. They had everything. They were cheap, they were readily available, they were easy to store, and easy to cook. And now we know they are good for us. Despite certain aspects of eating them, which has made them the subject of many crude jokes, it is the fiber that causes "that"-- in case you wonder. Here is a good version of dry beans.

COWBOY BEANS

1 lb dry pinto beans
¼ lb salt pork, in one piece
1 large onion chopped
1 tsp ground cumin
2 cloves of garlic, peeled and chopped
1 pod of dry red pepper
water to cover and salt to taste

Wash beans and cover them with water in a heavy pot. Bring to a full boil, remove from heat and allow to cool in the pan. Drain. In a heavy pot, fry the salt pork until brown and some oil has cooked out into the pot. Remove and reserve the meat. Stir onion and garlic into the oil and cook until soft and starting to brown. Add cumin and red pepper and return pork to the pan. Add the drained beans and water to cover. Cook slowly until tender adding water as necessary. Add salt to taste.

Walter N. Lambert, Noonday Chef

ANNE'S (AND THEREFORE WALTER'S) FAVORITE (TV 312)

    6 egg whites
    ½ tsp each cream of tartar and white vinegar
    ¾ tsp vanilla
    1 cup sugar

Beat egg whites until frothy. Add cream of tartar, vinegar, and vanilla. Continue to beat until fluffy. Slowly add sugar until completely added. Continue to beat until very stiff peaks form. Using a piping bag or spoons, shape into desired shapes on brown paper or parchment paper. Bake at about 250 deg for 45 minutes to an hour. Turn off oven, and allow to cool at least two hours before removing to fill as desired.

Meringues are basically egg white, sugar and air. A little acid, like cream of tartar or vinegar, helps break down the egg whites and therefore gets them fluffier. They are basically used as a base for almost any kind of dessert. Meringue shells, made by shaping a circle of meringue which is higher on the outside than on the inside, makes a great receptacle for sliced strawberries which have stood for a while with sugar. A little whipped cream on top makes a perfect combination. A small scoop of ice cream with fresh strawberries or blueberries is not bad.

Now I want to give you a recipe which is a lot of trouble but worth it.

LEMON MERINGUE TORTE

    4 eggs, separated
    1 ¾ cups sugar, separated
    ½ cup fresh lemon juice
    2 cups whipping cream
    1 tsp vanilla, separated
    ½ tsp each cream of tartar and white vinegar

Put the four egg whites, cream of tartar, ½ tsp vanilla, and vinegar in a large mixer and beat until fluffy. Slowly add ¾ cup sugar to make a stiff meringue. On parchment paper placed on baking sheets, make three 8" circles. Divide the meringue evenly between the circles and flatten to make even circles. Bake as described for meringues above. In a heavy sauce pan, place ¾ cup sugar, lemon juice, and egg yolks. Mix thoroughly and place over medium heat. Cook, stirring constantly until thick and clear. Allow to cool. Whip cream with remaining sugar and vanilla. Fold lemon mixture into whipped cream. Stack meringue layers with whipped cream mixture starting, ending with a meringue layer. Chill several hours before serving.

Walter N. Lambert, Noonday Chef

CHOCOLATE POTATO CAKE (TV 313)

    1 cup (2 sticks) margarine or butter
    2 cups each, sugar and flour
    2 eggs
    1 cup cold mashed potatoes
    1 tsp each, vanilla and baking soda
    ¼ cup cocoa
    1 cup milk
    1 cup chopped nuts (optional)

In a heavy mixer, cream butter and sugar completely. Add eggs one at a time. Beat in potatoes and vanilla. Mix flour, cocoa, and soda. Add alternately with milk to the creamed mixture. Fold in nuts. Bake at 350 deg for 45 minutes in a 9x13" baking dish. In a large bundt pan, bake at 325 deg for 1 hour and 15 minutes. Allow to cool in the pan.

Once again, we start adding unexpected ingredients to cake. This time, we give you a whole new way to use up left over mashed potatoes. In fact, if I had just called this a potato cake, you would have expected onions and cheese, right? Well surprise. This makes a very moist, very delicate cake. It will not support icing, and really doesn't need it. A slice of this cake with a glass of milk (or even a cup of hot coffee) is a delight not to be missed. But be warned it is very delicate and if handled harshly, will fall to pieces. Don't say I didn't warn you.

It does look pretty with a little glaze on it. You can make a nice glaze by mixing ½ cup confectioners sugar with ½ tsp vanilla and enough milk (about 2 TBSP) to make it just dribble off a spoon. Drizzle it around in a nice pattern on either the sheet cake or on the bundt cake to look pretty. It also looks nice to simply dust the cake with a little powdered sugar from a sifter.

Now while we are using up left over mashed potatoes, let me give you a fine, traditional potato cake.

FRIED POTATO CAKES

    2 cups (approx) left over cold mashed potatoes
    1 egg
    ¼ cup finely grated onion (or thinly sliced green onion)
    ¼ cup finely grated cheese
    flour for coating

Blend the potatoes, egg, onion, and cheese. Shape into patties and coat each side in flour. On a greased, heated griddle, fry each cake until brown. Turn on fry other side. Serve hot.

Walter N. Lambert, Noonday Chef

CHICKEN IN A SKILLET (TV 314)

1 to 1½ lb chicken breast, cut into chunks
2 TBSP cooking oil
1 cup each, onion and celery, chopped
1 tsp each, chopped garlic and oregano
1 14.5 oz can chopped tomatoes
1 cup Uncle Ben's Converted Rice
1½ cup water
salt to taste (about 1 tsp)

In a heavy skillet with a tight fitting lid, heat oil until hot. Add chicken and stir fry until just brown. Remove from skillet. Add the onion, celery, garlic, and oregano to the skillet. Stir fry until onion is wilted. Return the chicken to the skillet and add tomatoes and water. Bring to a full boil. Add rice and stir to mix. Reduce heat, cover and allow to simmer for 20 minutes.. Turn off heat and allow to stand 5 minutes to absorb all liquids. Serve hot.

A couple of weeks ago, we did **Anne's** favorite dish. This may be mine. Not just because I like the flavors in the basic recipe, which I have given you. But because this method of cooking chicken with rice allows you to give it almost any flavor you like and quickly produce a hot, nutritious dish. When combined with a green salad, it gives you a complete meal. Now about those variations.

If you like bacon, for example, fry about 5 or 6 strips of bacon until crisp in your skillet. Remove and reserve the bacon. Discard all but about 2 TBSP of the fat, and proceed with the recipe exactly like it is above. When finished, pile the chicken and rice on a platter and crumble the bacon over the top. If you like mushrooms, add about a half pound of sliced button mushrooms with the onions and proceed exactly like you have it described. Oh, by the way, this dish looks pretty and it is compatible with the flavor to sprinkle the top of the dish with chopped parsley just before serving.

Now about a whole different thing but still using the same recipe. Use the same amount of chicken and cook as described above. When you have removed the chicken, add the onion and garlic to the oil. Cook until the onion is soft and starts to brown. Add ½ lb of sliced mushrooms and continue to stir until the mushrooms start to brown. Add one can of cream of mushroom soup and stir to blend. Add 1½ cup water and bring to a full boil. Return the chicken to the pan and add the rice. Stir to blend. Reduce heat, cover, and allow to cook twenty minutes. Then let stand for five minutes before serving. This is creamy and good.

100

Walter N. Lambert, Noonday Chef

VIDALIA ONION PIE (TV 315)

    1 cup saltine cracker crumbs
    5 TBSP margarine (or butter), melted
    2½ cup thinly sliced Vidalia onions
    1 TBSP cooking oil
    2 eggs
    ¾ cup milk
    ½ cup cheddar cheese, grated
    salt and pepper to taste

Combine cracker crumbs with butter and press into an 8" pie pan. Bake a 350 deg for 8 to 10 minutes. Put oil into a heavy skillet and get hot. Add onion and stirring constantly, cook hot until soft and lightly browned. Turn into pie shell. Sprinkle cheese evenly over top. Beat together remaining ingredients and pour over onions. Bake at 350 deg for 45 minutes.

Vidalia onions have two things going for them. First they have a naturally high sugar content. This makes them taste the way we like things to taste. It also makes them cook nicely. The second thing they have going for them is a great press agent. The name of the small Georgia town has become associated so completely with big, sweet onions that we assume they have an exclusive tie. This is not quite so, but who am I to mess with success.

This recipe which is basically a quiche with emphasis on the onions rather than the custard makes maximum use of the sweetness of these onions. Note that I ask you not just to cook the onions until they are soft, but until they are browned. What you are doing is caramelizing the sugar in the onion. This deepens the flavor and adds greatly to the finished dish. The more sugar an onion has, the greater the effect of this.

Now let me tell you about an interesting variation on this pie. Instead of regular saltine crackers, use **Cheez-it** hot and spicy crackers for the crust. Use about 1 ½ cup of fine crumbs and only about 4 TBSP of butter to make the crust. It will be messy and hard to handle, but will be worth it.

Now let me tell you about one of my favorite ways to serve these sweet onions. Peel medium sized Vidalia onions and cut off the bottom so they will sit flat in a baking dish. Carve the top down slightly to make an indentation about ½" deep on the top. Put a pat of butter into this indentation with a pinch of salt. Place in a baking dish and cover with foil. Bake at 350 deg about 30 minutes. Remove foil and bake another 15 minutes to brown. Serve hot.

Walter N. Lambert, Noonday Chef

PEACHES AND CREAM PIE (TV 316)

        1 8" deep dish pie shell, unbaked
        2½ cups fresh peaches, sliced thin
        4 oz cream cheese
        ¾ cup brown sugar, firmly packed
        2 eggs
        1 cup sour cream
        1 tsp vanilla

Place peaches in the pie shell and distribute evenly. Mix together all remaining ingredients thoroughly and pour over peaches. Bake in a 350 deg oven about 45 minutes or until puffed and brown. Allow to cool before serving.

My favorite dessert in the whole wide world is the inspiration for this pie. It consists of placing sliced, fresh peaches in a bowl (blueberries will do) and adding a large dollop of sour cream. Then you sprinkle brown sugar over the top. Then you eat and enjoy. I love that combination of flavors and live for fresh peaches to have it.

I have developed this cheesecake like pie to take advantage of those same flavors. I like it a lot. It is fat. It is sweet. It is all those things that we like, but should not. I'm sorry. But I have tried yogurt. It didn't work. Save up some fat grams and live a little. By the way, use only fresh peaches. No cans.

Now let me give you another peach pie recipe which is much more traditional and wonderful.

PEACH BATTER PIE

        3 cups fresh peaches, sliced
        ¾ cup sugar, divided
        ½ tsp nutmeg
        ½ cup self-rising flour
        ½ cup milk
        4 TBSP butter

In an 8" square pan, melt butter in a preheated 350 deg oven. In a heavy saucepan, place the peaches, nutmeg, and ¼ cup sugar. Bring slowly to a boil to allow the natural juices of the peaches to form. Stir often. While the peaches are cooking, mix the remaining ½ cup sugar, flour, and milk to form a batter. Pour the batter into the butter in the pan. Spoon the hot peaches over the batter evenly. Place in the preheated oven and cook about 35 to 40 minutes or until brown. Serve hot with some good vanilla ice cream.

Walter N. Lambert, Noonday Chef

YELLOW RICE AND PEAS (TV 317)

2 TBSP olive oil
1 medium onion, chopped (about 1 cup)
1 tsp turmeric
1¼ cup **Uncle Ben's Converted Rice**
2½ cups water
1 cup sugar snap peas, broken
salt and pepper to taste

In a heavy saucepan, heat oil and cook onion until soft. Add turmeric and cook briefly. Add rice, stirring constantly; cook for a minute or two. Add water and bring to a full boil. Boil about 20 minutes. Remove from heat and stir in peas. Allow to stand for 5 minutes. Add salt and pepper to taste. Serve hot.

This simple but tasty rice side dish is a welcome addition to any simple meal. I recommend it with broiled chicken for a wonderful, light summer supper. Turmeric is a much neglected spice. When I was growing up, my grandmother used it to color and flavor some kinds of pickles. Otherwise, you didn't see much of it. In this dish, it takes the place of the extraordinarily expensive saffron which is used in many places to color and flavor rice. By adding the sugar snap peas this way, they keep their crisp, fresh taste. If you do not find sugar snaps, snow peas will do. If they are not available, those little green marbles which pass for frozen peas are alright. But they are my last resort. Now this dish lends itself to all kinds of additions. If you want to convert it to a main dish, stir in about a pound of poached chicken with the peas. Cubed ham will also work nicely with this dish. And I have even used a combination of ham and chicken. Another nice variation is to use this as the base for black beans to make a nearly nutritionally perfect vegetarian meal. Here is a recipe for good black beans if you want to go that direction.

BLACK BEANS

1 lb black beans
¼ cup olive oil
1 large onion, chopped
4 cloves garlic, minced
1 TBSP each, chili powder and cider vinegar
1 tsp Tabasco (or other hot pepper sauce
salt and pepper to taste

Cook beans according to package directions. Leave some water in beans. Heat oil in a heavy pan, and cook onions and garlic. Add all remaining ingredients including beans. Bring to a full boil. Reduce heat, cover, and cook for 30 minutes. Serve hot.

Walter N. Lambert, Noonday Chef

SUMMER SQUASH SAUSAGE CASSEROLE (TV 318)

    4 to 5 cups thinly sliced zucchini or yellow squash
    1 lb **Tennessee Pride Sausage**, fried, crumbled and drained
    8 oz grated cheddar cheese
    1 can cream of celery soup
    2 eggs
    1 cup milk
    ½ cup Bisquick

Spread squash evenly in a 9x13" baking dish which you have sprayed with a non-stick spray. Spread the sausage over the squash and the cheese over the sausage. Beat all remaining ingredients together thoroughly. Spread evenly over the top. Bake in a 350 deg oven about 45 minutes or until browned.

This dish combines some of my favorite flavors and is a great way to use all that squash that is around in the summer. I often mix the zucchini and yellow squash for the bottom layer. If you like things fairly salty, you may want to sprinkle about 1 tsp salt over the squash before completing the dish.

As always, you can decide if you like mild or hot sausage. My personal favorite is the sage sausage. It tastes more like sausage did when I was a child (which as everyone knows was only a short time ago). The celery soup is also a personal choice. Mushroom soup works very well. Originally, this dish used a cup and ½ of milk which made the batter considerably thinner. You may want to try that way. It causes the batter to go through the sausage and has a texture almost like the impossible pies we made some months ago.

Now you may remember that we made a dish very similar to this some time ago. If you want to try it, check in ***Cooking With the Noonday Chef, Volume 2***. The major difference was that it used tomato sauce (canned spaghetti sauce actually). **Anne** is not that fond of tomato sauce, so we developed this version to take its place. She approves.

I will tell you again that I learned my favorite easy way of cooking summer squash if you simply want it as a side dish for meat. Grate your zucchini or yellow squash coarsely. Sprinkle it with salt and allow to stand at room temperature at least one hour. Squeeze out all the excess water from the squash. In a heavy skillet, heat 1 TBSP each of butter and olive oil. Add the squash, and stir fry hot just until cooked (about 5 minutes). Stir in finely chopped fresh basil and serve immediately. This is also good with chopped, peeled, seeded tomatoes cooked with it. Just cook the tomatoes first and then add the squash.

Walter N. Lambert, Noonday Chef

BUTTERMILK BREAD PUDDING (TV 319)

 7 to 7½ cups sourdough French bread (torn into 1" pieces)
 ¼ cup butter
 4 cups buttermilk
 1 cup raisins
 4 eggs, beaten
 1½ cup brown sugar, firmly packed
 1 TBSP vanilla

Melt butter in a 9x13" dish; tilt pan to coat with butter. Toss the bread and raisins together in a large bowl. Mix all remaining ingredients together thoroughly; mix with the bread. Pour into buttered pan. Bake in a 350 deg oven about one hour or until puffed and brown.

I love bread pudding. I especially love it made with good French bread. Two things distinguish this one. First, it is made with brown sugar rather than white, and second it is made with buttermilk. That is what caused me to try it with good sourdough bread. The sour taste of the bread combines with the buttermilk and brown sugar for a great taste. Now about the raisins. I have never been crazy about them in bread pudding. **Anne** loves them. If you are not a raisin fancier, use a cup of flake coconut instead. Or use one half cup of each if you have trouble deciding. This will work with any French bread, but do give it a try using **Kroger's** good in-store baked sourdough French bread.

As you know, traditional New Orleans bread pudding (I gave you a recipe for that some time back) is generally served with whiskey sauce. I also gave you that recipe. With this one, let me suggest a rum sauce instead.

RUM SAUCE FOR BREAD PUDDING

 ½ cup butter
 ½ cup sugar
 1 egg yolk
 ¼ cup water
 ¼ cup rum

In a heavy saucepan, melt butter. Remove from heat, and stir in first the sugar, then the egg yolk, then the water. Return to medium heat, stirring constantly; cook until the sugar melts and the mixture begins to thicken. Do not allow to boil. Remove from heat, and stir in rum. The sauce will continue to thicken as it cools. In case you have lost your whiskey sauce recipe, it's the same as this with bourbon whiskey rather than the rum.

105

Walter N. Lambert, Noonday Chef

SAFE PASTA SALAD (TV 320)

1 16 oz pkg salad rotini, cooked according to pkg directions
5 cups (approx) broccoli florets, lightly blanched
1 cup each, chopped onion and parsley
2 cups peeled, chopped tomatoes
6 green onions, coarsely chopped
¾ cup fresh basil
½ cup each extra virgin olive oil and red wine vinegar
2 tsp salt
1 tsp chopped garlic

Toss the pasta, broccoli, onions, parsley, and tomatoes lightly. Place all remaining ingredients in container of blender. Blend until thoroughly mixed. Pour over pasta mixture and toss to mix completely. Allow to stand several hours covered in the refrigerator before serving.

One of the recurrent problems of summer is how to get food to picnics without getting food poisoning and dying. One of the great dangers is salads mixed with mayonnaise or sour cream. This light, flavorful salad depends on fresh herbs and good olive oil and vinegar to give it plenty of flavor without any mayonnaise at all. It has the added advantage of being better after it stands for a while. Make the night before, chill in a **Tupperware** bowl, and off you go.

Now since this is a salad, you should note that all measurements are approximate. What kind of pasta you use is also your choice. I think the rotini looks interesting, and it has lots of holes for the sauce to hide in. If you like shells better, go to it. Also, this works nicely with a mixture of broccoli, cauliflower, carrots, cucumber, celery, or any combination thereof. The broccoli, cauliflower, and carrots will do better if they are blanched before adding.

Oh, you don't know how to <u>blanch vegetables</u>. Then you have come to the right place. Put a heavy kettle on with a couple of quarts of water. Bring to a full boil. Dump in vegetables. Bring back to a boil. Pour immediately through a colander to get rid of the hot water and immediately run cold water over the vegetables to stop the cooking. This intensifies the flavor and color of the vegetables.

One last word, if you think that pasta or any other salad needs a creamy dressing to be good., then fine. Make this salad exactly by this recipe. When you arrive at your picnic, church supper, etc., and just before you start serving, stir in about ½ cup mayonnaise, sour cream, or fat free yogurt. Serve immediately.

Walter N. Lambert, Noonday Chef

CALICO BAKED BEANS (TV 321)

> 1 15 oz can each, white, black, chili hot and lima beans
> ½ cup catsup
> ½ cup molasses
> 2 TBSP mustard
> 1 cup onion, finely chopped

Mix all ingredients and turn into a 9x13" pan which has been sprayed with a non-stick spray. Bake at 300 deg for 2 to 2½ hours or until thick and browned on top. Serve at room temperature.

Everyone has their own way of doing baked beans. My problem is that I like all of them. This variation draws its interest from the use of the various colored and flavored beans. The ingredients which you mix in are pretty standard. Please note that any combination of beans will work. The only one which I always include are the chili hot beans because I like the little bit of added flavor they give. If you don't want to go to this much trouble, an equal mix of pork and beans and chili hots make good baked beans.

An old time favorite in my family is made with pork and beans. Place the pork and beans in a 2 quart casserole to within about an inch of the top. Peel a couple of onions and slice them paper thin. Spread on top of the beans. Over that, spread a bottle of chili sauce. (Look in the same section with the barbeque sauce). Bake, uncovered, at 350 deg for about an hour.

Finally, we should at least mention the baked beans which started us on all this.

NEW ENGLAND BAKED BEANS

> 1 lb navy beans
> ¼ lb salt bacon
> 1 cup tomatoes, peeled, seeded and chopped fine
> ½ cup molasses
> 1 cup onion, chopped fine
> salt and pepper to taste

Wash the beans, and bring to a full boil in water which covers the beans by about 2 inches. Drain beans; reserve liquid. Cut the bacon into very small pieces. Mix the bacon, beans, and all remaining ingredients with about 2 cups of the bean liquid, and turn into a heavy baking dish with a tight fitting lid. Bake about one hour. Stir and add an additional cup of liquid. Bake another hour. Stir again, and add more liquid if needed. Uncover and bake another hour. Serve hot.

Walter N. Lambert, Noonday Chef

SUMMER STIR FRY (TV 328)

2 to 3 TBSP cooking oil
10 to 12 oz chicken cut into uniform pieces
1 green pepper, cut into slices
2 cups other vegetables (snow peas, mushrooms, zucchini,
 bean sprouts, broccoli etc.)
½ cup green onions, sliced thin
3 TBSP soy sauce
½ cup chicken stock
1 TBSP cornstarch
¼ tsp hot pepper flakes (optional)

Mix together soy sauce, stock, cornstarch, and pepper (if using) and set aside. In a wok or large skillet, heat oil and add chicken. Stir fry about 1 minute or until it changes color. Stir in green peppers and other vegetables which need longer to cook. Stir fry one minute. Stir in snow peas and green onions; cook about one minute. Re-stir the cornstarch mixture, and pour over meat and vegetable. Stir fry until the mixture is thick and clear. Serve hot.

This is a basic stir fry, and I have called it summer stir fry because I have kept it simple to take advantage of good summer vegetables which are available. In every case, the amounts given are approximate. Any combination of vegetables that look particularly good that day can be used. If you are using vegetables like zucchini, yellow squash, or broccoli, be sure to add it first and give it a couple of extra minutes to cook. Then add vegetables in order of how much cooking they need. Beans sprouts always go in last. You want them to stay crisp.

Now you should understand that nothing is sacred in this recipe. If you want it to be vegetarian, leave out the chicken and add an equal amount of tofu. Simply rinse it off, cut it into squares, dry it with paper towels, and proceed as above. If you like the flavor of garlic, add minced garlic to the sauce. If you do not want a sauce, simply sprinkle the soy sauce onto the vegetable mixture at the end of the cooking time, and cook about 30 seconds.

I personally like stir fry a little stronger flavored than this. I do that by increasing the amount of soy sauce, adding some minced ginger, and some garlic. Again, we are dealing with something that you will need to experiment with until you have it tasting the way you want it. And lest I forget, if you do not want to use chicken, use turkey. I have made a great stir fry with turkey, ginger, soya sauce, and asparagus. Try it.

Walter N. Lambert, Noonday Chef

MACAROON CAKE (TV 329)
ZELMA CATE, MASCOT, TN.

2 cups each, sugar and flour
1 cup **Wesson** oil
6 eggs
1 tsp orange flavoring
2 tsp almond flavoring

Mix together sugar, flour, and oil. Add eggs one at a time, beating after each. Add flavorings. Spray a tube pan with a non-stick spray and line the bottom with waxed paper. Do not flour. Turn batter into pan, and bake at 300 deg for 45 minutes and then 325 deg for 15 minutes. Allow to cool in pan about 10 or 15 minutes before removing from the pan.

The name of this cake comes from the texture of the crust on the top of the cake. Not flouring the pan gives a firmer, browner crust which adds to the cake. If you do not like almond flavor (I do not) use vanilla instead. In fact, my favorite (and **Zelma** agreed) is lemon instead of the orange and vanilla instead of the almond.

HOT SAUSAGE BALLS
LILA PROPHATER, HARRIMAN, TN.

2 lb hot sausage
½ cup each, brown sugar, red wine vinegar, and catsup
2 TBSP soy sauce
1 tsp ginger

Shape the sausage into balls of desired size, and cook in a 350 deg oven for 30 minutes turning once. Drain. Heat all remaining ingredients in a heavy sauce pan until sugar is melted. Place drained sausage in a covered dish, and pour sauce over. Cover and refrigerate at least overnight. Reheat and serve hot.

Lila says that the size of the meatballs depends on how she is going to use them. If they are for a tea she makes them very small. If part of a meal, she makes them larger. If you are going to use these for a party, it is especially nice that they are done the day ahead, and all you have to do is heat them. By the way, if you store them in a glass dish with a lid, all you have to do is pop them into the oven for about 20 minutes, and you are ready to go.

Walter N. Lambert, Noonday Chef

CLASSIC BANANAS FOSTER
GREG MANGAN, KNOXVILLE, TN.

    4 TBSP butter
    1 ¼ cup brown sugar
    1 tsp cinnamon
    juice of ½ orange and ½ lemon
    3 bananas, peeled, cut into half lengthwise and then across
    1 oz creme de banana liquor
    ¾ oz rum

Melt butter and brown sugar together until smooth and all lumps are gone. Add cinnamon, orange juice, and lemon juice. Stir constantly! Add bananas and banana liquor. Cook until bananas soften slightly. Carefully add rum and ignite. Serve over vanilla ice cream.

You will be surprised at how easy it is to do this classic, fancy looking dessert. Just lay all your ingredients out before the meal except your bananas. Slice them at the last minute so they will stay light in color.

TOM'S TURKEY CHILI
TOM CHAFFINS, KNOXVILLE, TN

    2 lb ground turkey
    2 16 oz jars salsa (mild, medium or hot)
    1 16 oz jar picante sauce
    1 TBSP each, chopped garlic, ground cumin, coarse ground
     black pepper
    2 TBSP chili powder
    1 tsp dried mint (crushed)
    2 tsp sugar
    1 cup chopped onion
    1 quart bloody Mary mix

In a large pot over medium heat, place all ingredients except turkey, onion, sugar, and bloody Mary mix. In a large non-stick saute pan brown turkey. Drain; add to chili pot. In the same pan, saute the onion, sprinkled with the sugar, until brown. Add to the pot. Add Bloody Mary mix until chili has desired consistency. You are going to be amazed at how tasty this is without added fat. Unfortunately, Tom chooses to serve it with good, fat cornbread. He does it a new way which I think you would enjoy. Make your favorite cornbread and bake it until it is almost done. Remove from the oven and spread on the top a jar of salsa which you have drained thoroughly. Over this, spread a mixture of grated Monterey jack and cheddar cheese. Return to the oven and leave until the salsa is heated through and cheese is melted.

Walter N. Lambert, Noonday Chef

HAM DELIGHTS
DIXIE CRUZE, STRAWBERRY PLAINS

      2 lb precooked ham, ground
      1 large onion, grated
      7 oz Swiss cheese, grated
      6 tsp each, mustard and poppy seeds
      2½ sticks butter or margarine, melted
      1 tsp worcestershire sauce
      4 pkg Pepperidge Farm Party rolls

Mix all ingredients (except rolls) together well. Slice tops off the rolls and spread the bottoms (still in the foil pan) generously with the ham mixture. Replace tops on rolls. Cover tightly with foil. Bake 15 minutes at 350 deg. Serve hot.

Dixie, who is quite a cook, tells us that these freeze nicely if you are doing them for a party. Prepare the rolls up to the point that you seal them with foil. Place in the freezer. About an hour before you plan to serve them, remove from the freezer and allow to partially thaw. Bake for about 25 minutes at 350 deg.

Walter N. Lambert, Noonday Chef

TENNESSEE APPLE SWIRLS (TV 330)

    4 cups apples, peeled and sliced thin
    1½ cup sugar, divided
    ¼ cup water
    1½ cup **White Lily** self-rising flour
    2 TBSP cooking oil
    milk to make ½ cup
    4 TBSP butter, softened
    cinnamon to taste

In a heavy sauce pan, place the apples, 1 cup sugar, and ¼ cup water; stir to mix. Bring to a boil and cook until tender. When the apples are almost cooked, mix flour and ¼ cup sugar with the oil and milk to form a dough. Knead lightly on waxed paper. Roll into an 8 x 10" rectangle. Spread evenly with the butter. Sprinkle with remaining sugar and cinnamon. Roll up along long edge, seal edge, and cut crosswise into ½" slices. Pour apples into an 8" square pan which is sprayed with a non-stick spray. Place cinnamon roll slices on top of hot apples. Bake in a 350 deg oven for about 25 minutes or until brown on top. Serve hot.

With this recipe, we begin pick **Tennessee Products Month**. Each August, the **Tennessee Department of Agriculture** reminds folks in Tennessee that a good way to eat good and to benefit the economy of the state is to buy products grown or made in Tennessee. Here in East Tennessee, one of the best of these is apples. Whether you get them at **The Apple Barn** between Sevierville and Pigeon Forge or you drive to visit the **Baxters at Cosby**, you can get great apples. For this recipe, I like an apple which cooks without cooking up. I think it looks pretty.

The top crust of this dish is made with **White Lily Flour**. I use self-rising because it is easy. If you like, use plain and add a pinch of salt and about 1½ tsp baking powder. If you do not want to go to the trouble of making the cinnamon rolls as I have described above, simply mix all the sugar, cinnamon, and butter into the biscuit dough. Roll it out, and place it on top of the apples. It will not look as pretty, but it will be very good.

This kind of biscuit cinnamon roll is the basis of one of my favorite childhood treats. To do it, simply forget about the apples. Spray an 8" pan with a non-stick spray, and make the cinnamon rolls exactly as described above. Sprinkle the bottom of the pan with about ½ cup sugar and some cinnamon. Place the rolls evenly over the sugar and cinnamon. Pour about ¾ cup water over the rolls and bake at 350 deg for about 30 minutes, or until done. Spoon out onto individual serving dishes and you have "stickies". Remember, you heard it here.

Walter N. Lambert, Noonday Chef

TENNESSEE PASTA (TV 331)

2 TBSP cooking oil
½ to ¾ lb lean country ham, coarsely chopped
1 cup onion, chopped
3 cups tomato, peeled, seeded and chopped
8 oz pasta
1 cup grated Monterey Jack cheese

Cook pasta according to package directions and drain. In a heavy skillet, heat the oil and cook the onion until it starts to brown. Add the country ham and cook about 1 minutes, stirring constantly. Add the tomato and continue to cook on high, stirring. When the sauce starts to thicken, pour in the pasta and toss to mix. Turn into bowls to serve and sprinkle with the cheese. Serve hot.

Remember, we are picking **Tennessee products**. In this recipe, I sometimes use the **UT-shaped pasta** which is made by a company in Nashville. I use **Clifty Farm** ham and of course, I use only **Grainger County tomatoes**. My current favorite cheese is made by **Tennessee Valley Cheese Company** of Morrison, TN. If you write to them they will send you a catalog. If you live in the Knoxville area, you can find a full selection of **Tennessee Valley Cheese** at the **Knox County Farmer's Market** on Washington Pike.

By the way, my favorite way to have **Clifty Farm** country ham is just fried with some good **White Lily** flour biscuits. When I fry country ham, I first cut off as much fat as possible. I then fry that fat in a skillet on fairly high heat. When you have cooked the fat meat until it is brown and the grease is cooked out, lift the meat out and discard it. You can then proceed to fry the ham in the fat you have rendered. This keeps the lean ham from sticking and keeps the flavor of the ham fairly strong. I fry country ham hot. I like it brown on the outside and soft on the inside. I fry ham one layer at a time in the pan just as if I were frying bacon. When I have fried all the ham I need, I make red eye gravy by pouring the fat off into a heat-proof dish. I then get the skillet very hot and add about 1 cup of water or black coffee and let it cook down until it starts to thicken a little. I then pour that into the grease and serve it with hot biscuits.

Good **White Lily** biscuits are easy to make. To 2 cups of **White Lily** self-rising flour add ¼ cup of cooking oil and ¾ cup of milk. Work it into the flour to make a fairly soft dough. Knead three or four turns on a piece of waxed paper. Pat out to about ½" thick and cut into biscuits. Reshape and pat out any remaining dough and cut more biscuits. Bake at 400 deg about 15 minutes.

Walter N. Lambert, Noonday Chef

STUFFED TENNESSEE CORNBREAD (TV 332)

    3 cups **White Lily Cornmeal** mix
    2 cups milk
    8 oz country sausage
    1 cup onion, chopped
    8 oz mushrooms sliced

In a heavy skillet on high heat, cook and crumble the sausage until browned. Add the onion, and continue to stir and cook. Stir in the mushrooms. Continue to cook until the mushrooms start to brown. While this mixture is cooking, mix the cornmeal mix and milk and turn about ⅔ of the cornmeal mix into a well greased 10" spring form pan. Drain any liquid from the sausage mixture and spread it on the cornbread batter leaving about ½ inch clear around the outside. Pour the remaining batter evenly around the sausage mixture. Bake in a 400 deg oven about 35 minutes or until brown on top. Remove from oven and remove the outer rim of the pan. Serve immediately.

I call this dish a symphony of Tennessee Products. I don't need to tell you about **White Lily** products. If **White Lily** makes it, it is good. I have come to prefer **Tennessee Pride** sausage. I personally like the sage flavor best, but that is a matter of taste. The mushrooms I use almost exclusively are **Monterey Brand** mushrooms which are grown in Lenoir City, Tennessee. If you like, about 10 minutes before it finishes baking, generously sprinkle the top with a good grated cheddar cheese. If you remember, I told you last week about the good cheese from **Tennessee Valley Cheese Company** in Morrison, Tennessee. They have it at **Knox County Farmer's Market**.

Now just a word about **Monterey Brand mushrooms**. I use them constantly. There may be some way to do them that I don't like, but I haven't found it yet. The following is one of my favorites.

CHICKEN AND MUSHROOMS

    1 lb Monterey mushrooms, sliced
    1 lb chicken breasts, cooked and cut into cubes
    2 TBSP each, butter and flour
    1 cup of chicken stock

Heat butter in a heavy skillet and saute mushrooms on high heat until wilted and starting to brown. Stir in the flour and stir to mix completely. Add chicken stock; stir until it comes to a boil and thickens. Add the chicken and cook a couple of minutes until it is hot through. Add salt and pepper to taste. Serve over toast points or rice.

Walter N. Lambert, Noonday Chef

GREEN TOMATO CAKE (TV 333)

2¼ cups sugar
3 eggs
2 cups plain flour
1 tsp each, salt, soda, cinnamon, nutmeg
1 cup each, shortening, raisins, nuts
2 tsp vanilla
2½ cups diced green tomatoes

Cream together shortening and sugar. Add eggs one at a time; cream together. Beat in vanilla. Mix together flour, salt, soda, cinnamon, and nutmeg. Blend into the egg mixture. Beat in tomatoes, nuts, and raisins. Turn into a greased and floured, 9X13" dish and bake in a 350 deg oven for 1 hour.

I can't help it. I am just a sucker for recipes that are a little peculiar. And what could be more peculiar than a cake with chopped up green tomatoes in it. In mean, after all, everyone knows that green tomatoes are good fried. Or made into relish.

Well actually, this did not come as a real surprise to me. I have an uncle who was raised over in North Carolina, and his family made green tomato pie. From them, my aunt learned, and from her, I learned. I now will teach you.

GREEN TOMATO PIE

pie crust for a double crust pie
sliced green tomatoes
1 cup sugar
1 TBSP flour
¾ tsp cinnamon
2 TBSP vinegar
1 TBSP water
2 TBSP butter

Place the unbaked bottom crust in a deep 9-inch pie pan. Thinly slice enough green tomatoes to fill the crust. Combine sugar, flour and cinnamon and spread evenly over the tomatoes. Sprinkle with water and vinegar. Dot with butter. Cover with the top crust and seal. Bake in a hot oven (400 deg) for 10 minutes. Reduce heat to 350 deg and cook for 30 to 35 minutes more or until brown. Do Not undercook.

This recipe is from our cookbook **_Kinfolks and Custard Pie_** which is available at your neighborhood bookstore. Or I hope it is.

Walter N. Lambert, Noonday Chef

TEMPTING TOFFEE TREATS (TV 334)

    6 TBSP butter, melted
    ¾ cup brown sugar
    ¼ tsp salt
    2 TBSP milk
    1 tsp vanilla
    2 cups rolled oats

Mix butter, brown sugar, salt, milk and vanilla. Stir in the oats. Mix well. Divide evenly into 24 greased tiny muffins tins. Bake at 325 deg for 20 minutes. Allow to cool in the pan at least five minutes. Loosen with a thin knife and turn out.

This is one of many variations now circulating to make a toffee tasting treat without all the trouble, fuss and mess of making true English Toffee. **Anne** has a great recipe and sometime maybe we can get her to share it. However, I must tell you that it requires lots of time and equipment. This requires almost nothing. By the way, do use the little gem muffin tins. If you try it in regular pans, the pieces are simply too large.

Now if you want to dress these little goodies up a little, it is very easy. When these are turned out, the bottoms are nice and brown and pretty. The tops don't look like much. Therefore, I like to dip the tops in chocolate and sometimes in finely chopped nuts.

If you want to go to the trouble, you can use regular chocolate chips for this. Simply place 6 oz of the chips in a microwave dish and heat about one minute. Stir. Continue to heat in 15 second intervals, stirring between each until the chocolate is soft. To get a firm chocolate, you may want to add about 1 TBSP of finely cut paraffin with the chocolate chips.

There is an easier way. Go to Kroger and in the sugar and spice section, you will find chocolate flavored "bark" mix. This is a chocolate which has been premixed to make it easy to melt and use. Again, for one recipe of these goodies, melt two of the squares of the bark mix following the instructions above for chocolate. Then holding the little gems by the sides dip about ¼ inch of the top into the melted chocolate and place, chocolate side up, on waxed paper to cool. If you want nuts, have the nuts chopped fine on a saucer and dip the toffee treats into the chocolate and immediately into the nuts.

Any time you are using chocolate, be careful not to overheat it. It will become a lumpy mess if you do. Also, be careful that no water gets into the melted chocolate.

Walter N. Lambert, Noonday Chef

HANDY PUMPKIN MUFFINS (TV335)

    1½ cups sugar
    3 eggs
    1 cup cooking oil
    1 tsp vanilla
    1 16 oz can pumpkin (about 2 cups)
    2¼ cups plain flour
    1½ tsp each, salt, baking powder, soda, and cinnamon
    ½ cup chopped nuts
    1 cup raisins

Beat together the sugar, eggs, oil, and vanilla. Stir together the flour, salt, baking powder, soda and cinnamon. Mix with the oil mixture just enough to blend. Stir in nuts and raisins. Fill cups of muffin pans about ⅔ full. Bake in a 350 deg oven about 15 minutes or until lightly browned. Makes about 2 dozen.

One of the ways that I know it is fall is that I start to think about pumpkin and sweet potatoes. I haven't started to see fresh pumpkin in the market yet, but it won't be long. In fact, for these little gems, canned pumpkin works just as well. If you want to use your own fresh pumpkin for these, be sure to cook it down very thick and mash it well. Otherwise, the batter will be too thin, and the muffins will fall apart. A nice thing about these muffins is that the batter will keep very nicely in the refrigerator. Simply place it in a bowl with a tight cover and keep it cold. When you are ready for muffins, give it a quick stir, put it in the pans, and away you go. **Anne** and I have muffin pans with four cups and that way we can have fresh rather than warmed over muffins whenever we want them. Years ago, we used to do bran muffins the same way. For some reason we stopped that. Perhaps it was that we ate too many muffins. At any rate here is the recipe.

HANDY BRAN MUFFINS

    1 cup each all-bran cereal and hot water
    1½ cup sugar
    ¾ cup cooking oil
    2 eggs
    2 cups buttermilk
    2 1/2 cup plain flour
    2 1/2 tsp baking soda
    1 tsp salt
    2 cups raisin bran cereal

Pour hot water over all-bran; allow to stand. In large bowl, mix sugar, oil, eggs, and buttermilk. Mix together all dry ingredients. Stir dry ingredients into milk mixture. Add raisin bran. Bake in 375 deg oven about 20 minutes or until brown.

Walter N. Lambert, Noonday Chef

SAVORY SWEET POTATO CASSEROLE (TV 336)

4 medium sweet potatoes
1 lb **Tennessee Pride Country Sausage**, fried and drained
3 cups milk
2 TBSP flour
4 eggs
1 tsp salt
sprinkle of nutmeg

Boil sweet potatoes until barely tender, peel and slice. Arrange half of the slices in the bottom of a greased 9x13" pan. Sprinkle sausage over potatoes. Cover top with the remaining potato slices. Beat together eggs, salt, and flour. Beat in the milk. Pour over potatoes evenly. Sprinkle with nutmeg. Bake in a 350 deg oven about 45 minutes or until lightly browned.

Some of us tend to get into a rut about certain things. Sweet potatoes would certainly be one such thing. We know that you can boil them and put butter and sugar over them to bake for candied sweet potatoes. You know that you can cook them, mash them, add eggs, brown sugar, nutmeg and milk and make a nice sweet potato pudding. Some marshmallows on top when it is almost finished baking is not a bad touch. It is also nice to mix together some coconut, pecans and butter and sprinkle that over the top of the sweet potato pudding for the last 10 minutes of baking. And then there is sweet potato pie. We all remember **Grandpa Jones** singing about "Pie, Pie, 'tater Pie". And it is good. And easy. Again, boil your sweet potatoes, peel and mash them. For four potatoes, add about 1 stick of butter, ¾ cup brown sugar, 1 tsp nutmeg, 2 eggs, and about ½ cup of heavy cream. If you want the filling to be very firm, beat in about 3 or 4 TBSP flour. Pour into an unbaked 9" deep dish pie shell and bake in a 350 deg oven about 1 hour or until puffed and brown. Allow to cool before serving.

But this recipe is not about that. This is about sweet potatoes cooked for their natural flavor into a savory casserole. By the way, if you scorn country sausage, use about 1 lb of left over ham cut into small cubes. It is great. If you are vegetarian, leave out the sausage and use only the sliced sweet potatoes with the custard. Cut the milk back to about 2 cups and use 3 eggs. This makes a great side dish with baked chicken or roast pork.

And besides, I taught you that sweet potatoes didn't have to be sweet a long time ago. Look on page 76 of ***Cooking With the Noonday Chef Volume 2.*** for a great potato salad made with sweet potatoes. Go look it up!

Walter N. Lambert, Noonday Chef

CHOCOLATE CHOCOLATE CHUNK COOKIES (TV 337)

1 cup **Crisco** butter flavored shortening (or butter)
1½ cups sugar
2 large eggs
1 tsp vanilla
2 cups plain flour
⅔ cup cocoa
¾ tsp soda
¼ tsp salt
1 10 oz pkg semisweet chocolate chunks
½ cup chopped almonds

Cream shortening and sugar until fluffy. Beat in eggs and vanilla. Mix flour, cocoa, soda, and salt. Beat into the egg mixture. Beat in nuts and chocolate chunks. Drop by teaspoonful onto an ungreased baking sheet, and bake at 350 deg for 10 to 12 minutes. Allow to cool on the pan before removing to a rack to cool completely.

I love cookies. I love chocolate. So what could make more sense than chocolate cookies. Especially if you double up on the chocolate. These are great for the busy times of the fall with parties and all that stuff. They go into the holidays just fine as well. In fact, they can be made ahead, layered with wax paper in a tight container, and frozen. When you are ready to serve them, allow to come to room temperature (in a single layer, still on the waxed paper) and away you go.

One word of caution. When these come from the oven, they are very, very soft. It is impossible to pick them up before they cool for a couple of minutes. Other than that, it is the only slight word of caution.

Now let me tell you about a couple of variations. If you have trouble finding chocolate chunks, use the miniature kisses which are now available. The milk chocolate in them is great. **M & M's** also work just fine. But I will have to tell you my all time favorite with these cookies. Instead of the chocolate chunks and the almonds, add a 10 or 12 oz bag of **Reese's peanut butter chips** and ½ cup chopped peanuts. If you use salted peanuts, leave the salt out of the batter. Trust me, these are excellent. Again, all these will freeze just fine if you can keep folks hands out of them long enough to have any to freeze.

Now next week, we are going to get back onto our fall treats of apples, sweet potatoes, pumpkin and the like. But I had not done chocolate in weeks, and I was starting to shake a little. After all, we must comfort each other with chocolate.

Walter N. Lambert, Noonday Chef

HALLOWEEN CASSEROLE (TV 338)

1 small pumpkin
1 onion, chopped
2 TBSP oil
2 lb lean ground beef
¼ cup soy sauce
1 can cream of mushroom soup
2 cups cooked rice
1 8 oz can sliced water chestnuts, drained

Cut off top of the pumpkin and remove the seeds and pulp. In a heavy skillet, heat oil until hot and cook onion until soft. Add the beef and brown. Drain completely. Mix in all remaining ingredients and bring to a boil. Spoon mixture into the pumpkin shell. Replace top, and place on a baking sheet in a preheated 350 deg oven. Bake 1½ hours or until the pumpkin is tender. Scoop out the pumpkin and the meat together to serve.

This is a casserole which is strictly for fun. I mean nobody has to cook a casserole in a pumpkin. But think of the delight to be had by serving this as a Halloween night supper. And in addition to all that, it is very good. Now let me warn you. The cooking process is a balancing act. If you do not cook it long enough, the pumpkin will be hard. If you cook it too long, the pumpkin will collapse and you will have problems. So be careful, you hear.

I personally grew up with pumpkin being something which you made pies of. I talk about this at some length in **_Kinfolks and Custard Pie_**. Which is my cookbook done by the UT press several years ago. If you do not have it, get it and it will tell you considerably more than you want to know about pumpkin pies. If you do not find it, give me a call and I will tell you how to order it.

120

Walter N. Lambert, Noonday Chef

FRESH APPLE BREAD (TV 339)

2¼ cups self-rising flour
1 cup sour cream
1 cup granulated sugar
2 eggs
1 cup fresh apple, chopped fine
1 cup grated cheddar cheese
½ cup chopped nuts
1 tsp vanilla

Place sugar and apples in a food processor with the metal blade. Run about 30 seconds or until the apple is ground fine. Mix in all remaining ingredients except the flour. Stir the apple mixture into the flour just to mix. Turn into an 8" cake pan which has been sprayed with a cooking spray. Bake one hour in a 350 deg oven. Serve hot.

This is one of those recipes which is just made to be served on a cold morning. Fry some good country sausage, or even country ham, scramble some eggs and dig in. Try the bread spread with some apple butter just to gild the lily a little. Because of the cheese, you will not need butter, but some of you will want to anyway. This is designed to take advantage of the good apples we have in Tennessee at this time of year. By the way, if you do not have a food processor, simply grind the apples in a food mill or even in the blender. If you use the blender, add the apples, eggs, and sour cream to have enough liquid to grind them. The important thing is to grind the apples fine for the flavor they will give the bread.

Here is another good recipe for apples at breakfast:

APPLE-OAT PANCAKES

2 cups flour
1 TBSP baking powder
½ tsp salt
1 cup uncooked regular oats
2 TBSP sugar
2 eggs, beaten
2 cups milk
1 cup raw apple, finely ground
6 TBSP butter, melted

Mix all dry ingredients. Form a well and pour in all other ingredients; stir just to mix. Pour about ⅓ cup of batter for each pancake onto hot, greased griddle. Turn when pancake bubbles. Serve with syrup or just sprinkle with powdered sugar.

Walter N. Lambert, Noonday Chef

SAUSAGE-APPLE CASSEROLE (TV 340)

1 lb **Tennessee Pride Sausage**
1 large apple, peeled and thinly sliced
4 cups bread cubed
1 cup grated sharp cheddar cheese
4 eggs
2 cups milk

Fry sausage and drain on paper towels. Fry apple slices in sausage fat. Remove to the towels with the sausage. Place sausage and apples into an 8" square pan which has been sprayed with a cooking spray. Toss with the bread cubes and cheese. Mix together eggs and milk and pour over all. Bake at 350 deg for about 45 minutes or until set in the center. Serve hot.

This is the umpteenth variation on this wonderful dish which I have given you through the years. Now let me tell you a secret about it. It works great to completely put this casserole together the night before you plan to serve it. Cover tightly with plastic wrap, and refrigerate overnight. In the morning, pop it into the oven, allow to bake, and dazzle your guests at breakfast or brunch.

If you particularly like onions, you can chop an onion fine, cook it in with the sausage, and proceed as described above. You can also increase the amount of apples if you like a sweeter flavor. If you want to cut down on the fat even more than you do already, fry the apple slices in a non-stick skillet which you spray with a cooking spray. This will allow you to drain off the sausage fat and use absolutely none of it.

You will also notice that I specified **Tennessee Pride** sausage. That is because I like it best. It is completely a matter of taste whether you use mild, hot, or sage flavors. Sometimes I double this recipe and bake it in a 9x13" dish. When I do, I often use one pound of mild and one pound of hot sausage.

A final word about this casserole. We sometimes call it Sunday Morning Souffle. This is because as it bakes it will puff up and then fall as it cools. We have at one time or another baked almost everything into it. It is good with cubed ham instead of the sausage. It is good with a mixture of sausage and ground beef if you want to lighten the flavor a little. It is good just with cheese if you want to get rid of the meat. We have done it with half cheddar and half **Velvetta** (how is that for down to earth) which gives you the good taste of the cheddar and the creaminess of the Velvetta. Did someone say something about versatile?

Walter N. Lambert, Noonday Chef

CURRIED CHICKEN AND APPLE SALAD (TV 341)

2 to 2½ cups cooked, cubed chicken
2 apples, cored and cut into cubes
½ cup each, green onions chopped fine, raisins, and
unsalted peanuts
1 cup fat free yogurt
1 TBSP mild curry powder
salt to taste

Mix curry powder and salt with yogurt. Toss together all remaining ingredients except the peanuts. Add yogurt and toss again. Chill several hours or overnight. Add the peanuts. Toss and serve.

This is a super easy, low fat recipe which takes advantage of the natural affinity between apples, onions, and curry powder. The raisins are just for the fun of it.

Now I am about to make history. The following is a complicated version of an apples and chicken salad which I secured for you by "surfing the net". This recipe comes from a feature on the World Wide Web provided by the egg council. Don't ask me why it doesn't have eggs in it.

TOUCH OF APPLE CHICKEN SALAD

1 whole broiler-fryer chicken
2 cups apple juice
1 piece lemon peel
1 cup golden raisins
1 small onion, chopped
1 cup bean sprouts
1 cup chopped pecans
1 cup mayonnaise
¼ cup each, chopped green olives and sweet pepper relish
1 cup grated white cheese
spinach leaves

In a deep saucepan, place the chicken. Add the apple juice and lemon peel. Cover and simmer about 45 minutes or until fork tender. Remove chicken and cool; reserve broth. Add raisins to broth and allow to stand 20 minutes or until raisins are plumped. Remove chicken meat from the bones; discard skin and bones. Chop the chicken, place in a large bowl; drain the raisins and mix with the chicken. Add the onion, bean sprouts, pecans, mayonnaise, olives, and pepper relish; stir to mix well. Chill in the refrigerator. Arrange spinach leaves on a serving dish; add the chicken mixture and sprinkle with cheese.

Walter N. Lambert, Noonday Chef

TURNIP GREENS (TV 342)

Thoroughly wash greens to be cooked. Nothing is worse than grit in greens. I personally mix turnip greens with curly mustard, kale and anything else which I happen to have available. It is better not to use spinach, because it cooks too quickly, and collards because they cook too slowly.

Once you have the greens clean, you have two choices. First is the parboil method. To do this, place about three times as many greens as you want when you are finished into a large pot and pour on cold water to almost cover. Bring to a boil and boil about 15 minutes. Drain. Fry bacon (preferably salt bacon) in a heavy skillet with a lid. If you have 6 to 8 cups of cooked greens, you will need about ½ pound bacon. Remove bacon, and place greens into the hot fat with a little of the water in which they parboiled. Cover and cook, stirring occasionally, about 30 minutes. Remove lid and cook out any excess water. Salt to taste and serve hot.

Another method for green cooking, I call the "pot liquor" method. In this method, the washed greens are placed in a heavy pot with a ham hock or a chunk of salt bacon and just a small amount of water. They are covered and brought slowly to a boil. The heat is then decreased just to the point that the greens will continue to boil. They then are allowed to cook slowly for a couple of hours. The cover is then removed, and excess water is cooked out until the remaining liquid starts to thicken and turn very dark (this is pot liquor). Salt to taste and serve with cornbread.

Now you should know that we got off onto all of this because of **Tanna Nicely** and her second grade class at Sunnyview School. They had a garden full of greens and wanted to know what to do with them. I then did a survey of females I know and discovered that none of them had ever cooked greens from scratch. Now you have no excuse. Also, just so you will know, this is how I make cornbread. Notice it has no eggs and certainly NO sugar.

CORNBREAD

      3 cups cornmeal
      1 cup plain flour
      2 TBSP baking powder
      1 tsp baking soda
      1 1/2 to 2 cups buttermilk

Heavily grease (and I do mean heavily) a heavy skillet. Mix the dry ingredients, then stir in buttermilk to make a batter that is about the consistency of heavy cream. Pour into skillet, and bake about 30 minutes at 375 deg until brown.

124

Walter N. Lambert, Noonday Chef

WEEK OF TURKEY TIPS (TV 343)

MONDAY

<u>ALWAYS be sure that turkey is COMPLETELY THAWED</u>

Remove neck from inside cavity and giblets from under skin at breast. Place in a saucepan with several cups of water; cook until tender. Set aside for dressing and gravy.

Rinse turkey completely (inside as well) with warm water. Dry off outside of turkey, rub with vegetable oil (or spray with a cooking spray), and sprinkle with salt. Place on a rack over a roasting pan with 2 or 3 cups of water poured into the pan.

Roast uncovered in a 325 deg oven about 15 to 20 minutes per pound. That is about 3 hours for a 12 pound turkey. If the turkey starts to brown too much cover with a loose tent of foil.

Pour the pan drippings from the turkey roaster into the giblets above. Allow to stand at least 30 minutes before slicing.

TUESDAY

DRESSING

    4 cups each, cornbread and biscuit crumbs
    2 medium onions, minced
    4 stalks celery, cut small
    2 tsp each, black pepper and salt
    1 tsp ground cayenne pepper
    1 to 2 TBSP rubbed sage
    2 cups water
    4 cups (approx) turkey broth

Place onion and celery in a saucepan with water and bring to a boil. Place the rest of the ingredients, except broth in large mixing bowl. Mix thoroughly and pour onion-celery mixture over. Add broth and stir until the mixture is soft but still hold its shape. Taste and adjust seasonings as necessary. Place in a greased, large, flat baking dish and bake in a 350 deg oven until browned and firm (about 1 hour).

Walter N. Lambert, Noonday Chef

Week of Turkey Tips Continued

WEDNESDAY
PRALINE TOPPING FOR PUMPKIN PIE

    1 cup coarsely chopped pecans
    ¾ cup brown sugar
    ¼ tsp nutmeg
    4 TBSP butter, softened

Bake your favorite 9" pumpkin pie and allow to cool. Mix all ingredients together, and sprinkle evenly over the top of the pie. Place about 4 inches from the preheated broiler; cook until the top is glazed and bubbly. Allow to cool and serve at room temperature.

TRADITIONAL CRANBERRY ORANGE RELISH

    1 pound cranberries, washed
    2 small oranges, quartered and the seeds removed
    2 cups sugar

In a food processor or food grinder, grind cranberries and oranges (including the peel) together. Stir in sugar. Put into a container with a tight fitting cover. Refrigerate at least overnight before serving.

THURSDAY
GIBLET GRAVY

    6 cups rich turkey stock (approx)
    giblets cut into small pieces
    2 cups milk
    ½ cup plain flour
    salt and black pepper to taste

Mix flour completely with the milk. (I shake it in a tightly closed quart jar). Bring the stock and giblets to a full boil. Stir in milk mixture. Stir continuously until thick. Add salt and pepper to taste. Serve hot.

Gravy is a very personal thing. This is turkey gravy made the way my mother and grandmother did. It is white gravy. If you wish it to be browner, use water instead of milk and add a couple of TBSP soy sauce. It will be just as good and a nice caramel brown. If you wish to do so, and do not mind the added fat, you can make a roue from a stick of butter which you melt in your saucepan. Stir in flour and cook until lightly browned. Then add your hot broth and giblets. This will make a rich, creamy gravy. It will be FAT.

126

Walter N. Lambert, Noonday Chef

Week of Turkey Tips Continued

FRIDAY
TURKEY STIR FRY

> 4 to 6 cups leftover turkey cubed
> 1 medium onion, peeled and cut into strips
> 6 to 8 cups mixed vegetables (I prefer broccoli, cauliflower, and carrots), lightly cooked
> 2 TBSP cooking oil
> ½ cup soya sauce
> 1 bottle commercial oyster sauce

In a wok or a heavy skillet, heat oil and cook onion until it starts to brown, stirring constantly. Add the turkey and cook for a couple of minutes until hot. Add vegetables and stir to toss. Stir in soy sauce and oyster sauce; cook another couple of minutes. Serve hot with rice.

Walter N. Lambert, Noonday Chef

ANOTHER EASY MEAT LOAF (TV 344)

½ LB **Tennessee Pride Country Sausage**
1½ LB lean ground beef
1 medium onion, chopped fine
1½ cups fine cracker crumbs
¼ cup worchestershire sauce
1 8 oz can tomato sauce
2 eggs
2 tsp each, salt and black pepper

Knead all ingredients together thoroughly. Shape into one large or two small loaves and place into a 9x13" pan, which has been sprayed with a cooking spray. Bake in a 350 deg oven about one hour. Remove from the oven and move immediately to a serving platter. Allow to stand at least ½ hour before serving.

I absolutely love meat loaf. There may be some ways to cook it that I do not like, but I have not found it yet. There are as many ways to do it as there are cooks. I like this way because it makes a fairly coarse, fairly soft meat loaf which is good hot or cold. As far as I am concerned, the real reason for making meat loaf is to have some cold for sandwiches.

If you promise not to tell anyone, I will let you in on a secret. I love meat loaf sandwiches on whole wheat bread with mayonnaise and **American** Cheese.

Now let me give you a tip about this meat loaf. You can make nice potatoes with it without messing up another dish. Once you have placed your loaves into the pan, cut about 3 or 4 potatoes into quarters or eights and spray them lightly with a cooking spray. You may choose whether or not you want to peel them. I do not. Arrange potatoes around meat loaf and let them roast while the meat loaf is cooking. Do not stack them any more than you have to. When the meat loaf is done, the potatoes will be also. Remove the meat loaf from the pan, arrange the potatoes around it, sprinkle with a little chopped parsley, and it will look like the Ritz.

Now one last word about meat loaf. I like just a little tomato flavor in it, but do not want the tomato to predominate. Hence the tomato sauce blended into the meat loaf. If you like a stronger tomato flavor, you have a couple of easy choices. First, you may use catsup instead of the tomato sauce. Second, you can wait until the meat is almost done and spread the top with more catsup and allow it to brown. Finally, you can soak about a cup of sun dried tomatoes in warm water until soft. Drain and chop the tomatoes and add to the meat mixture.

Walter N. Lambert, Noonday Chef

CRUNCHY PEANUT BROWNIES (TV 345)

　　¾ cup smooth peanut butter
　　½ cup butter or margarine
　　1½ cups brown sugar, firmly packed
　　2 eggs
　　2 tsp vanilla
　　1½ cups flour
　　1½ tsp baking powder
　　pinch of salt
　　½ cup chopped peanuts

Cream peanut butter, butter, and brown sugar until mixed and fluffy. Beat in eggs and vanilla until smooth. Mix dry ingredients and beat into the creamed mixture. Spread in a 9x13" pan which has been lined with aluminum foil and the foil greased. Sprinkle with peanuts. Bake in a preheated 375 deg oven about 15 minutes, or until lightly browned. Allow to cool 10 minutes in pan. Lift out with the aluminum foil and cut into squares. Allow to cool.

These brownies have no chocolate and you will not care. These are the kind of brownies which are so rich and moist that they are more like candy than cake. The peanut and peanut butter taste is perfect. I recommend lining the pan with the foil because these come out of the oven very soft. If you try to turn them out, it will be a disaster. Of course, you could just allow them to cool in the pan and then cut them, but the chance of sticking is great. Now I know most of you believe that to be good, brownies must have chocolate. Fine. Let me suggest an easy solution to this. Make the brownies exactly as above. At the end, stir in a 12 oz pkg of chocolate chips and proceed as described. Instant chocolate chip peanut brownies.

BUTTERSCOTCH BROWNIES

　　½ cup butter or margarine
　　2 cups firmly packed brown sugar
　　2 eggs
　　1½ tsp vanilla
　　1 ¾ cup flour
　　1½ tsp baking powder
　　¼ tsp each, soda and salt
　　1 cup chopped pecans

Cream butter and brown sugar. Add eggs and vanilla and beat together. Mix all dry ingredients and beat into creamed mixture. Beat in pecans. Turn into a greased 9x13 dish and bake in a 350 deg oven about 25 minutes. Cool in the pan. While warm, cut into squares. Cool completely in pan.

Walter N. Lambert, Noonday Chef

SNAPPY SAUSAGE BALLS (TV 346)

    1 lb **Tennessee Pride Sausage**
    1 lb grated sharp cheddar cheese
    3 cups Bisquick
    1 cup **Cheez-it Hot and Spicy cracker crumbs**

Blend all ingredients together thoroughly, kneading to mix. Shape into 1" balls, and bake on a rack which you have sprayed with a cooking spray for 30 minutes at 350 deg. Serve hot.

I love sausage balls. They are the ultimate handy treat. In fact, if you really want to be lazy about these, let me give you a tip. Make them, bake them, cool them, seal them in a tight container, and freeze. When you are ready to serve, pop into a hot (375 deg) oven for about 10 minutes, and you are ready to go.

Now a couple of words about sausage variations. The first and easiest is just to leave out the cracker crumbs and you have sausage balls as I first ate them. I think the crackers give just a little extra kick. However, if you do not like the pepper, a suggestion you might like (and which we did on the show several years ago) is to use one cup of chopped peanuts instead of the cracker crumbs. A third variation is to make them in any of the ways described above, wrap the unbaked dough around a well drained, pitted olive and bake. Call them sausage surprises.

Now you know me well enough to know that I would never gild the lily. However, I have been known to make this famous (infamous) sauce and serve it on the side with cubes of ham or sausage balls. You may decide for yourself if you think it is too much.

JEZEBEL SAUCE

    1 12 oz jar apple jelly
    1 12 oz jar pineapple preserves
    1 5 oz bottle grated horseradish
    1 1½ oz can dry mustard

Blend all ingredients thoroughly. Place in a tightly covered container and allow to stand in the refrigerator at least overnight to blend the flavors. Serve at room temperature.

Be warned. This is hot as....! It is not named for this wicked woman for nothing. In small amounts with plain meats of almost any kind, it is a wonderful treat. I personally like it with the plain sausage balls described above, but do not put them into the sauce. Serve on the side and dip gently.

Walter N. Lambert, Noonday Chef

POTATO LATKE (TV 347)

    4 large potatoes, peeled and grated fine
    1 medium onion, peeled and grated fine
    ½ to 1 tsp salt
    1 tsp baking powder
    4 TBSP flour
    2 eggs, beaten
    oil for frying

Squeeze and drain any excess moisture from the grated potatoes. Mix in all remaining ingredients (except oil);blend well. Heat about ½" oil in a heavy skillet. Drop potato mixture into hot oil by tablespoons, and fry until crisp and brown on each side. Serve hot with applesauce.

Sometimes in the rush toward **Christmas**, we in the majority in the **United States** sometimes forget that we are a nation which is made up of many religions. Not only is December the time of Christmas, it is the time of **Hanukkah** (or Chanukah or the feast of lights). This holiday commemorates the intervention of **God** to keep the lamp on the temple alter burning for eight days with only oil enough for one. And guess what! At Hanukkah, gifts are given, and food is eaten.

When I called the ever wonderful **Addie Shersky** at **Harold's Kosher Foods** on Gay Street to tell her I wanted to do something to mark Hanukkah, there was no hesitation. Latke, she said. And she gave me the recipe. By the way. If you have not eaten with these folks, you do not know what you have missed. Get on down there. Holiday or not.

Now, let me give you one more little treat from the wealth of **Jewish** foods.

NOODLE KUGEL

    8 oz broad noodles
    ¼ lb butter, melted
    6 eggs, beaten
    ¼ lb cream cheese (or 1 cup cottage cheese)
    ½ cup sugar
    1 cup sour cream

Cook noodles according to package directions. Beat in all remaining ingredients. Turn into a 9x13" dish, which has been sprayed with a cooking spray. Bake in a 375 deg oven about 45 minutes. If you like, you can mix about half the butter with butter cracker crumbs and sprinkle on top of the noodles before baking.

Walter N. Lambert, Noonday Chef

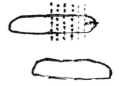

BREAD SCULPTURE (TV 348)

In **_Cooking With the Noonday Chef Volume 2_**, **Anne** talked at some length about bread sculpture. On pages 170 and 171, she talked about a number of sculptures she had done using **Rich's** brand pre-done bread dough. On the show, on Thursday, we sculpted a bread <u>teddy bear</u> from two loaves of the bread. To do this, you will need to shape one loaf into a flattened ball to make the body. Place the completed piece on a flat baking sheet. The second loaf is cut into halves with one half shaped into a flattened ball to be the head. It is placed against one side of the body. The remaining half is cut into six pieces. Four of the pieces are placed at appropriate places to serve as the four paws. The fifth piece is flattened and shaped to be the snout of the bear and placed on the head. The sixth piece is cut in two and the two pieces shaped to make the ears. If the pieces are placed against the adjoining part, they will stick as the bear rises and bakes. If, however, a piece comes loose, it can be reattached after baking with toothpicks. Allow the dough to rise until double in bulk and bake according to package directions. Decorate as desired.

You should not be limited to the teddy bear design. Be original. Simply use the dough as you would modeling clay, remembering that you must allow for it to rise, and because rising is not uniform, the finished piece is always a surprise.

DEVILED HAM SPREAD

    2 4 ½ oz cans deviled ham
    4 oz cream cheese
    2 TBSP green onion, chopped fine
    2 TBSP sweet pickle relish

Mix all ingredients together thoroughly. Line a small container with **Saran Wrap**. Pack mixture tightly into container, cover and chill. Unfold and decorate. Serve with thin crackers.

This is an example of a completely simple little dish that can be made look very fancy. One of our favorite ways of doing this is to use a small square or rectangular dish to mold the spread. Then using strips of green onion top, it is decorated to look like a package. Alternatively, it can be molded into a round container and turned out onto a serving plate. Another four ounces of cream cheese can be softened with a little sour cream and whipped so it will spread. Frost the outside of the spread and you have a snow ball. By the way, if you don't like deviled ham, use crab meat mixed with the cream cheese and add a little lemon juice for flavor. If you want it as a dip, thin with enough sour cream to make it the right consistency.

Walter N. Lambert, Noonday Chef

FRUITY GRANOLA BARS (TV 349)

3 cups miniature marshmallows
½ cup smooth peanut butter
3 TBSP butter or margarine
1 tsp almond extract
2 cups granola cereal
½ cup chopped apricots
½ cup chopped dates

Butter an 8 or 9 inch baking pan. In a microwave proof mixing bowl, combine marshmallows, peanut butter, butter, and extract. Heat on high about one minute or until all ingredients are melted. Stir in remaining ingredients. Wet your fingers, and press the mixture evenly into the pan. Allow to cool. Cut into sixteen squares.

If you are looking for a quick, easy, high energy snack, these little goodies are hard to beat. As we are doing more and more outdoor activities even in winter, these are handy as a pocket in a shirt. If you have family members who ski, individually wrap these squares in **Saran Wrap** to put into a pocket for nourishment on the ski slopes.

Another advantage of these squares is that there is an almost infinite variety of modifications which you can make to meet individual tastes. I have used **Sun-Maid mixed dried fruit** which I chopped fine and included instead of the apricots and the dates. In case you are not familiar with this fine product, it is a mixture of dried apples, pears, apricots, prunes, etc., which is excellent eaten straight from the bag.

You can also use raisins, or prunes, chopped, instead of the dates. If you will not tell anyone, I sometimes used the apricots with a ½ cup chopped walnuts instead of other fruit. This seems to be cheating since we call them fruity, but you are in charge.

Now just in case you are the type who would gild the lily, you can melt a couple of squares of semisweet chocolate and spread over the top of the squares immediately after placing them in the pan. By the time the squares are set, the chocolate will be too.

Now, one last variation which you may want to try. Some folks are offended by the high amount of sugar in these squares. Fine. You can reduce it markedly by leaving out the marshmallows. To do this, melt butter and mix with all remaining ingredients and two beaten eggs. Pack into an 8 or 9 inch pan which you have sprayed with a cooking spray. Bake about twenty five minutes; cut into squares while still warm.

Walter N. Lambert, Noonday Chef

LOW FAT CHICKEN (TV 350)

    4 boneless, skinless chicken breast halves
    1 cup each, chopped celery and chopped onion
    1 6 oz can vegetable juice (V-8)
    salt and pepper to taste
    juice of one lemon

Spray a non-stick skillet with cooking spray. Saute onion until soft. Stir in celery and vegetable juice. Bring to a full boil. Place the chicken breasts on top of the vegetables; pour the lemon juice over them. Reduce heat but keep mixture boiling. Cover and cook about 25 minutes or until chicken is done through. Remove chicken to a serving plate. Correct salt and pepper. Spoon vegetables over chicken and serve hot.

Well, it is January. Time to get back to a healthy lifestyle. You already know the rules. If you greatly reduce fat and sugar in your diet, you will go a long way toward reducing calories and increasing things you ought to have. However, if you are not careful, you can remove all taste along with the fat. This recipe shows that you can avoid that.

What you see above is what I would call the basic recipe for this. It has an almost infinite number of variations possible. For example, if you want it to be spicy, simply use the hot and spicy V-8 juice. Or liven regular vegetable juice (I personally use **Kroger** brand. It is just as good, and a lot cheaper.) up with hot sauce to taste. It seems to me these days that everyone has their own favorite hot sauce. I personally like **Durkee's** brand. If you do not want hot, use herbs instead. A combination of oregano and basil works nicely. Fresh basil is great on its own. Dill, either fresh or dried, works well. Use about 2 tsp of dried herbs, total, or about 1 TBSP or more of fresh. You also need not be limited by the vegetables. I use onion and celery because almost everyone likes them. However, if you like, add green pepper. A great combination would be 1 cup onion, ½ cup celery, and ½ cup green pepper. This also works great with onion and mushrooms. To do this, use 1 cup of onion and 1½ cups sliced fresh mushrooms. After you have cooked the onions, add the mushrooms and cook until most of the liquid has cooked out. Then add the juice and move ahead. And if you do not want tomatoes, just leave out the juice and add about ½ cup water (or white wine) to the poaching mixture.

Now a last word. This works even better with fish fillets. Simply cook the vegetable mixture down about 10 minutes before you lay the fish fillets on top. Cover and poach about 10 to 15 minutes.

Walter N. Lambert, Noonday Chef

CHICKEN AND GREENS (TV 351)

1 lb collard greens
2 tsp salt
water for boiling
4 chicken breast halves
1 TBSP olive oil
2 TBSP hot sauce
⅓ cup peanuts

Wash greens, remove heavy stems, and slice crosswise into thin slices. You should have about 10 or 12 cups. Heat 4 or 5 cups water to boiling. Add salt and greens; stir. Bring back to a boil and cook for 5 minutes. Drain. Cut chicken into 1" cubes. Heat olive oil in a large skillet and cook chicken 4 or 5 minutes, stirring constantly. Add collards and stir to heat thoroughly. Stir in hot sauce. Serve at once, sprinkled with the peanuts.

Today, we celebrate **America's** newest holiday, **Dr. Martin Luther King Jr.'s** birthday. I once had the pleasure to hear Dr. King speak. This was long before he became famous, but the spark was already there. This dish is done in honor of all those great **African-American women** who taught us all so much about good food. Now I doubt that any of them ever stir fried collard greens. But that is also what is happening today. We are taking the best of the old, like collards, chicken, and peanuts, and putting them together in all new ways.

Now if you were raised in **East Tennessee** rather than **South Georgia** and are not sure about collard greens, don't worry yourself about them. Use turnip greens, curly mustard, or kale, or any combination thereof.

I will also tell you that if you do not like hot sauce, you can do a very good oriental sauce version of this dish. To do this, chop about 1 tsp fresh ginger very fine. Add it with the chicken and allow it to cook. Then when you have added the greens, add about 3 or 4 TBSP of soy sauce with them. I have even been known to add both the soy sauce and the hot pepper sauce.

Now a word to all the vegetarians out there. This can become the basis of a nearly perfect vegetarian dish. Start by preparing the greens just as we described above. However instead of adding cubes of chicken, add cubes of tofu. Cut it into about ½ inch cubes and saute in oil very carefully so as not to break them up too much. Then add the soy sauce and hot pepper sauce to the tofu. At the very last, carefully toss in the parboiled greens and sprinkle with peanuts. Enjoy.

Walter N. Lambert, Noonday Chef

REUBEN CASSEROLE (TV 352)

    2 lb sauerkraut, drained
    8 oz medium noodles, uncooked
    2 cans cream of mushroom soup
    1 cup milk
    2 TBSP mustard
    ½ cup onion, finely chopped
    1½ lb polish sausage, sliced
    2 cups shredded Swiss cheese
    ¾ cup Ritz cracker crumbs

In a 9x13" dish sprayed with a cooking spray, spread the sauerkraut evenly. Sprinkle the UNCOOKED noodles over the kraut. Mix the soup, milk, mustard, and onions; spoon over noodles. Spread sausage slices over soup and sprinkle the top with cheese, then with the cracker crumbs. Seal tightly with foil. Bake in a 350 deg oven 1 hour. Serve hot.

Here, I have for you the ultimate **Superbowl Sunday dish**. You can prepare it ahead, pop it into the oven just before kickoff, and be ready to serve dinner at half time. With this, all you will need is a salad and a light dessert and you are ready to go. This will serve six with very large servings or serve 8 normal people. Now what could be easier than that? Let me say a word about the cheese in this dish. I give you the standard recipe above. But sometimes, **Swiss** cheese is hard to find. Especially pre-grated. Therefore, I often use **Sargento** brand 6 cheese mixture. It comes in 2 cup, pre-grated packages and is a great mixture for this dish. Here's more kraut.

ESCALLOPED KRAUT CASSEROLE

    1½ pound Polish sausage, sliced thin
    6 medium potatoes, peeled and sliced thin
    1 large onion, peeled and sliced very thin
    2 ribs of celery, sliced thin
    4 TBSP butter
    1 cup water
    1 quart sauerkraut, undrained
    1 can cream of celery soup, diluted with ½ can water

Spray a 9x13" baking dish with cooking spray and layer in order, sausage, potatoes, onion, and celery. Dot with butter and pour water over. Cover with foil and bake at 350 deg about 35 minutes or until potatoes are tender. Remove from oven and spread kraut over top. Beat together the soup and water and pour over the kraut. Bake about 30 minutes more. Serve hot.

Walter N. Lambert, Noonday Chef

DO-SI-DOES CHEESECAKE (TV 353)

1 pkg **Girl Scout** Do-Si-Does cookies
1 lb cream cheese, room temperature
2 cups cottage cheese
1 cup sugar
3 TBSP flour
4 eggs
2 tsp vanilla
2 squares baking chocolate, melted

Crush cookies and press the crumbs into the bottom of a 10" spring form pan. Bake at 350 deg for 10 minutes. Remove from oven and cool. Beat together the cream cheese and cottage cheese until completely blended and cottage cheese is mashed small. Beat in sugar, flour, and vanilla. Beat in eggs, one at a time. Stir in melted chocolate. Pour over crust and bake at 350 deg for one hour. Turn off and allow to cool in the oven 1 hour before removing. Cover and chill overnight before serving.

It is Girl Scout Cookie time again. For several years now, I have given you a recipe each year that used up all those extra cookies you wanted to order but could not eat immediately. This one gives you the prime combination of peanut butter and chocolate and is delightful.

The cottage cheese lightens the cheesecake a little and gives it a nice texture. If you object to the tiny pieces of cottage cheese which you will still have in this, either use ricotta cheese or run the cottage cheese in the food processor before using it. However, this cheese cake has a nicer texture if you mix it in a heavy mixer rather than in the food processor.

Now let me tell you how I really prefer to do this. Make the cheesecake exactly as we did above up to adding the chocolate. Pour about ¾ of the batter (without chocolate) into the crust. Stir the melted chocolate into the remaining batter and spoon onto the batter in the pan. Swirl through the white batter with a knife, and you have a great looking chocolate marble cheese cake which will impress all the folks.

By the way, this cheesecake will crack while it is in the oven for the cooling hour. The steam will cause it. However, it also greatly improves the texture of the finished product. As you allow it to stand overnight, the cracks will become less obvious. And let me reemphasize the overnight cooling. The cheese cake will be good as soon as it cools. It will be far better when it has stood. Now go on out there and order those Girl Scout cookies! I know of no organization which does any more good.

137

Walter N. Lambert, Noonday Chef

SNOWY DAYS SOUP (TV 354)

1 lb pkg **Kroger** 15 bean soup mix
¾ to 1 lb country ham pieces (or a ham hock)
1 16 oz jar chunky salsa
5 to 6 cups water

Wash beans, cover with hot water, and allow to soak overnight. Trim off any excess fat on the ham and discard. Place ham and salsa in a heavy saucepan with a tight fitting lid. Drain beans and mix with the ham. Add water. Bring to a boil and reduce heat to maintain a simmer. Cook at least three hours or until beans are tender. Serve hot.

Now I could just have called this quick and easy bean soup, but don't you like this name better? After all, all these ingredients can be kept on hand all the time. The dry beans and canned salsa will keep on the pantry shelf. Country ham ends and pieces or ham hock will keep almost indefinitely if wrapped tightly and frozen.

Now let me tell you a couple of changes you may want to try. First, if you prefer to have the salsa ingredients still intact and not just cooked up to flavor the beans, cook the beans and ham a couple of hours, then stir in the salsa. I personally prefer it the way I have described, but try it for yourself.

This makes a lot of soup, and if it is too much, allow any left over to cool, place it in a tight fitting dish and freeze. Simply thaw, heat, and you are ready to go. In fact, it might not be a bad idea to double the recipe to have some to freeze.

Now about the ham. For convenience, I sometimes buy the **Clifty Farm** ham pieces to use in this kind of dish. I also always have the hock cut off whole when I buy a country ham to have it to use in soup. You can make that choice. Another perfectly acceptable choice is to leave the ham out altogether. This produces a tasty vegetarian soup which is very nice.

If you want to make this a more general vegetable soup, that is also easy. Simply chop up carrots, celery, cabbage, turnips, or any combination thereof into pieces of about equal size. About one hour before the soup finishes cooking, add about 4 cups of any combination of these ingredients with a couple of cups of hot vegetable stock. Bring back to a boil and simmer until the vegetables are very tender. Now one last word, I think it should be illegal to eat this soup without cornbread, but **Anne** disagrees wholeheartedly. She actually eats it with crackers. You can try it, but at least give the cornbread a try.

Walter N. Lambert, Noonday Chef

DRIED CHERRY MUFFINS (TV 355)

1 cup sugar
½ cup cooking oil
2 eggs
1 cup buttermilk
2 tsp vanilla
2 cups all purpose flour
½ tsp salt
1 tsp soda
¾ cup dried cherries, chopped
zest of 1 orange

Mix sugar, oil, eggs, buttermilk, and vanilla thoroughly. Mix flour, salt, and soda; stir into the sugar mixture just enough to mix. Stir in cherries and orange zest. Divide evenly into 12 muffins pan which you have sprayed with a cooking spray. Bake at 350 for about 20 minutes or until brown.

It is the season of **Valentines** and **George Washington** and all those things that are supposed to make us think of cherries. I have recently found something that I like a lot. Dried cherries. These muffins, which I have adapted from a nice recipe **Louise Durman**, Foods Editor of the **Knoxville News- Sentinel**, shared with me, is a great use for them.

If you want to make these a little prettier, try this. Squeeze the juice from the orange which you took the zest from earlier. When the muffins are fresh from the oven and still in the pan, brush the top of each muffin with the orange juice and sprinkle with a little granulated sugar. About a TBSP should be enough for all twelve muffins.

Now these are not the only muffins which the dried cherries are good in. In fact, in any muffins which call for raisins, try chopped cherries. I especially like them in oatmeal muffins.

Now a last word about these good cherries. They make a great sauce to serve with pork. For example, prepare the roast pork which is on page 132 of Volume 2 of ***Cooking with the Noonday Chef***. When you have finished, pour vegetables and broth, which will have gathered in the bottom of the pan, through a sieve to remove the carrots and onions. Stir a package, about ¾ cup, of dried cherries into the liquid and bring it to a full boil. Allow to reduce until it begins to thicken. Slice the pork and pour the cherry sauce over the slices. It is a great taste. By the way, you will find dried cherries in the produce section of **Kroger**. I mean, you didn't think I was going to send you to some specialty shop did you?

Walter N. Lambert, Noonday Chef

CHEERY CHERRY COOKIES (TV 356)

2 stacks **Oreo Cookies** (about 35 or 36 cookies), crumbled
8 TBSP butter (1 stick), melted
1 16 oz bottle maraschino cherries, drained and chopped
1 cup coconut
1 10 oz pkg white chocolate chips
1 can sweetened condensed milk

Mix cookies crumbs and melted butter. Press onto the bottom of a 9x13" pan. Bake at 350 deg for 10 minutes. Cool. Spread milk evenly over the crust. Mix remaining ingredients and sprinkle evenly over milk. Bake at 350 for 30 minutes. Cool and cut into squares.

I continue to be amazed at how recipes seem to go in cycles. If these look similar to the seven layer cookies (or five, three, or more layer cookies) which we have talked about and done before, it is because they are. Suddenly these cookies, which are based on a cookie crust, sweetened with condensed milk (most commonly known as **Eagle Brand** milk, but **Kroger** private brand is cheaper-- and just as good), and stuff sprinkled on top are everywhere. The magazine **Chocolatier** which is known for fancy, hard to make delights just had a whole feature on them. By the way, it did not include this cherry version. It is my own concoction. After all, it is **President's day** and we don't want to forget old **George**.

Now, these good little bars can be done with an infinite variety of cookies and toppings. Some examples follow.

Make the bottom crust out of vanilla wafers and butter. Spread the milk and top with a mixture of 1 cup pecans, 1 cup coconut, and 1 10 oz pkg of butterscotch chips. You can make the bottom crust out of chocolate coated graham cracker crumbs and butter. After you spread on the milk, top it with 1 cup coconut, 1 cup roasted, unsalted peanuts, and 1 pkg of peanut butter chips. You can do a nice variation on either of these by using half of the regular chips and half Butter brickle chips. In other words, let your self go. Try combinations which you like.

Now a couple of procedural tips. I make the crumbs by placing the cookies in a heavy plastic bag and rolling them with a rolling pin. Roll, shake the bag, roll again, etc. until you have the consistency you like. You can use the food processor, but you will tend to get very fine crumbs. And finally about the baking. If you do not bake the crust, you get a softer, crumblier crust. If you bake, it is crunchy. You choose.

140

Walter N. Lambert, Noonday Chef

FIVE SPICE BISCUITS (TV 357)

2 cups **White Lily Self-rising** flour
½ tsp baking soda
1 tsp **Chinese five spice powder**
2 TBSP sugar
⅓ cup salad oil
⅔ cup buttermilk

Mix the flour, soda, sugar, and spice powder. Mix oil and buttermilk and blend into the dry ingredients. Turn out onto a lightly floured board and knead three or four turn. Roll to about ½ inch thick, and cut and place onto biscuit pan. Bake at 400 deg about fifteen minutes or until brown. Serve hot.

Gung Hsi Fa Tsai. If you happen to be **Chinese**, I have just wished you **Happy New Year** as we begin the **Year of the Rat**. We are just leaving my birth year in the Chinese calendar which is the **Year of the Pig**. I am not kidding and I do not like folks who snicker behind their hand.

Rather than do a real Chinese recipe, I thought I would share this little goodie with you. We find it delightful either with ham or with some sort of good tart something like apricot jam. In case you are interested, you can find Chinese Five Spice powder in the spice section at **Kroger**. Let me also tell you that if you want to make these really fancy, after you have placed them on the baking sheet, brush the top with beaten egg; sprinkle with <u>sesame seeds</u>. That is my favorite way.

Now a word about <u>biscuits</u>. Do not make them unless you can get **White Lily flour**. Made from scratch here in **Knoxville**, it is the only true soft wheat flour left in America. The self rising flour which is mentioned for this recipe already has salt and baking powder added. If you use plain flour for this recipe, simply add 1 tsp salt and 2 tsp baking powder if you are using soda and buttermilk. If you want to use sweet milk instead, leave out the soda, use 1 TBSP of baking powder and proceed exactly the same.

Now a word about that cooking oil instead of shortening. I like it. It changes the texture of the biscuits a little, but they are still good and it reduces the saturated fat a lot. If you want to be a purist, use a good solid shortening, like Crisco. Use about ¼ cup and work it into the flour mixture before adding about ¾ cup milk. Use a little more flour on the board if you are doing it this way because it will be a little stickier. If you want regular biscuits, leave out the sugar and 5 spice. Enjoy.

Walter N. Lambert, Noonday Chef

CHILDREN'S PIZZA PARTY (TV 358)

Spaghetti sauce and/or picante sauce
assorted shredded cheeses
ham, pepperoni, or other sliced deli meats
chopped vegetables
onions or green onions
green or red peppers
mushrooms
assorted pizza crusts
flour tortillas
pita bread
canned pizza crust from the dairy case
pre-made pizza crust
English muffins

Arrange various crusts and fillings on a table. Have children choose a crust and place it on a cookie sheet. They then should spread it thinly with either picante sauce or spaghetti sauce. They then sprinkle cheese evenly over the sauce. You then add any desired toppings. Bake about 8 to 10 minutes in a 375 to 400 deg oven or until the cheese is bubbling. Allow to cool a little before slicing and serving.

Pizza makes an ideal project for young children on a slow afternoon. The only problem with pizza ever was the crust, and now that need not be a problem. There are pre-made pizza crusts available at **Kroger**. They are not cheap. And you need not use them unless you wish. Pita bread does nicely. So do English muffins for individual pizza. I love to make Mexican pizza by using flour tortillas which I spread with a little picante sauce, sprinkled generously with cheese, and added various chopped vegetables or meats to taste. You can do a nice meat pizza by frying about a pound of lean hamburger until it is fully cooked. Drain thoroughly and stir in about 1 TBSP chili powder and 1 tsp ground cumin. Allow to cool, then prepare the pizza by spreading on the sauce, sprinkling with the hamburger and then adding cheese.

One word of caution if you are using tortillas or pita bread or other things which do not have a natural edge, be sure not to overdo the toppings. If you do, it will run off the edge and you will have a major mess. Leave at least a half inch all around the edge of each one.

A final suggestion. Use various toppings to form faces. Small tomato slices topped with a black olive makes nice eyes. Cut a nose of green pepper and a mouth of pepperoni or red sweet pepper. Be creative. And remember it is fun.

Walter N. Lambert, Noonday Chef

IRISH YEAST BREAD (TV 359)

1 cup milk
1 pkg yeast
1 TBSP sugar
½ tsp salt
2 TBSP butter, melted
1 egg, beaten
2 cups all purpose flour

Warm milk (about 105 deg) and stir in yeast, sugar, and salt. Allow to stand about 5 minutes or until it starts to bubble. Stir in butter, egg, and flour until smooth. Turn into a well greased 8" or 9" cake pan or skillet. Allow to rise until doubled in bulk (about 30 minutes). Bake at 350 deg for about 30 minutes or until brown. Serve hot with butter.

Once again, **St. Patrick's day** is upon us. In memory of my Irish **Grandmother Freeman**, I try to never forget it. Everyone knows about **Irish Soda Bread**. This is the yeast version of it. Because the batter is so much thinner than the soda bread, it must be baked in a pan with sides. I use the same 8" skillet that I use for cornbread. The traditional way to serve this bread was to slice it crosswise and butter the whole loaf. It was then cut into 8 wedges to serve.

In fact, this is a bread which is quick enough and simple enough to make for almost any meal and it lends itself nicely to all sorts of variations. Our favorite is to make whole wheat bread of it. Use 1 cup of white flour and one cup of whole wheat flour and you will get a good bread. If you like, you can use honey or molasses for the sugar in whole wheat. If you like breakfast breads which are a little sweet but not too much so, try this variation. Make the batter exactly as described above. Turn about ⅔ of the batter into the pan and spread it smoothly. Sprinkle about ½ cup of sugar and a couple of tsp of cinnamon over the batter. If you like, drizzle about ¼ cup melted butter over it. Carefully spoon the remaining batter over the top to cover the sugar and cinnamon. Proceed to allow the bread to rise and bake as above. First, it will smell wonderful and it will taste just as good.

I have also made this into herb bread by adding about 2 or 3 tsp of dry herbs with the flour. I like a mixture of basil, oregano, and thyme. I have also done it with mint and oregano for a **Middle Eastern** sort of flavor. With crushed rosemary, it makes a great accompaniment for lamb. And if you want a great Irish Stew, try the baked Irish stew on page 50 of Volume 2 of ***Cooking with the Noonday Chef***.

Walter N. Lambert, Noonday Chef

PEANUT BUTTER FUDGE PIE (TV 360)

  1 stick butter, melted
  1⅓ cup sugar
  3 eggs, beaten
  2 tsp vanilla
  ¼ cup cocoa
  ½ cup smooth peanut butter
  1 unbaked 9" pie shell

Mix the butter, sugar, eggs, and vanilla completely. Stir in the cocoa and peanut butter. Pour into pie crust, and bake in a 350 deg oven for about 45 minutes. Allow to completely cool before serving.

Everybody in the world has a peanut butter pie recipe. Our friend **Frankie Wade** makes one that is like cream pie with peanut butter and jelly spread over it (or under it or something). Others mix the peanut butter in with cool whip and other things. In fact, let me give you one of those.

CHOCOLATE PEANUT BUTTER PIE

¾ cup chunky peanut butter
1 small container (4 oz) frozen whipped topping, thawed
1 quart chocolate ice cream, softened
1 chocolate crumb pie shell

Mix peanut butter, whipped topping, and ice cream completely. Turn into the chocolate pie shell. Cover loosely and freeze overnight. Thaw slightly before serving. If you want to make your own chocolate pie shell, use 1½ cup chocolate wafer crumbs, ¼ cup melted butter, and 2 TBSP sugar. Blend and press onto the bottom and sides of a 9" pie plate.

Now let me give you another version of a similar pie which is absolutely decadent:

WHIPPED CREAM PEANUT BUTTER PIE

1 cup whipping cream
3 ½ oz cream cheese, softened
¾ cup peanut butter
⅓ cup sugar

Whip the cream until stiff. Set aside. Blend cream cheese, peanut butter, and sugar. Beat until creamy. Fold in whipped cream, spread in a chocolate or graham cracker shell, and chill at least one hour before serving.

Walter N. Lambert, Noonday Chef

LULU'S CLAFOUTI (TV 361)

2 cups fresh raspberries, blackberries, or pitted cherries
¼ cup each, sugar and cherry liquor
1 tsp lemon juice
1½ cup flour
¼ tsp salt
6 eggs
2 cups half and half
6 TBSP butter, melted

Place fruit, sugar, cherry liquor, and lemon juice in a glass container, and allow to stand at least one hour or overnight. Drain and reserve the liquid from the fruit. Pour half the butter into a glass casserole. Pour the fruit over the butter. Beat together all remaining ingredients with the reserved liquid. Pour over the fruit, and bake in a 425 deg oven about 25 minutes or until puffed and brown. Serve warm sprinkled with powdered sugar.

This recipe comes from a fine cookbook, **Cuisine for all Seasons** prepared for the **Meals on Wheels** operation by the **Seagram's Classic Wine Corp.** Ten dollars of the $18 purchase price goes to the local **mobile meals** program. It is an absolutely beautiful cook book filled with elaborate and delightful recipes from famous chefs from all over California. Call **The Knox County Mobile Meals program** at 524-2786 from your copy.

While you are at it, you might want to talk to **Barbara Monty** about volunteering for this wonderful program. Through the help of mobile meals, hundreds of people in this area are able to continue to live at home. You know that you would get great satisfaction from such a worthwhile enterprise.

Now about this recipe. It is a modern variation on a classic **French** recipe. Traditionally, a rich pastry was made, pressed into a pan, and filled with fresh cherries which had been sprinkled with sugar and liquor. It was baked, served warm sprinkled with powdered sugar.

This version depends on a batter which is flavored with the liquid from any one of several fruits. At one time, we had to wait for spring for the fruit to make this sort of treat, which simply must have fresh fruit if it is to be good. But now, throughout the worst of winter (that means January, February, and March), a whole assortment of fine fruits are available from Chile. If you have not been taking advantage of the fresh berries which you start seeing about the middle of January, you are missing a treat. Whether you make clafouti or just eat them.

Walter N. Lambert, Noonday Chef

CHEF WALTER'S FRUIT AND VEGGIE SALAD (TV 362)

1 cup each diced red and green apples
1 cup each chopped broccoli and celery
¼ cup each chopped onion and slivered almonds
½ cup raisins
¼ cup sugar
1 TBSP white vinegar
1 cup fat-free mayonnaise

In a small bowl, mix sugar, vinegar, and mayonnaise. Place remaining ingredients, except almonds, into a large bowl and toss with dressing. Chill in a covered bowl for several hours or overnight. Mix in almonds and serve.

Well, let's hear it for Hamblen County. **Dolores Coffey**, who is the food service manager for the **Hamblen County schools**, has been responsible for that county being one of six (yes, I said six) schools chosen from all across the country in a test program to use the school lunch program to teach good nutrition. This is a year long program, and we will be seeing more of it as the year progresses.

We went to the **Russellville Elementary School** to make the healthy salad which you see above and had a great time visiting with the teachers and students. I know this looks like a strange set of ingredients, but give it a try. It is high in fiber, vitamins, and nutrients and low in fat and sodium. Good stuff that is good for you. As her centerpiece, **Anne** choose to carve some veggies but also to make a fresh fruit pizza. This is how she did it.

FRESH FRUIT PIZZA

1 pre-baked pizza shell
1 lb fat free cream cheese
¼ cup sugar
1 cup approx. apple jelly
assorted sliced fresh fruit (like Kiwi, strawberries, grapes)

In a microwave safe dish, heat the jelly until it is melted. Brush the pizza shell with jelly and chill until set. While the crust is chilling, mix the cream cheese and sugar. Spread it evenly in the shell. Arrange the fresh fruit attractively over the cream cheese. Brush with the melted jelly until it is completely covered. Chill for about one hour. Slice and serve. By the way, if you do not tell anyone that I told you, this is excellent if you make your crust by pressing sugar cookie dough into a pizza pan and baking it. But don't tell.

Walter N. Lambert, Noonday Chef

AFTER EASTER PIE (TV 363)

1 cup each, ham, and cooked asparagus, chopped
1 cup grated cheddar cheese
3 hard cooked eggs, chopped
½ cup green onion, chopped
1 cup milk
3 eggs
1 TBSP salad mustard
½ tsp salt
1 tsp black pepper
1 unbaked 9" deep dish pie shell

Toss together the ham, asparagus, cheese, hard cooked eggs, and green onions. Place in pie shell. Beat together the eggs, milk, mustard, salt and pepper. Pour over other ingredients to fill the shell. Bake in a 350 deg oven about one hour or until puffed and brown. Serve hot.

It is the day after **Easter** and in keeping with custom, we supply a recipe which will use up leftover eggs and ham. This year we throw in the leftover asparagus. This assumes that you feel as I do that it is not Easter without asparagus. If you ate all the asparagus just forget it. If you just have to, you can use canned asparagus which has been well drained. Or even lightly poach a 10 oz pkg of chopped frozen asparagus (or even broccoli) and drain it thoroughly to use in the dish. Now you may well ask if this is not just a quiche under an assumed name. You would be right. But one can only eat so much egg salad, and this will get rid of a few of those left over eggs for you.

For years, we made a casserole which involved cooked asparagus or broccoli chopped and placed into a greased casserole dish. A layer of chopped hard cooked eggs was placed over this and a layer of chopped ham was put over that. Then a nice cheese sauce was made and poured over the whole thing and the top generously sprinkled with crumbled **Ritz** crackers. This was then baked about 40 minutes in a 350 deg oven until the top was browned and the casserole was bubbly. If you want to do this, the following makes a nice cheese sauce to pour over the dish.

WHITE SAUCE WITH CHEESE

In a heavy sauce pan, melt 6 TBSP butter. Stir in 6 TBSP flour and stir on low heat about 5 minutes to cook but not brown the flour. Stir in 2 cups of milk and continuing stirring until the mixture comes to a boil and is thick. Stir in ½ lb of cubed **Velvetta** cheese and ½ lb grated cheddar cheese. Stir until cheese is melted. Serve hot over almost anything or in the recipe above.

Walter N. Lambert, Noonday Chef

MARY CLEMENT'S HOMINY CASSEROLE (TV 364)

    2 regular (or 1 large) cans of hominy, drained
    1 4 oz jar pimento, drained
    ½ stick butter, melted
    8 oz sour cream
    6 to 8 oz grated cheddar cheese (about 2 cups)

Mix hominy, pimento, butter, and sour cream, and place in a casserole which you have sprayed with a cooking spray. Sprinkle the cheese evenly on the top. Bake in a 350 deg oven about 30 minutes or until bubbly and brown.

I stole this recipe outright from **Mary Clement** who placed it in the wonderful **Congressional Club Cookbook**. But when did you last eat hominy? And this is good. It is fat as everything, but with a simple piece of broiled chicken, it will make the meal festive. In case you have not guessed by now, **Mary Clement**, who is a fine lady in her own right, is married to **Congressman Bob Clement**. And she was kind enough to send **Anne** a copy of this cookbook, which has been done by the Congressional Club (which is made up of spouses of members of Congress) since the 1940's. Mary is now President of this distinguished group. The book is a treasure trove of good recipes and liberal doses of history.

Now just to show how bipartisan we are around here, this recipe is from **Cecile Cox Quillen**, whose husband, **James Quillen**, has just announced his retirement.

WHITE CHOCOLATE CAKE

    ¼ lb white chocolate
    1 cup butter
    2 cups sugar
    4 eggs
    2¼ cups cake flour
    ¼ tsp baking powder
    1 cup, each, buttermilk, chopped pecans, and coconut
    1 tsp vanilla

Melt chocolate over hot water and cool slightly. Cream together butter and sugar until light. Add eggs one at a time. Stir dry ingredients together and add alternately with buttermilk. Fold in vanilla, pecans, and coconut. Pour into greased and floured 9" pans and bake 45 minutes at 350 deg.

You can ice this with your favorite white frosting for a real treat. You might want to try the white chocolate frosting from the **Mary Starr** cookbook which would be great with it.

148

Walter N. Lambert, Noonday Chef

BUTTERSCOTCH GOODIES (TV 365)

½ cup butter (or shortening)
½ cup brown sugar, firmly packed
1 pkg butterscotch pudding (not instant)
1 egg
1½ cups plain flour
½ tsp soda
½ cup (approx) flaked coconut

Cream the butter and sugar. Cream in the pudding and egg. Mix soda into the flour, and blend into the creamed mixture. Shape into 1 inch balls and roll in coconut. Place on an ungreased cookie sheet and flatten slightly. Leave room for the cookies to spread. Bake at 350 deg for 10 minutes. Allow to cool a couple of minutes before placing on a rack to cool.

A friend of ours in Nashville, **Shirley Bridges**, gave us this recipe and the one which follows. They came from pudding boxes in the 1940's. They have a number of good qualities. Foremost, they are easy to make. Second, they keep well. Third, they are good. I find the butterscotch taste to be very pleasant and a nice change.

Now it is possible to work nuts into these cookies if you like. I personally prefer this recipe just as it is, but I find that the one below works especially well with chopped pecans or walnuts. If you want to do that, add about ½ cup to the recipe as the final step before making the cookies into balls. It just occurred to me that this would probably work well to roll the cookies in finely chopped pecans, but I have not tried that. Now here is the other version. By the way, I personally prefer to let these stand overnight in a tightly closed tin before eating them.

BUTTERSCOTCH OATMEAL COOKIES

¾ cup shortening
1 TBSP sugar
1 egg
1 tsp vanilla
1 pkg butterscotch pudding (not instant)
1½ cups oats
1 cup plain flour
½ tsp each, salt and baking soda
1½ tsp cream of tartar

Mix all dry ingredients. Cream shortening with the sugar, egg, and vanilla. Blend in the dry ingredients. Roll the mixture into 1½ inch balls, and flatten slightly onto a greased cookie sheet. Bake at 350 deg about 10 minutes.

Walter N. Lambert, Noonday Chef

LOW FAT BROWNIES (TV 366)

¾ cup vegetable oil
3 ¾ cups sugar
1½ tsp each salt and vanilla
2½ cups applesauce
1½ cups eggbeaters (or egg whites)
3½ cups flour
1½ cups cocoa
1 TBSP baking powder
1 cup nuts, chopped (optional)

Cream oil, sugar, salt, vanilla, and applesauce for several minutes until completely blended. Add egg beaters, and beat on medium speed until well blended. Stir together the flour, cocoa, and baking powder. Add to wet ingredients and blend thoroughly, beating for 3 or 4 minutes. Spread in an 18x13" pan or into two 9x13" pans and sprinkle nuts on top if desired. Bake in a preheated 350 deg oven for 25 to 30 minutes or until lightly browned. Makes 50.

We continue our happy relationship with **Ms. Delores Coffey** and the good folks in the **Hamblen County Schools**. As you remember, these folks have one of six grants in the country to use the school lunch program to educate the students about healthy eating. They have brought us this fine recipe which greatly reduces the fat (about 3.8 gram of total fat and .8 grams of saturated fat in a brownie about 1½" by 2"), and eliminates the cholesterol in these great little cookies. Be warned that they are still high in carbohydrates and have about 135 calories in one piece. But you can't have everything.

In case you wonder, it is the applesauce which keeps the brownies soft and rich tasting with the oil cut back. You may wonder why I gave you such a big recipe. Well, that is the way Delores gave it to me. You can half all the ingredients and it will work fine. In fact everything divides evenly except the oil (use ⅓ cup) and the sugar (use 1 ¾ cup plus a TBSP). Another alternative is to make the whole recipe and freeze them. They freeze just fine, thank you. Or you could share them with the neighbors. Now if you must have your brownies iced, use this recipe.

BROWNIE ICING

Beat together 1 lb powdered sugar with ¾ cup cocoa. Beat in 3 TBSP butter, ½ cup low fat milk, and 1 TBSP vanilla. Beat about 5 minutes or until smooth. Spread on brownies while just barely warm. Makes enough for the 50 serving recipe above.

Walter N. Lambert, Noonday Chef

BAKED COMPANY CHICKEN (TV 367)

    8 chicken breasts boned
    8 slices Swiss cheese
    1 can cream of chicken soup
    ¼ cup milk
    1 cup herb seasoned stuffing mix
    ¼ cup butter, melted

Arrange chicken breast in a single layer in a 9x13" pan which you have sprayed with a cooking spray. Place a slice of cheese on top of each chicken breast. Beat the soup and milk together and spoon evenly over the chicken. Sprinkle the stuffing mix over each chicken breast and drizzle with the butter. Bake for 45 to 50 minutes in a preheated 350 deg oven.

A young friend of ours has become a fine, trained chef. On a recent visit home, his mother asked how you tell if a recipe was truly for a gourmet. Well, he allowed, if it is really for a gourmet, it will not contain a can of chicken soup. So there. He is right, of course, but I like it. What can I say. If you want to clear your conscience a little, use ¼ cup white wine instead of the milk. If that ain't gourmet, what could be?

Now while we are into this mood, why not go all the way. Here is a casserole version of an elegant old dish which used broccoli spears and sliced chicken and a Mornay sauce. What can I tell you. There is not room enough on this page for all those recipes, but you can make:

CHICKEN DIVAN CASSEROLE

    2 whole chicken breasts
    1 small onion
    1 stalk of celery, chopped into 1" pieces
    salt and pepper to taste
    1 can cream of chicken soup
    ½ cup JFG mayonnaise
    1 tsp mild curry powder
    1 TBSP lemon juice
    1 pkg frozen chopped broccoli, cooked and drained
    ½ cup grated cheddar cheese

Boil the chicken with the onion, celery, salt, and pepper about 10 minutes. Remove from heat and allow to cool in water. Discard water and cut the chicken into cubes. Mix the soup, mayonnaise, curry powder, and lemon juice. In a 2 quart casserole, which you have sprayed with a cooking spray, layer the broccoli, chicken, the soup mix, and the cheese. Bake at 350 deg for 45 minutes or until brown and bubbly.

Walter N. Lambert, Noonday Chef

TURTLE CAKE (TV 368)

    1 pkg chocolate cake mix
    ¾ cup butter or margarine
    ½ cup sweetened condensed milk
    14 oz caramels
    1 cup chocolate morsels
    1 cup chopped nuts
    chocolate frosting (optional)

Prepare cake according to package directions. Pour half of batter into lightly greased 9x13" pan. Bake 15 minutes at 350 degrees. Melt butter, caramels, and milk in heavy saucepan. Pour on hot, partially-baked cake. Sprinkle chocolate morsels and nuts over top. Add remaining batter. Bake 20 to 25 minutes longer at 350 deg. Remove from oven, and let set 1 hour. Frost if desired.

This recipe is from my friend and editor, **Louise Durman's** new book **Lessons with Louise**. The book is based on Louise's popular series in **The Knoxville News-Sentinel**. If you are looking for a fine basic book, you cannot beat this one. Louise credits this nice recipe to **Amy McRary**. Good work Amy!

You can watch for Louise at book stores, in area **Kroger** stores, and wherever two or three are gathered together in the next few months. Get her to sign a copy of the book for you. She is a super lady, and I feel privileged to get to work with her. Of course, if you are so inclined, you can watch for the coupon in the News-Sentinel and order the book by mail.

Now about that frosting question. I personally think this cake is so excessive that you might as well go ahead and frost it. I have been known to use commercial frosting and Louise admits that as well. See, sometimes what is easy is acceptable. But just in case you want no part of that, here is a creamy chocolate frosting recipe which is also from **Lessons with Louise**. I have doubled the recipe for this size cake as Louise suggests.

CREAMY CHOCOLATE FROSTING

    4 cups confections' sugar
    5 TBSP unsweetened cocoa
    4 TBSP butter or margarine, softened
    4 TBSP evaporated milk
    1 tsp vanilla
    pinch of salt

Beat ingredients together with electric mixer until smooth. Spread on cooled cake.

Walter N. Lambert, Noonday Chef

PICNIC PIZZAZZ (TV 369)

PORTABELLA MUSHROOM RELISH - MONDAY, May 20

2 TBSP olive oil
1 cup onion, chopped
2 - 3 cloves garlic (about ½ tsp), chopped
1 lb portabella mushrooms chopped coarsely
¼ cup soy sauce
¼ cup white wine vinegar

In a heavy non-stick skillet, heat olive oil until hot. Add onion, and cook stirring constantly about 5 minutes or until onion starts to brown. Stir in garlic, and cook just a few seconds before adding the mushrooms. Continue to stir constantly about 2 or 3 minutes until mushrooms start to lose their liquid. Add soy sauce and vinegar, and continue to cook on high heat, stirring constantly, until the liquid is evaporated. Allow to cool.

This relish is good either hot or cold. If you want to make a really fancy dish at home, top a broiled or baked chicken breast with a couple of TBSPs of the relish, place a slice of cheese on top and broil it until the cheese is melted. For a picnic, take it along to serve with hamburgers

SWEET AND SOUR SALAD - Tuesday, May 21

1½ lb red potatoes, cooked, cooled and cubed
1 cup celery, chopped
1 medium red apple, chopped (Do Not Peel)
½ lb Swiss cheese, chopped
½ cup olive oil
¼ cup white wine vinegar
1 TBSP Dijon mustard
2 tsp salt
1 tsp black pepper
¼ cup parsley
¼ medium onion, chopped

Toss potatoes, apples, celery, and cheese in a large mixing bowl. In the blender, place the oil, vinegar, mustard, salt, pepper, parsley, and onion. Run until completely blended. Pour over the potato and apple mixture. Refrigerate, covered, overnight.

This is a great alternative to regular potato salad. It has no mayonnaise to be dangerous on a picnic. If you like almonds, slivered almonds make a nice crunchy addition to this salad. Dried cherries or cranberries are also nice. You can add about a cup of either.

Walter N. Lambert, Noonday Chef

PICNIC PIZZAZ CONTINUED

BLACK BEAN SALAD - Wednesday, May 22

    1 lb dry black beans
    1 8 oz bottle salsa
    1 medium onion, chopped
    1 cup tomato, peeled, seeded and chopped
    ½ cup olive oil
    ¼ cup white wine vinegar
    ½ cup cilantro, chopped

Cook black beans according to package directions, being careful not to over cook. Immediately drain the beans, and pour cold water over to stop cooking. Drain thoroughly. Mix olive oil and vinegar and toss with all other ingredients with the beans. Allow to chill.

Let me say a word about cooking the beans. I soak the beans overnight, and then cook them almost exactly an hour. Immediately drain the beans, pour cold water through them to cool, and allow to drain again. If you are not careful, black beans cook up.

Here is another nice dish to take along on a picnic or to have at home on a hot summer night. I throw it in free:

BAKED BLACK AND WHITE BEANS

    1 can black beans
    1 can great Northern beans
    1 8 oz jar salsa
    ½ lb bulk, country sausage
    1 small onion, chopped
    ½ cup fresh parsley, chopped

Fry the sausage and drain. Stir onion into the sausage and continue to cook, stirring constantly until the onion is soft and starts to brown. Mix the undrained beans with all remaining ingredients, and turn into a 2 quart casserole which has been sprayed with a cooking spray. Bake, uncovered, in a 350 deg oven for about 1½ hours or until thick and brown. Serve warm, hot, or cold.

Walter N. Lambert, Noonday Chef

PICNIC PIZZAZZ CONTINUED

PICNIC CUPCAKES - Thursday, May 23

      1 devils food cake mix
      8 oz pkg cream cheese
      ½ cup sugar
      1 egg
      1 tsp vanilla

Mix together cream cheese, sugar, egg, and vanilla. Set aside. Mix cake mix according to package directions. Divide evenly into cupcake liners placed in muffin tins. Spoon about one ample teaspoon of the cream cheese mixture on top of each unbaked cupcake. Bake in a preheated 350 deg oven about 25 minutes. Allow to cool completely before packing into a tight container.

CAJUN BROILED CHICKEN - Friday, May 24

Dip chicken pieces, I prefer skinless, boneless breasts, into lemon juice, and coat generously with Cajun seasoning. Drop into a plastic bag, seal, and refrigerate at least a couple of hours before cooking. If you are going on a picnic, prepare, pack on ice, and cook on a medium hot charcoal grill at the site. You can use a commercial Cajun seasoning or make your own. Here is a fairly tame version which we like very much.

Mix together thoroughly 3 TBSP each paprika, cayenne pepper, and salt, with 2 TBSP each black pepper, garlic powder, onion powder, and crumbled thyme. I sometimes use lemon pepper or add 2 TBSP of dry lemon peel, if I can find it. If you like it hotter, simply add more cayenne pepper and keep everything else the same. This is good for fish or chicken.

155

Walter N. Lambert, Noonday Chef

TRADITIONAL SHORTCAKE (TV 370)

> 2 cups plain flour
> 1 TBSP baking powder
> ½ cup butter
> 1 tsp salt
> ½ cup sugar
> ¾ cup half and half cream

Blend flour, sugar, baking powder, and salt. Cut in butter with a pastry blender or a fork until well mixed. Stir in cream to make a firm dough. Turn out onto a floured board and knead lightly for a few turns. Flatten onto the board and roll into an oval about ½ inch thick. Cut with a biscuit cutter, and place on an ungreased baking sheet with the edges not touching. Re-roll and cut any scraps until all the dough has been used. Bake in a 375 deg oven about 15 minutes or until lightly browned.

To make shortcakes, allow the cakes to cool to room temperature. To serve, split the shortbread and fill with sliced, sugared strawberries which have been refrigerated overnight. Top with more strawberries and whipped cream.

You have just watched history being made. For the first time, we are repeating a recipe on Noonday. I did this because strawberries are now available all the time and because some of you good folks continue to ask about cookbooks. This recipe comes from ***Cooking with the Noonday Chef Volume 1.*** Volume 2 is also available.

Walter N. Lambert, Noonday Chef

QUICK CHOCOLATE MERINGUES (TV 371)

4 egg whites
1 cup chocolate flavored powdered sugar
¼ tsp cream of tartar
2 tsp vanilla
¾ cup, each, chopped nuts and mini chocolate chips

In a heavy mixer, beat egg whites and cream of tartar until foamy. Turn to highest speed of mixer and add the vanilla. Slowly add the powdered sugar. Beat until stiff peaks form. Carefully fold in the nuts and chips. Drop onto ungreased cookies sheets which has been lined with parchment paper or aluminum foil. Bake at 325 deg for 30 minutes. Turn off and allow to cool in the oven without opening the door.

For 35 years, today (June 3, 1996), I have had the pleasure of being married to my wife, **Anne**. We were married on top of a mountain in **Pittman Center**. The cabin is long since gone, but we are still here. One of the things that Anne absolutely loves is meringues. In whatever form, she loves them. So I have done these for her.

I have found that the new flavored powdered sugars make lovely meringues. I have done the chocolate, which you see above, and lemon meringues. When I do lemon, I break up lemon drops and stir them into the meringue instead of the nuts and chocolate chips.

You should know that meringues are great whether or not they are flavored. I do meringues with plain sugar, add a little vanilla, and spread them into circles about 4 inches across. I shape them a little thicker at the outer edge than in the center and use them as the base for a fresh fruit dessert or for pudding or for almost any other filling.

You can also do them the same way and spread them into about 8 inch circles which is smooth. Make three or four such circles and bake them as above. When they are cool, place one layer on a plate, and spread it with fresh fruit and whipped cream. Place the next layer on and repeat the fruit and cream. End with a meringue layer on top. Allow to stand about an hour, refrigerated, before serving. This is great with peaches, strawberries, or blueberries. You can even combine the three if you wish.

One final idea for meringue layers is to whip a pint of cream with about ¼ cup sugar and 1 tsp vanilla. Fold in about 1 cup of lemon curd into the whipped cream. Spread between the layers as you did the fruit and cream. I have also made individual circles as I described above for this lemon cream.

Walter N. Lambert, Noonday Chef

PEACHY CHICKEN SALAD (TV 372)

    2 cups cooked chicken, cubed
    2 cups peaches, cubed
    1 cup each, celery and snow peas, chopped
    ¼ cup green onions
    ½ cup each, mayonnaise and peach yogurt
    ¼ cup peach puree
    1 tsp salt

Blend together the mayonnaise, yogurt, peach puree, and salt for dressing. Toss together gently all remaining ingredients. Pour dressing over salad and toss to blend. Serve on crisp leaf lettuce.

I know that peaches are supposed to be used in peach pie. In fact, peaches may be used in any number of different peach pies. Or in peach muffins or some other peach dessert. However, I also know that we broil peach halves with a little raspberry jelly in the center to use as an accompaniment for roast pork. So why not marry them to some nice chicken with a light dressing for a delightful summer salad entree?

Just a couple of words about this salad. As usual, if you do not like these proportions, change them to suit your taste. In the original recipe which I adapted this from, it had one cup of peaches for each two cups of chicken. I could barely taste the peaches and so I increased them. It also did not have the dressing as a mixture of mayonnaise and yogurt. I like it a lot better this way than just with mayo. But suit yourself. By the way, if you happen not to have peach yogurt, plain works just as well. Now while we are into slightly different chicken salads, let me give you another one. Again, it mixes chicken with fruits.

CARIBBEAN CHICKEN SALAD

    2 cups cooked chicken, cubed
    1 cup chopped celery
    1 cup pineapple chunks, canned or fresh
    1 can mandarin orange sections, drained
    1 banana, peeled and cut into chunks
    ½ cup each, mayonnaise and plain yogurt
    1 tsp mild curry powder
    ¾ cup salted peanuts

Mix the mayo, yogurt, and curry. Lightly toss all other ingredients and toss with dressing. Salt to taste and sprinkle with peanuts before serving.

Walter N. Lambert, Noonday Chef

COOL SUMMER SALAD (TV 375)

8 oz pasta, uncooked
6 cups mixed vegetables, broccoli, snow peas, celery, green
 onions, green peppers, cucumbers, tomatoes, etc.
2 TBSP toasted sesame seeds
¼ cup each, olive oil, white wine vinegar, soy sauce
1 TBSP sesame oil
2 cloves garlic, minced
salt and red pepper flakes is desired

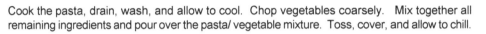

Cook the pasta, drain, wash, and allow to cool. Chop vegetables coarsely. Mix together all remaining ingredients and pour over the pasta/ vegetable mixture. Toss, cover, and allow to chill.

This is sort of a do it yourself venture. You get to choose whatever you like to mix into this salad. If you can find them, I like to use Japanese soba noodles for the pasta. They are buckwheat noodles which have a good texture and a nice nutty taste. If they are not available, Japanese odon noodles or even plain spaghetti works well. Break any of these up into fairly short pieces. This also works well with shells, and I have used the mixed veggie macaroni from **Kroger's** with it nicely.

The vegetables are as versatile. My favorites are broccoli, snow peas, celery, and sweet peppers. However, use whatever looks best at the market that day. If you add tomatoes, which I like to do very much, add them at the last minute. Otherwise, if they stand, they can cause too much moisture in the salad. Using red pepper flakes or even tabasco sauce is a matter of choice. We usually do not. I do look on the garlic and the sesame oil as essential, but that also is optional.

This noodle salad is a first cousin to a noodle dish which I have given you before. It has only one major difference in ingredients. In fact, I would suggest that you prepare the salad exactly as I have had you do it above. Except that you leave the sesame seeds out and add ½ cup creamy peanut butter to the dressing. Mix thoroughly and pour over the salad. This will give a creamy texture to the sauce.

I should tell you that in either case, this salad does not hold very well for long periods of time. If you want a cold noodle dish to serve at picnics, cook 16 oz of noodles and add about one cup of cucumbers which have been peeled, seeded, and grated, and about 1 cup of grated carrots. Then prepare the peanut butter dressing just as we did above. Pour it over the noodles and the veggies and allow to chill overnight before serving.

Walter N. Lambert, Noonday Chef

SWEET BERRY DELIGHT (TV 376)

1½ cup milk
1 cup self-rising corn meal mix
3 eggs
½ cup butter
⅔ cup sugar
⅓ cup lemon juice
grated lemon rind from one lemon
sweetened, chilled berries (about 2 cups)

Heat milk to boiling, and stir in corn meal. Cook, stirring, until thickened. Remove from heat; stir in sugar and butter. Continue beating until butter is melted. Beat in lemon juice and rind. Beat in eggs, one at a time and continue beating until fluffy. Turn into a greased 2 quart baking dish for 35 to 40 minutes in a preheated 375 deg oven. Serve hot with chilled berries spooned over the top.

I know! All these years, I have raved on about how bad it is to put sugar into cornbread and here I am advocating sweetened spoon bread. Well, we all change with the times. This recipe was originally developed by a home economist in Nashville. I loved it. I do it with strawberries, but **Anne** much prefers blackberries. Use your own judgment. What is really nice to me is the contrast of the hot lemon spoon bread with the cold berries.

Now you may want to try a variation which we have used a couple of times. If you are using frozen berries, they do not have a good texture to put over the top. Fine. Fold two cups of the thawed berries into the mixture after the eggs and bake as described. This will give you a softer bread which is really like a berry flavored Indian pudding. I serve it warm with powdered sugar sprinkled on top and it is very good.

Now let me give you one final variation which makes this excellent but requires a little work. Use the recipe just as I have given it to you above. However, separate the eggs and beat only the yolks into the cornmeal mush. Beat the egg whites until stiff and folks them into the mixture at the very end. Turn into the bowl and bake. This will not change the flavor of the dish, but will make it lighter and more delicate.

Now in case you are not familiar with traditional spoon bread, check your copy of ***Cooking with the Noonday Chef Volume 2*** on page 24 and you will find a recipe for the traditional spoon bread as well as a savory spicy cheese version. The point here is that spoon bread makes a nice place to start not end. Try it!

Walter N. Lambert, Noonday Chef

SPECIAL SUMMER SALAD (TV 377)

> 6 cups (approx) spinach, washed, stemmed and broken
> 2 oranges peeled and sliced thinly
> ½ to 1 cup each, fresh raspberries and red onions
> 4 oz feta cheese, crumbled
> ¼ cup each extra virgin olive oil and raspberry vinegar
> 1 TBSP honey
> 4 chicken breast, salted lightly and broiled or grilled

Toss together the spinach, oranges, raspberries, onion, and cheese. Thoroughly mix olive oil, vinegar, and honey. Pour over the salad and toss to mix. Spoon out onto 4 salad plates. Slice the hot chicken breast crosswise and place on top of the salad. Serve at once.

This is the ultimate ladies luncheon salad. It has everything going for it. It has spinach and onions as you would have in any salad. It then has orange sections and raspberries added for a sweet taste and feta cheese for a little tang. The dressing is light and refreshing. Then the hot chicken breast placed on top of the salad makes it a meal.

I must tell you that I like this salad very much as a side salad without the chicken. This recipe will make about 6 good-sized side salads. It is great served with cold roast beef and good hot rolls or hot sliced bread for lunch or dinner. We have also served it with roast pork and dressing.

Again, the strength of this salad lies in the several contrasts within it. That is why I like to put the chilled salad on a plate and put the hot chicken breast onto it.

You may have noticed that I do not include any salt or pepper in either the salad or the dressing. That is a matter of personal taste. If you like a taste of salt or pepper, add them to the dressing. Oh, and by the way, if you really want to make this elegant looking, after you put on the chicken, sprinkle the top with toasted walnuts or even pine nuts if you want to go whole hog.

A good bread to serve with this salad is the beer bread which is on page 40 of ***Cooking With The Noonday Chef Volume 1***. .

161

Walter N. Lambert, Noonday Chef

FRIED GREEN TOMATOES (TV 378)

        1 cup buttermilk
        2 eggs
        1½ cups self rising flour or self rising meal mix
        1 tsp salt
        1 tsp black pepper
        3 or 4 green tomatoes, cored and sliced
        oil for frying

In a fairly large bowl, beat together the buttermilk and eggs. Put tomato slices into milk mixture. In a heavy skillet, heat about ½ inch cooking oil until it is hot. Lift a tomato slice out of the milk mixture, and coat thoroughly on both sides with either the flour or meal mixture. Drop into the hot oil and fry until brown on the bottom. Turn and allow to brown. Lift out and place on paper towel to drain. Serve warm.

Everywhere I go these days, somebody is doing fried green tomatoes. They are one of those "**New Southern**" dishes that is hot. No doubt they will cool off, but for some of us they have been a standard part of our diet for years.

Now, let me tell you that there are as many ways to do fried green tomatoes as there are cooks to fix them. My **mother** put just a little bit of fat in an iron skillet (it was usually bacon grease), sliced the tomatoes, rolled them in flour and fried them. I have fixed them just the same way, except I liked them rolled in corn meal instead. My mother always shakes her head and says, "Everybody to their own taste". I agree. Then they started appearing everywhere with all kinds of coatings.

However, you are going to coat them, I like to start with the buttermilk and eggs. Some folks dust the slices of tomato with a little flour before putting them into the buttermilk. This will make the batter stick a little better, but I usually don't go to the trouble. Then after the buttermilk and egg mixture, dip the slices into either of the suggestions above. Fine cracker crumbs or even fine cheese cracker crumbs are also very good.

We like to serve fried green tomatoes with either corn relish or with good chow chow. You can find both of these at **Kroger**.

Now let me tell you about another variation which I told you about so long ago that you have probably forgotten: You can make a nice fritter by chopping green tomatoes fairly small and mixing about 2½ cups of chopped tomatoes with ¼ cup corn meal mix, ¼ cup buttermilk, 1 egg, and ½ tsp each of salt and Tabasco sauce. Drop this in about tablespoonfuls into hot oil and cook until brown, turning once. Great little fritters as a side dish.

162

Walter N. Lambert, Noonday Chef

UPSIDE DOWN CORNBREAD (TV 379)

2 TBSP Crisco (or other solid shortening)
1 onion, coarsely chopped
2 cups **White Lily** self-rising corn meal
1 to 1¼ cup **Mayfield** buttermilk
1 cup shredded **Tennessee Valley** cheddar cheese
½ cup **Tennessee Chow Chow** relish, drained

In a heavy 10" cast iron skillet, heat oil and cook onion, stirring constantly, until brown. Mix together the remaining ingredients and pour over the browned onion. Bake in a 425 deg oven about thirty minutes until brown. Turn out onto a plate and serve hot.

After a great kick off last Thursday with Tennessee's First Lady, **Mrs. Martha Sundquist**, we start our month long **Pick Tennessee Products** production here on **Noonday**. **Tennessee** is a major food producing state in this country, and we must not forget that we grow lots of food and process even more.

You will notice in almost every ingredient listed above there is a brand name. That is to show the range of foods which are processed in this state. Let me tell you that **Tennessee Brand Chow Chow** tastes most like my **mother** used to make. It comes either hot or mild and either works nicely in this recipe. If you happen to like it, and want to stretch this a little drain a can of **Bush's** golden hominy and stir it into the bread as well.

I originally intended to call this cornbread **"Pinto Bean Bread"**, but was talked out of it. I was told that if I called it that you would expect it to have Pinto Beans in it. Wrong! I would have called it that because it is perfect to eat with pinto beans. Or white beans. Or a mixture of the two. Now if you want to have perfect dried beans in a short time, let me make a suggestion. Buy some seasoning pieces of **Clifty Farm** ham at **Kroger**. In a heavy pan, fry the ham until it is cooked. Dump in as many cans of **Bush's Best Canned Beans** as you need to feed your crowd. Heat until they are boiling and then keep your mouth shut.

Now if you want to cook the beans from scratch, there is not much to that. Wash a pound of pinto, great Northern, or mixed beans and place in a sauce pan with water to cover. Bring to a boil, remove from the heat, and allow to stand at least an hour. Drain off the water and wash again in cold water. Place into a heavy pot with plenty of room to expand with a ham hock for seasoning. Cover with water and bring to a boil. Reduce heat as low as possible to keep the boil. Cook until tender. Salt to taste.

163

Walter N. Lambert, Noonday Chef

CHICKEN AND MUSHROOMS (TV 380)

3 TBSP cooking oil
1 medium onion, chopped
4 chicken breast halves, cut into bite sized pieces
½ lb mushrooms, sliced
4 TBSP flour
2 cups milk
½ cup water
salt and pepper to taste

Heat the oil in a heavy ovenproof skillet, and cook onions on high until they start to brown. Stir the chicken and stir fry until it changes color. Stir in mushrooms and continue stirring until they are almost cooked. Stir in flour and stir until the flour starts to brown. Stir in milk and water and continue to stir constantly until the mixture boils and thickens. Place biscuits on top of boiling chicken mixture, and bake in a 350 deg oven about 20 minutes until brown.

As we continue with **Pick Tennessee Products**, we use several of the major items produced in **Tennessee.** Chicken farming has been a major industry for years. **Tyson Chicken Corp.** has large production facilities in **West Tennessee. Monterey Mushrooms** of Lenoir City is known throughout the Southeast. These good folks grow a variety of mushrooms. For this recipe, I like plain little button mushrooms, but you may want to try some of their other varieties. We have recently used portabellos several times. These big beauties are now grown in their own building at Lenoir City.

The biscuits on the top of this dish are optional, but they add a lot to the dish. I use the mother of all biscuit flours, **White Lily**, to make biscuits. For this dish I general only use half a recipe, but you can make up a full recipe and bake half on the chicken and the rest to have for later. Did you know that you can bake biscuits just until they start to brown, remove from the oven and allow to cool. Wrap the biscuits completely and place in the freezer. To serve, place on a cookie sheet, still frozen, and pop into a 375 deg oven. By the time the biscuits are brown, they will be hot through and nearly as good as fresh.

For quick biscuits, use my secret biscuit recipe. Mix two cups of **White Lily** self rising flour with ¼ cup cooking oil and ¾ cup milk. Stir to blend. Knead lightly on a lightly floured sheet of waxed paper. Press or roll out to about ½" thick and cut into biscuits. Reshape the scraps and cut again until all are used. Bake at 400 deg about 15 minutes or until brown. This will make about 10 medium sized (2½") biscuits.

Walter N. Lambert, Noonday Chef

COUNTRY HAM QUICHE (TV 381)

1 9" deep dish pie shell, unbaked
1 cup (approx) country ham, chopped
1 cup (approx) cheddar cheese, grated
½ cup onion chopped
4 TBSP flour
3 eggs
1 cup buttermilk

Place ham, cheese, onion and flour in a mixing bowl. Toss to mix. Turn into the unbaked pie shell. Beat together the eggs and buttermilk. Pour slowly over the country ham mixture. Place in a 425 degree oven for 10 minutes. Turn oven down to 350 deg, and cook for about 35 minutes more until quiche is puffed and brown. Serve hot, warm, or cold.

For me, country ham may well be the premiere **Tennessee** product. At one time, the curing of hams was a very personal activity. It was often treated as a deep, dark secret as to just how much salt, sugar, pepper, or whatever made up the rub which was put on the fresh ham. Fights could break out over whether hams should be smoked and how long they needed to hang in the smoke house before being eaten. Now you get good country ham by going to **Kroger** and buying a **Clifty Farm Ham**. Or you can go up to Clinton and buy a ham from the great folks at **Cold Stream Farms**. Or you can mail order **Mar-Tenn** hams from Martin, Tennessee.

Now traditionally, country ham was fried, put on a biscuit and enjoyed. I still like that a lot. If you have not tried this, by all means do so. When I fry ham, I trim off all the fat. I heat a heavy skillet hot, and fry the fat until it is brown and all the grease is out. I then discard the fat meat. In the grease in the pan, I drop slices of country ham and cook them hot and quick until brown. I then place them on paper towels to drain. If I think my arteries can stand it, I then make red gravy (sometimes called red eye gravy) by pouring the hot fat into a heat resistant bowl. I then pour about ½ cup black coffee into the skillet and stir it around until all the brown bits in the skillet cook off and the mixture starts to thicken a little. Pour this into the hot fat and enjoy. If you are not frying much ham and you want to cheat a little, after you have poured off the fat, sprinkle a couple of TBSP of sugar into the pan. Let it caramelize before pouring in the coffee. This make the gravy look and taste better.

But do not limit yourself to plain old fried ham. Try it in this quiche or get last year's country ham pasta sauce recipe. Or even try baking one. I will tell you how sometime.

Walter N. Lambert, Noonday Chef

EASY APPLE PUDDING (TV 382)

1 cup **White Lily** self-rising flour
¾ cup each, white sugar and brown sugar
½ cup milk
3 TBSP cooking oil
2 cups **Cocke County Apples**, peeled, cored and sliced thin
2 tsp cinnamon
1 cup boiling water

In an ungreased 8" square pan, spread apples evenly over the bottom. Mix the flour and white sugar. Mix milk and cooking oil and stir into the flour mixture. Pour evenly over the apples. Sprinkle brown sugar over the top and sprinkle the cinnamon evenly over the brown sugar. Carefully pour the boiling water over the top. Place into a 350 deg oven, and bake for one hour. Serve warm.

This week concludes our **"Pick Tennessee Products Month"**. We are proud to have been part of this venture with the **Tennessee Department of Agriculture** and appreciate the hard work which **Mrs. Don Sundquist, First Lady of Tennessee**, has done to help folks know about the importance of the food industry in Tennessee.

One of my favorite Tennessee products is apples. It has been great fun to watch the success of the **Apple Barn** complex near **Sevierville,** and for years I have gone with my mother to **Baxter's Apple Farm** near **Cosby**. A friend of mine observed that they do not even charge you extra to drive up there to get them.

Now you may have noticed that this pudding looks a lot like the old lemon cake top puddings which we used to do. Or even the **Jack Daniels** pudding that is on page 62 in _**Volume 1 of Cooking with the Noonday Chef**_. It is exactly the same principal. This same recipe will work nicely with slices of fresh plum or fresh peaches. Simply peel the peaches, (there is no need to peel the plums) slice thin, and place in the bottom of the pan. This pudding works quite nicely with ice cream on the top.

If you have not done so, you might like to do what we have always called poor man's pie with some of the good **Tennessee apples**. Slice about 3 cups of apples. Place in a heavy saucepan with ½ cup sugar and ½ cup water. Bring to a full boil, and cook until apples are barely tender. Pour into an 8" square pan in which you have melted 4 TBSP butter. Sprinkle with cinnamon to taste. Mix ½ cup **White Lily Self-rising flour** with one half cup sugar and ½ cup milk and pour over the fruit. Bake in a 350 deg oven about 35 minutes. Serve warm.

Walter N. Lambert, Noonday Chef

PINTO BEAN PIE (TV 383)

    1 cup cooked pinto beans
    1 cup each, white sugar and brown sugar
    ½ cup butter, melted
    2 eggs, beaten
    1 tsp vanilla
    ¾ cup chopped pecans
    1 9" deep dish pie shell, unbaked

Puree beans with mixer. Blend in sugars, butter, eggs, and vanilla thoroughly. Pour into pie shell, and sprinkle pecans evenly on the top. Place into a preheated 350 deg oven and bake about 45 minutes. Cool before serving.

First off, let me tell you that I take no blame for this pie. Our good friend and good cook **Jean Millis** gave us the recipe. You will remember Jean. She gave us the recipe for beet salad which pleased **Alan Williams,** so!

This recipe, like others we have done, is based on the unusual nature of using something which we do not think of as dessert material in a dessert. What the beans really do in this pie is add bulk and moisture. Their high fiber nature, which is what makes them so good for us, and incidentally, what gives them their bad reputation, keeps the filling of the pie moist and firm.

Some of you may remember the pork and bean cake of a few years ago. That cake uses a can of pork and beans which are pureed. In fact, why don't I just give you that recipe again.

WHAT'S IN IT CAKE

    2 cups self-rising flour
    2 cups sugar
    1 cup oil
    4 eggs
    2 tsp cinnamon
    1 8 oz can crushed pineapple (drained)
    1 16 oz can pork and beans (drained)
    1 cup walnuts or pecans

Grease and flour a bundt pan or a tube pan. With a heavy mixer, beat the pork and beans until completely mashed. Add all remaining ingredients except nuts and beat together thoroughly. Beat in the nuts. Turn into a bundt pan, and bake in a preheated 350 deg oven about 45 minutes or until cake tests done. Allow to cool about fifteen minutes before turning out.

Walter N. Lambert, Noonday Chef

LEWIS COSBY'S BREAKFAST CASSEROLE (TV 384)

8 slices white bread
1 lb hot pork sausage
3 cups shredded cheddar cheese
6 eggs
2 cups milk
½ tsp salt
1 tsp dry mustard

Spray a 9x13" pan with a cooking spray. Break the bread into large pieces in the pan. Cut sausage into approximately 1" chunks and fry until browned. Drain. Layer sausage evenly over the bread. Sprinkle with cheese. Beat together the milk, eggs, salt, and mustard, and pour evenly over the top. Cover tightly, and allow to stand in the refrigerator overnight. Bake in a preheated 350 deg oven about 40 to 45 minutes or until puffed and brown. Serve hot.

Lewis Cosby has been the general manager of **Channel 8** as long as there has been a Channel 8. I wouldn't want him to know it, but I think he is a very nice man. I regularly tell him that I am nice to him only because he is the boss. But that is not true. I am nice to him because I like him and I admire his wife, Lydia. Recently, he asked why I had never asked him to cook. That was hint enough for me. I asked. You see the result above.

This is a variation on a recipe which I gave you earlier in which you toss the cheese, sausage (or ham), and bread together and pour the milk and egg mixture over it before baking. It not only looks prettier this way, I think it tastes better as well.

This base of bread, milk, and eggs is very versatile. You can make this savory or sweet casserole. You can use your own creativity to get a taste you like. For example, it is very good to use ham instead of the sausage and substitute 1 cup of crumbled blue cheese for 1 cup of the cheddar cheese. If you like, you can sprinkle the top of that with some chopped walnuts. Their flavor blends nicely with the blue cheese. A friend does a similar dish instead of a cinnamon roll variation. He uses about a dozen slices of bread which he puts into a 9x13" pan. He then whips together 6 eggs with 2½ cups milk and ¾ cup sugar. He pours this over the bread and covers and refrigerates overnight. Just before he bakes it, he drizzles 1 stick of butter, melted over the top and then sprinkles ¾ cup brown sugar mixed with ½ cup of chopped pecans and 1 tsp cinnamon over the top. Bake for 40 to 45 minutes in a 325 deg oven. Watch carefully to see that the sugar does not burn. You now have baked French Toast. You also have permission to try your own variations. Good luck, Lewis!

Walter N. Lambert, Noonday Chef

MARY MILLS MACARONI SALAD (TV 385)

1 8 oz box macaroni, cooked, drained, rinsed and drained
1 large tomato, peeled and diced
1 small onion, finely chopped
1 TBSP each green pepper and celery, finely chopped
½ cup shredded cheese
2 hard boiled eggs, chopped
1 small cucumber
3 TBSP sugar
¼ cup sweet pickle syrup (4 or 5 TBSP)
1 tsp vinegar
½ cup mayonnaise
salt and pepper to taste

In a jar or small bowl, combine mayonnaise, salt, pepper, vinegar, sugar, and pickle syrup. Mix until smooth. In a large bowl, place all remaining ingredients except the cucumber. Pour the dressing over, and toss to mix. Place in a covered dish and refrigerate overnight. Just before serving, chop the cucumber and toss in the salad.

Now let me admit right off that this recipe is a little longer than I usually give you. However, this recipe came to me from **Mrs. Mary Mills** of **Morristown** ,who with her daughter **Mary Geneva Mills,** has been to several of our demonstrations. Mary Geneva told me that this is the only macaroni salad she ever liked. I have liked many, but I like this one best. You may well ask why you add the cucumber at the last minute. Well, to keep it crisp of course. Mrs. Mills also gave me a fine looking zucchini relish recipe which I have not tried, but pass it along to you with full confidence. This lady knows what she is doing.

ZUCCHINI RELISH

10 cups zucchini, peeled, seeded and shredded
2 cups sweet peppers, chopped (Use one red and one green)
4 onions, chopped
4 cups sugar
2 cups vinegar
1 tsp celery seed
1 tsp black pepper
1½ TBSP cornstarch

Mix well zucchini, pepper and onions. Let stand 4 hours. Drain, squeeze out lightly with hands. Mix sugar, vinegar, celery seed, pepper, and cornstarch. Let come to a boil and pour over vegetables. Return to heat and let boil for 5 minutes. Put into sterilized jars and seal.

Walter N. Lambert, Noonday Chef

MISS PIGGY SQUARES (TV 386)

> 1 lb **Rudy's Farm country sausage** (mild)
> 1½ cups chopped raisins
> 2 cups water
> 2½ cups flour
> 2 cups light brown sugar
> 1 tsp each, baking powder, baking soda, and cinnamon
> 1 cup finely chopped nuts

Bring raisins and water to a boil and simmer for 20 minutes. Drain, reserving 1 cup of the cooking water. Sift together dry ingredients. Using your hands, work the sausage into the flour mixture until it is evenly distributed. Add raisins and the cooking liquid, then stir in the nuts. Pour into a lightly buttered and floured 9x13" pan, and bake in a preheated 350 deg oven for 45 minutes. Cool and frost with caramel topping.

I hope you have not let the idea of **Rudy's Farm sausage** in a nice dessert square scare you off. This great little treat is the brain child of **Joyce Clevenger of Newport, Tennessee** who used it to win the Rudy's Farm sausage cooking contest at the **Tennessee Valley Fair** this year. **Anne** and I had the privilege of being two of the judges at this event and there was never a doubt that this was the winner. You should keep your eye out for the whole range of cooking contests that are now part of the Fair. Get yourself out there and compete!

Now Joyce frosts these squares with a fine caramel frosting, and we are giving you the recipe below. Remember, caramel icing is not the easiest thing in the world to do, but this is a fine recipe.

CARAMEL TOPPING

> 1 cup each sugar and dark brown sugar
> ½ cup milk
> 2 TBSP butter, softened
> 1 tsp vanilla

Put sugar, milk, and butter into a saucepan and, stirring constantly, cook over low heat until the sugar has dissolved. Do not allow mixture to boil. When the mixture is well blended, increase heat and boil until the soft ball stage has been reached. Remove from heat, let cool 5 minutes, then stir in the vanilla. Beat until the surface is not shiny and it is cool enough to spread. **Note**: soft ball stage is when a drop of the mixture dropped into cold water forms a soft ball which can be picked up.

Walter N. Lambert, Noonday Chef

AUTUMN CHOPS (TV 387)

6 to 8 lean pork chops
1 28 oz can sauerkraut, drained completely
2 cups each, chopped cabbage and peeled and chopped apples
2 cans cream of mushroom soup, undiluted
salt and pepper to taste

Mix kraut, cabbage, apples, and soup. Spread evenly in a 9x13" dish which has been sprayed with a cooking spray. Place pork chops on top of the kraut mixture, fitting them closely together to cover as much of the top as possible. Sprinkle lightly with salt and pepper. Cover tightly with aluminum foil, and bake in a preheated 350 deg oven one hour. Remove foil, and continue to bake for 30 minutes or until the chops are browned. Serve hot with rice.

This dish is one of our fall favorites. I think because it is SO easy and hearty. On the subject of heart, if you do not eat pork, place boned, skinned chicken breasts on top of the kraut mixture, and proceed exactly as you do with the chops. Someone always asks me what you can do if you do not like kraut. Well, I don't have a good answer to that, because I love it and cannot understand how someone would not. I especially like it cooked with apples. However, if you just must leave out the kraut, cook peeled and sliced potatoes until they are about half cooked. Mix them with the cabbage, apples, and soup and proceed as above.

Now let us talk a little about variations on this theme. I very much like to do this as a casserole using left over roast pork. To do that, trim off any fat or gristle from the pork and cut it into cubes. Mix about 3 or 4 cups of this pork into the kraut mixture. Pat into the 9x13" dish, and bake covered for about 30 minutes and uncovered for about 45. Again, this will work with cubes of chicken or turkey just as well.

I recommend this dish for covered dish suppers as well. Because you have added so little grease, the dish is good even at room temperature. But if you do this, be sure to use nice, lean chops or chicken. The fatter your chops are, the more grease you will have in the veggies.

One final word. This produces a lot of the kraut mixture for the amount of pork you have. That is because I like it a lot. If you find this is too much kraut and apples for you, use a smaller can of kraut. Also, the mushroom soup is added to give a creamy texture to the vegetables. If that does not matter to you, simply leave it out. Proceed as above.

Walter N. Lambert, Noonday Chef

TOFFEE POUND CAKE (TV 388)

3 cups flour
2 tsp baking powder
pinch of salt
6 1.4 oz Heath Bars, chopped
2 sticks butter
3 TBSP Crisco butter flavored shortening
2 cups sugar
4 eggs
1 TBSP vanilla
1 cup milk

Mix flour, baking powder, and salt. Sprinkle about 2 TBSP of flour mixture over candy bars, and stir to coat completely. Cream butter and shortening thoroughly. Cream in sugar. Add eggs, one egg at a time, beating between each addition. Beat in vanilla. Alternately add the flour and milk while beating at low speed. Stir in the toffee. Spoon into a greased and floured bundt pan and bake in a preheated 350 deg oven about 55 minutes or until done. Cool for 5 minutes in the pan before inverting onto a serving plate.

I absolutely love **English Toffee**. The best I have ever eaten is made by **Anne** when she decides to, which is not all that often. In a pinch, I pick up a **Heath bar**. For this cake, you will need six. Chop them up as fine as you want. I run them for just a short time in the food processor which gives you some fine crumbs and some bigger ones. This makes a nice contrast in the cake. I personally, think this cake is rich and moist enough that it does not need embellishment. If, however, you are the type which never leaves well enough alone, you might chop another candy bar or two very fine. Make some good whipped cream and put a dollop onto a slice of the cake, then sprinkle it with the toffee dust. Oh did I mention that I usually just sprinkle the top of the cake with confectioners sugar instead of even thinking about frosting.

Now let me give you another couple of quick tips for **Heath Bar desserts**. First, you can make a lovely parfait by layering ice cream and chopped Heath bars in a parfait glass. If this is not enough for you, pour a little **Kahlua** over the top. A particularly elegant friend of our makes English Toffee Mousse and never tells a soul how she does it. Don't tell her that I spilled the beans. Completely dissolve a package of un-flavored gelatin in about ¼ cup of water. Allow to cool. Fold the gelatin mixture into 2 cups of cream which has been whipped, and sweeten with about ½ cup confectioners sugar. Fold in 6 chopped Heath Bars. Pour into individual parfait glasses and chill. Serve cold and wait for the compliments!

Walter N. Lambert, Noonday Chef

PUMPKIN AMARETTO CHEESECAKE (TV 389)

2 8 oz pkgs cream cheese
1 cup canned pumpkin
3 eggs
1 can **Eagle Brand Amaretto flavored condensed milk**
1 8" crust in a spring form pan
½ tsp each, allspice and nutmeg
¼ cup sliced or slivered almonds

Cream the cream cheese in a heavy blender using the flat blade. Cream in the pumpkin and then add eggs one at a time, scraping the bowl after each addition. Beat in the **Eagle Brand** milk. Pour mixture into the prepared crust. Sprinkle the top with the spices and almonds. Bake in a 300 deg oven about 1 hour. Remove, allow to cool. Chill to serve.

I love cheesecake. And this one is so easy thanks to **Eagle Brand Milk**. I don't know who thought up the idea of Amaretto flavor for this fine old product, but they did good. I noticed in the **Knoxville News-Sentinel** recently that **Louise Durman** had a good looking recipe for an orange cheesecake using this product. It sounded great, but I was looking for pumpkin recipes and gave this one a try. Super! Next, I am going to try a pumpkin pie with it.

Now a word about the crust. I personally prefer a pastry crust for cheesecake in the style of the famous **Lindy's** Cheesecake in **New York**. If that is to your taste, roll a piece of **Pillsbury's** ready made crust from the cooler very thin, and fit it into an 8 or 9" spring form pan. If you prefer a crumb crust, try using **Zweiback Toast** crumbs instead of graham cracker crumbs. It gives a mild, delicate, nutty flavor to cheesecake which I like very much. Of Course, you can simply use a graham cracker crust. I have been known to use a prepared graham cracker pie crust. In fact, this filling will fill two graham cracker pie shells, and make one pumpkin cheese pie to eat and one to give the neighbors.

If I am making a crust from scratch, I use 2 to 2½ cups of fine crumbs, which I mix with ¼ cup sugar and ½ cup melted butter. I press this into the bottom of a spring form pan, and bake about 15 minutes in a 350 deg oven. Sometimes, I like to flavor the crust a little. In this one for example, you could finely chop some almonds, mix them in with the crumbs, and proceed as usual. I wouldn't use more than about ½ cup of the nuts. With a chocolate cheesecake, you might want to use pecans. Spices would also work very well in this one. If you use Zweiback crumbs, try adding about ½ tsp of nutmeg to the crumbs as well as sprinkling it on top. Enjoy.

Walter N. Lambert, Noonday Chef

SWEET POTATO STEW (TV 390)

1½ lb lean beef stew meat
½ cup flour
2 tsp each, salt and pepper
2 TBSP cooking oil
¼ cup soy sauce
1 16 oz can beef broth
3 onions, divided
1 medium sweet potato, peeled and cut into chunks
2 cups carrots and/or celery
1 medium pumpkin

Cut the top from the pumpkin and hollow out the inside. Set aside. In a heavy saucepan, heat oil until hot. Add one onion which you have chopped coarsely. Stir until onion starts to brown. Place the flour, salt, and pepper into a heavy plastic; shake to mix. Add meat, close the bag, and shake to coat the meat. Add to the hot oil and brown. Stir in the soy sauce. Add the beef broth, reduce heat, and allow to cook until tender. Cut the remaining two onions into quarters and add with the remaining vegetables. Cook until tender. While still boiling, pour into the pumpkin, replace cover and bake at 350 deg for 1½ hours or until pumpkin flesh is tender. Scoop out and serve.

I know this is a long and complicated recipe. But it is worth the trouble to carry this meal in a pumpkin onto the table on all hallows eve. Now I must admit that baking in the pumpkin is just for the fun of it. However, using sweet potato instead of Irish potatoes and adding the pumpkin is strictly for the flavor. If you do not want to go to the trouble of the extra cooking in the pumpkin, make the stew exactly as describe above. Then when it is done and just before you are to serve it, stir in about a cup of canned pumpkin and serve immediately. Great flavor, good color, fine dinner. Serve cornbread with it. That is about as international as you can get.

Let me say a word about the dredging of the meat in flour before browning it. This does several things at once. First, it improves the flavor of the beef. Second, it provides a browned flour to thicken the stew which is much, much better than adding flour at the end. And finally, about the broth. If you happen to not have it, just use water. The broth simply increases the richness of the flavor of the stew.

If you do decide to treat this as your Halloween supper, serve a good spinach salad, the stew and some hot cornbread. Then if you want to set the meal off just perfectly, have last weeks Pumpkin Amaretto cheesecake for dessert. And next week, pumpkin soup.

174

Walter N. Lambert, Noonday Chef

ROASTED PUMPKIN GINGER SOUP (TV 391)

    5 to 6 cups roasted pumpkin, cubed
    5 to 6 cups chicken stock
    1 inch piece of fresh ginger, thinly sliced
    1 large onion, chopped (about 1½ cups)
    3 TBSP olive oil
    salt to taste
    sour cream for garnish

In a large saucepan, heat the olive oil. Add the onion and cook until lightly browned, about 5 minutes. Add the ginger and stir a couple of times. Add the pumpkin and the chicken stock. Bring to a boil, reduce heat and cook about 30 minutes to blend flavors. Using a hand blender or the food processor, puree the soup. Add salt to taste. Serve hot with a dollop of sour cream.

Now before you can ask, let me tell you about roasting pumpkin. Cut a medium to small pumpkin into half, and remove the seeds and the stringy material on the inside. Cut the pumpkin into 4 or 5 pieces, and place in a baking pan with the cut side up. Bake at 400 deg for about 1½ hours or until lightly brown and tender. Allow to cool, cut away the peel, cut into chunks and proceed with the recipe.

This means of cooking pumpkin is important to this soup. For years, I have cooked pumpkin in the oven by cutting it in half, removing the inside and then covering the cut side with aluminum foil and baking the pumpkin halves slowly (at about 300 deg) until it was tender. You then scooped out the pumpkin and discarded the shell. Cooked this way, the pumpkin is fairly watery but very good. When you cook it hot and uncovered instead, the pumpkin comes out firm, with its flavor intensified instead of diluted.

Now ginger is the not the only choice of flavors for this soup. You may want to try powdered cumin instead. Or a mixture of cumin and nutmeg. Or even nutmeg alone. With either of these dry spices, add them to the soup after it has been pureed rather than letting them cook as the ginger does. Do not substitute dried, powdered ginger for fresh.

If you wish, you can stir the sour cream into the soup rather than using it as a garnish. If you do this, puree the soup first. Then stir about 2 cups of sour cream into the soup. Heat it slowly until it is just below boiling. Do not allow the soup to boil after the sour cream has been added. By the way, for a whole new taste, use half pumpkin and half a sweet potato in this soup. It is beautiful and very tasty.

Walter N. Lambert, Noonday Chef

SWEET POTATO NUT MUFFINS (TV 392)

    1 cup each, self-rising flour and self-rising meal
    ½ cup each, sugar and chopped pecans
    1 tsp nutmeg
    ½ cup milk
    2 eggs
    1 cup cooked, mashed sweet potato
    2 TBSP oil

Mix together the flour, meal, sugar, nuts, and nutmeg. In a separate bowl mix remaining ingredients. Mix wet mixture into the dry just until mixed. Spoon into twelve muffin cups in muffin tins which have been sprayed with a cooking spray. Bake in a 400 deg oven about 15 to 20 minutes or until lightly browned. Serve hot.

Since it is still fall and the holidays are ahead, I thought we needed to pay a little attention to sweet potatoes. They need not just be candied anymore. We love these muffins to accompany a simple lunch. We have been known to serve them for **Thanksgiving** brunch. They are just lightly sweet and have a little extra crunch from the corn-meal. Because you use self- rising flour and meal, they are super easy to do.

You may want to try these with peanuts rather than pecans. It is a different taste, but one I like. Second, you may want to use only ¼ cup of nuts with ¼ cup raisins for a little added sweetness and chew. These are also very nice to do a little nut topping for them. Use about ¼ cup additional nuts which you mix with ¼ cup sugar and ¼ cup softened butter. Sprinkle this mixture evenly over the muffins before you bake them. This adds a little to the flavor and a lot to the appearance of the muffins.

Finally, let me say a word about cooking sweet potatoes. Many recipes will suggest that for recipes like this or even for candied sweet potatoes that you peel the potatoes and boil and drain them. This is fine. They also cook nicely to boil them in the peeling and then drain and peel them before proceeding with whatever recipe you are doing. In fact, my mother used to cook them this way to make sweet potato pudding. Mash up boil sweet potatoes, mix in about a stick of butter for each 3 or 4 cups of cooked potatoes along with ½ cup brown sugar, a little milk and an egg. Bake in a greased dish topped with marshmallows for the last 15 minutes of cooking. I personally prefer sweet potatoes which are cooked by wrapping them in aluminum foil and baking hot (400 deg) for about 45 minutes to an hour depending on the size of the potato. Allow to cool in the foil, peel and proceed. Give this a try.

Walter N. Lambert, Noonday Chef

QUICK HOLIDAY COOKIES (TV)

    1 1 lb pound cake mix
    ¾ cup cooking oil
    2 eggs
    1 TBSP vanilla
    1 cup quick cooking oats
    1 cup raisins (dried cranberries)

In a heavy mixer, blend cake mix, oil, egg, and vanilla. Stir in oats and craisins. Drop by tablespoonfuls onto an ungreased cookie sheet about 2" apart. Bake in a preheated 375 deg oven about 8 to 10 minutes or until lightly brown. Gently lift off onto a rack to cool. Store in a tightly covered container.

Now I know you are wondering about raisins if you have not already discovered them in the specialty food section at **Kroger**. If not, you are in for a treat. They are presweetened, dried cranberries, and they can be used almost any way you would use raisins. Except I think they taste better.

I should tell you that this basic recipe lends itself to all sorts of variations and is, therefore, an ideal recipe to have around for the **holidays**. For example, if you should happen to have such bad taste that you don't like the dried cranberries, use raisins. Even better, use chocolate covered raisins. If you like things a little spicy, add ½ tsp nutmeg and ½ tsp cinnamon to the cake mixture. Then use 1 cup of chopped dates instead of raisins or raisins. You may want to use ½ cup chopped pecans and ½ cup chopped dates as well. See, once you start, there is almost no end to the variations.

Starting this week, we are doing things that make holiday preparations easy while still doing nice things. Next week, we will be using a cake mix to make fruit cake. Stay tuned.

Now some of you that joined us late may not remember when we did cookies once before that were based on a cake mix.

QUICK LEMON COOKIES

    1 pkg Betty Crocker Lemon Cake Mix
    2 cups Cool Whip, thawed
    1 egg

Blend all ingredients thoroughly. Drop by full teaspoonfuls onto a lightly greased cookie sheet. Bake at 350 deg for 12 to 15 minutes until puffed and lightly browned. Allow to cool on the pan for a couple of minutes before moving to a rack to cool.

Walter N. Lambert, Noonday Chef

FAST, FANCY FRUITCAKE (TV 394)

   1 pkg white cake mix
   ⅔ cup cooking oil
   ½ cup **Eagle Brand Milk**
   2 egg whites
   2 cups candied fruit (see note)
   1 cup chopped pecans

With a heavy mixer, beat cake mix, oil, milk, and egg whites until completely blended. Stir in the fruit and nuts. Pack into two greased and floured loaf pans. Bake in a 350 deg oven about 45 minutes or until cake tests done. Allow to cool in the pan at least ten minutes before turning out. Wrap tightly to store.

Do you like those dark fruitcake with all the strange stuff in it. I don't. Some long time ago I gave you a recipe for a favorite light fruitcake of mine. If you are interested, you can find it on page 37 of _**Cooking with the Noonday Chef, Volume 2.**_ It is a very nice cake, but it is a fair amount of trouble. This one is no trouble at all. It is also very pretty because of the white cake making the fruit and nuts stand out.

Now about that fruit mixture. If you like it, you can simply use two cups of the premixed, precut, candied fruit. I don't like it, therefore, I do not use it. I use one cup of candied pineapple and 1 cup candied cherries. To add to the appearance of the cake, I usually mix the cherries half and half with red and green. There is nothing sacred about this. If you like candied apricots by all means use them. I personally would cut them up before putting them into the cake. Be sure to use candied ones and not just dried ones for this purpose.

I have you baking this mixture in two large loaf pans. That is simply so you have one cake to eat and one to give as a gift. If you give gift baskets, use the small loaf pans, and bake it in four loaves. If you want one big, showy fruitcake for a buffet table, you can do that as well. Simply pack all the batter in a greased and floured bundt pan. Reduce the heat to 300 deg, and bake for about 1 hour and 15 minutes. Be sure to test to see if it is done, and allow it to cool in the pan before turning it out because it comes out of the oven very tender.

Last week, we baked cookies using a cake mix. When I was preparing this week's fruit cake, it occurred to me that a nice variation on last weeks cookies would be to chop candied fruits fairly fine and add a cup of mixed chopped fruit to the basic cookie dough. See, you have to be thinking all the time.

178

Walter N. Lambert, Noonday Chef

POOR MAN'S PECAN PIE (OATMEAL PIE) (TV 396)

1 cup oatmeal
⅔ cup each, sugar and maple flavored syrup
1 stick butter, melted
1 tsp vanilla butter nut flavoring
2 eggs
1 9" deep dish pie shell, unbaked

Mix oatmeal and sugar. In the bowl of a mixer mix the melted butter, syrup, flavoring, and eggs until fluffy. Beat in the oatmeal mixture and turn into the pie shell. Bake in a preheated 350 deg oven for 45 minutes or until barely set in the center. Cool before serving.

This recipe comes to us from the cookbook of the **Forks Grove Baptist Church** of **Lafollette,** Tennessee by way of a friend of ours named **Arie Hatmaker.** Arie is a sweet lady we met through the show, and we value her friendship.

Now we are walking a fine line on this one since we called it a pecan pie when it has no pecans in it at all. But it has the consistency and much of the taste of a pecan pie without the expense of the nuts. Thus the name. We think it is delightful made just this way. However, I should in the interest of truth tell you that **Arie** and her friend **Ellen Ivey,** who supplied this recipe to the book, do note that it is alright to add some pecans as well if you wish. I would suggest that you might want to use ½ cup of oatmeal and ½ cup of chopped pecans if you decide to go that route.

Now let me give you another of **Arie's** fine recipes. She brought us a piece of this cake and I know first hand that it is good. By the way, if you happen not to like prunes, add some applesauce instead.

"GLORY BE" CAKE

2 cups each, self-rising flour and sugar
1 cup cooking oil
3 eggs
2 jars plum baby food or one jar prune junior baby food
2 TBSP instant tea
1 tsp each, allspice and cinnamon
1 cup chopped pecans (optional)

Mix all ingredients. Pour into a grease, floured bundt pan, and bake for 1 hour in a 325 deg oven. Test for doneness. Allow to cool in the pan a few minutes before turning out to cool.

Walter N. Lambert, Noonday Chef

ALMOND CHUTNEY CHEESE BALL (TV 397)

2 8 oz pkgs. cream cheese, softened
½ cup mango chutney plus some for garnish
3 tsp mild curry powder
½ tsp dry mustard
blanched whole or slivered almonds

Combine the cream cheese, ½ cup chutney, curry, and mustard; blend together completely. Shape into a ball, wrap in **Saran Wrap,** and allow to chill overnight to firm and allow flavors to blend. Unwrap, and place on a serving plate. Cover the outside with the almonds and spoon some additional chutney onto the top of the ball. Serve with crackers.

I am not at all sure why, but I absolutely love cheese balls. They seem a necessary part of the holidays for me. This is a lightly spicy, almost sweet version with gives a different and interesting taste. When we do this, we generally press the almonds into the ball to stand out. It is also easy and attractive to roll the ball of cheese in the slivered almonds. Spoon about ½ cup of the chutney onto a small serving dish and set the ball in the center of it. The hallmark of all this is that it is easy, attractive and good.

I think that we gave you the recipe for our long standing cheese ball some long time ago. In case we did not, it follows. I should note that we generally make several pounds of this at the start of the season and give it as **Christmas** gifts. It was given to us by our good friend, the late **Eleanor Boyd Grace**, and I never make this without thinking of her.

ELEANOR'S CHEESE BALL

2 lb sharp cheddar cheese, grated
1 lb each, cream cheese and blue cheese
½ cup onion, grated very fine
3 TBSP Worcestershire sauce
½ tsp ground cayenne pepper

Have all cheeses at room temperature. Crumble the blue cheese. Blend all ingredients completely. Shape into balls, wrap tightly in **Saran Wrap,** and allow to stand in the refrigerator at least a day. To serve, you may roll the balls in pecans, paprika, dried parsley or some combination thereof. Serve at room temperature.

As always, this just gives you a base recipe. If you like blue cheese more, add more of it. If you like it less, leave it out altogether and increase the cream cheese.

Walter N. Lambert, Noonday Chef

SPICY CRANBERRY RELISH (TV 398)

    1 12 oz pkg fresh cranberries
    1 Granny Smith (or other sour) apple, cored and cut into
      chunks
    ½ cup each, sugar and orange marmalade
    1" piece of fresh ginger
    1 jalapeno pepper, with the stem and seeds removed cup fresh cilantro

Combine all ingredients in the bowl of a food processor, and process with the metal blade until fully blended and chopped fine. Place into a covered bowl, and refrigerate overnight before serving.

Well, here we go again. It's cranberry relish time and this time, I have stirred up a hornets nest. I developed this recipe after reading about a **Southwestern Christmas** dinner that featured cranberry salsa. No recipe was given. Therefore, liking the sound of the salsa, I set out to put flavors that I liked into some combination. This is the result. I love it. **Anne** hates it. In fact, she says it is the worst thing I have ever made in 35 years of trying. I disagree. So there decide for yourself what you think. By the way, I like this either with roast turkey or with roast pork.

If you do not want to be that adventuresome, make the old standby.

CRANBERRY ORANGE RELISH

    1 12 oz pkg fresh cranberries
    1 medium orange cut into sections and the seeds removed
    1 cup sugar
    2 TBSP lemon juice

Place all ingredients in a food processor (do not peel the orange) and process until fully blended and chopped fine. It may be necessary to scrape down the sides of the bowl a couple of times in the process. Place in a covered bowl and refrigerate overnight before serving. This is very pretty served in hollowed out orange peel.

For an altogether different cranberry relish, look on page 137 in *__Cooking with the Noonday Chef, Volume 2__* for a recipe for a sweet relish given to us by **Ruth DeFriese**, who is a great lady and a great cook.

Walter N. Lambert, Noonday Chef

QUICK SPICY NUTS (TV 399)

      2 egg whites, lightly whipped
      1 lb pecan halves
      1 pkg taco seasoning mix

Beat egg whites until they are just frothy. Stir in the pecans and then the seasoning mix. Pour onto a lightly oiled cookie sheet and spread evenly. Bake in a 250 deg oven about 1 hour stirring each 15 minutes. Allow to cool before storing in a tight container.

It is beginning to look a lot like **Christmas**. And if you are like me, you are looking for that last minute snack item which can be packed into a decorative plastic bag and used to fill out a gift basket. This is a good one. I don't know about you, but I tire a little of sweet about this time each year. This is a nice break. If you don't want to turn this much control over to someone else, mix your own spicy mix. Mix about 1 TBSP paprika, 1 TBSP chili powder, and 1 TBSP salt and use instead of the taco seasoning. If you like it hotter, add in about ¼ tsp ground cayenne pepper. Alternatively, you can beat about 1 tsp Tabasco sauce into the egg whites to add some heat. The point is that the egg whites hold the seasoning mixture into place while you roast the nuts.

The same technique can be used to make sweet, spicy nuts. Beat the egg whites and use to coat the nuts just as we did above. Then sprinkle the nuts with ½ cup sugar mixed with ½ tsp each, cinnamon, nutmeg and cloves. Roast as described above. I use only cinnamon and nutmeg. **Dianne Sharp** at my office brought us an interesting nut and cereal mixture which is also easy. Here is the recipe for that.

SWEET AND SPICY MIX

      4 TBSP butter
      3 cups each nuts (either pecans or walnuts) and waffle crisp
       cereal
      ½ cup each brown sugar and confectioners sugar
      1 tsp cinnamon

In a large baking pan with sides, melt the butter. Toss nuts in the butter to coat and sprinkle with the brown sugar and cinnamon, stirring to coat. Bake in a 300 deg oven about 30 minutes, stirring thoroughly half way through. When the nuts come out of the oven, stir to coat with melted sugar and stir in the cereal. Sprinkle on the confectioners sugar and toss to coat. Allow to cool before storing in a tight container.

Walter N. Lambert, Noonday Chef

NEW YEAR'S CHILI (TV 400)

¼ lb hog jowl bacon, diced (about 1 cup)
1 large onion, chopped
1 to 1½ lb lean ground beef
¼ cup chili powder
2 TBSP ground cumin
3 cans each chopped tomatoes and black eyed peas

In a large heavy pan, fry bacon until it is crisp. Add onions and cook, stirring, until they start to brown. Crumble in ground beef and cook, stirring, until it has lost all pink color. Drain off all fat. Stir in the chili powder and cumin; stir until completely mixed. Add tomatoes and black eyed peas. Bring to full boil, reduce heat and allow to simmer at least an hour before serving.

Now this is the dish for all those folks who know they should eat black eyed peas on **New Year's Day** for good luck, but just don't like them. In fact, if you are cooking for those folks, don't tell them and they will never know. This is good, simple, quick, **East Tennessee style chili**. About that hog jowl, you are supposed to eat it. If it happens that you are making this dish some time other than new years, don't worry about it. Just start with a couple of TBSP's of cooking oil. The chili powder, of course, is to taste. This will give you a medium hot chili. If you want hotter, add a little ground cayenne. The cumin is for flavor not for hot. I like it. If you leave it out, it will not be a tragedy.

The other thing you are supposed to eat on **New Year's** is greens. The black eyed peas are for luck, the greens are for money. There are as many ways to cook greens as there are cooks to cook them. My **mother** washes the greens well, puts them in a pot with some water, and boils them until they are almost tender--which will take about 20 minutes. She then drains them, chops them up coarsely, and adds them to a skillet in which she has fried out bacon. She then sautes them until they are tender. Another traditional way is to wash the greens, put them into a heavy pot with a piece of fat meat, bring to a boil, reduce the heat, and cook until they are tender. If there is still a lot of water, remove the lid. Increase the heat and "boil them down" until the remaining liquid starts to be thick. This is the infamous **"pot likker"** and is good with corn bread. This whole process may take more than an hour of cooking. At the new **Southbound at the L&N Restaurant**, they serve collard greens which have been chopped, blanched and then stir fried with a little red bell pepper. See, I told you there was a lot of ways to cook them. Now have a Happy New Year and thanks for watching 400 shows!

Walter N. Lambert, Noonday Chef

CRAZED COOKIES (TV 401)

    10 TBSP butter
    6 TBSP cocoa
    2 cups plain flour
    1 cup sugar
    2 tsps baking powder
    ½ tsp salt
    2 eggs
    1 tsp vanilla
    ½ cup nuts
    confectioners sugar

Melt butter and blend in the cocoa. Add all remaining ingredients except confectioners sugar. Stir to blend. Wrap dough tightly in **Saran Wrap** and chill overnight. Shape dough into 1" balls and roll in confectioners sugar. Place on a lightly greased cookie sheet about 2 inches apart. Bake at 325 deg about 12 minutes. Allow to cool on pan before removing to a rack to cool completely. Makes about 4 dozen.

I am not absolutely sure, but I believe these came from an old **Hershey's Cocoa book**. The powdered sugar coating crackles (or crazes) as the cookies bake to produce a very pretty cookie. I like them because they are so easy. In fact, these will keep for several days in the refrigerator, and you can have instant hot cookies. In case you are interested, black walnuts are my favorite for this recipe. Now I am going to tell you something. These little goodies can be cooked in the microwave if you are having a chocolate fit. Make the balls exactly as described above. Arrange 8 of them in a circle on waxed paper in the bottom of your microwave. Set the power at half power, and cook for about 2 minutes. The cookies should be almost dry on the outside but still soft. Allow to cool on the paper and chew away. These are related, non chocolate cookies:

CRINKLY MOLASSES COOKIES

    ½ cup butter and ¼ cup shortening
    1 cup sugar
    1 egg
    ¼ cup molasses
    2 ¼ cups flour
    1 tsp each soda, cinnamon and ginger
    ½ tsp salt

Cream butter, shortening, and sugar. Beat in molasses and egg. Mix remaining dry ingredients and work into butter mixture. Roll into 1" balls, and roll in additional sugar. Bake at 350 deg for 12 minutes.

Walter N. Lambert, Noonday Chef

PEANUT BUTTER STEW (TV 402)

    1 lb beef, in small cubes
    2 medium onions, chopped
    2 cans chopped tomatoes, undrained
    ½ inch piece fresh ginger, chopped
    ¾ cup peanut butter
    1 tsp hot pepper or Tabasco Sauce
    2 cups water

Brown beef in large, heavy skillet. Add onions and ginger, and continue to saute. Pour the tomatoes and the water over meat mixture and bring to a boil. Cover and simmer about 20 minutes. Mix some of the hot broth with the peanut butter and stir it into the meat mixture with the hot sauce. Simmer about 30 minutes, uncovered, stirring occasionally to prevent sticking.

This interesting recipe comes from a nice cookbook prepared by the good folks at **Highland Presbyterian Church in Maryville**. We were given the book as a **Christmas** gift and we are enjoying it a lot. This recipe was supplied by **Mr. Scott Brunger** who is a professor at **Maryville College** and spouse of the Pastor at the church. Mr. Brunger notes that this is a **West African** recipe. I was fascinated by the number of things it has in common with some Thai recipes which I have done--including using peanut butter as a major component of the stew. Scott does not specify, but we chose crunchy peanut butter and liked it a lot. I should also tell you that the original recipe called for 3 cups of chopped tomatoes and I simplified it by going with two cans. I have a strong feeling that the recipe would benefit from using good, fresh tomatoes. I will leave that up to you.

Just to show you that the book has some more conventional recipes, I give you:

OVEN BEEF STEW

    1 ½ lb lean beef stew
    3 to 4 potatoes, quartered
    3 carrots, cut into large pieces
    1 medium onion, quartered
    1 bell pepper, quartered
    1 bay leaf
    1 can tomato soup

Put all ingredients in covered casserole dish. Cook for 4½ hours at 275 deg. Enjoy.

Walter N. Lambert, Noonday Chef

STIR FRY CHICKEN WITH VEGETABLES (TV 403)

> 6 boneless, skinless chicken breast halves cut into½" cubes or thin slices
> 1 egg white
> 3 to 4 cups mixed vegetables (celery, mushrooms, bok choy)
> 1 tsp garlic
> ½ cup green onions, chopped
> ¼ cup soy sauce
> ¼ cup water
> 2 TBSP cornstarch
> 3 to 4 TBSP oil for frying

Heat a wok or a heavy skillet until hot. Add about 2 TBSP oil. Add onion to the oil and stir to mix. Mix chicken with the egg white and add to the hot oil and onion. Stir constantly about 3 minutes or until chicken is no longer pink. Remove to a plate. Add one TBSP additional oil. Add vegetables. Cook stirring until vegetables are tender crisp. Stir back in the chicken and add the garlic. Mix the soy sauce, water and cornstarch, and add to skillet. Stir until the sauce comes to a boil and thickens. Serve immediately.

Welcome to the **Year of the Ox. Lunar New Year** is a big deal all over the orient. It is commonly called **Chinese New Year**, but the Chinese have no monopoly on it. This dish is great with almost any vegetable mix. I like celery and mushroom. I also like celery and snow peas. I love bok choy with its bright green leaves and white stems. If you are using bok choy, wash, slice crosswise into about ½ inch pieces and wash again. Drain thoroughly before using.

In case you are interested, the egg white keeps the chicken moist as it cooks. Whole egg is also ok, but it does discolor the chicken some. This dish works as well with cubes or slices of pork as it does with chicken. With pork, I love bean sprouts. Just be careful to not overcook them. Now here is a bonus:

GOLD, JADE AND IVORY

> 3 to 4 cups broccoli florets
> 2 to 3 cups carrot, cut into chunks
> 2 cans sliced bamboo shoots, washed and drained
> 1 jar oyster sauce
> oil for frying

In a hot wok, cook carrots until tender crisp. Add broccoli and stir fry until it changes color. Add the bamboo shoots and stir until they are hot through. Stir in oyster sauce. Serve immediately.

186

Walter N. Lambert, Noonday Chef

SNAPPY PEACH DELIGHT (TV 404)

> 1 stick low fat margarine
> ¾ cup skim milk
> 1 large can sliced peaches (1 lb 13 oz)
> 1 cup flour
> 1 cup sugar
> 14 low fat snap cookies crumbled

In an 11x8 ½" pan, melt the margarine and mix with the milk. Pour peaches and juice into the pan and spread evenly. Mix all remaining ingredients, and spread evenly over the top. Bake in a 350 deg oven about 1 to 1½ hours until golden brown and bubbly. Serve warm garnished with additional snaps.

It is **Girl Scout Cookie** time again. As you can remember, through the years, we have always used the cookies in a recipe. This allows grandparents to buy more cookies than usual and still finish them before mid summer.

Once again, we have used the cookies as part of a crust. If you will look in ***Cooking with the Noonday Chef, Volumes 1 and 2,*** you will find this is a pattern. It is not, however, the only way that the cookies can be used. You can make a perfectly delightful parfait if you follow these instructions:

CHOCOLATE COOKIE PARFAIT

> 1 5.6 oz pkg **Jell-O** instant chocolate pudding mix
> 2 cups cold milk
> 1 cup cold sour cream
> 1 pkg **Girl Scout Thin Mint Cookies**

Break the cookies up fairly fine and set aside. In a large bowl, beat together the milk and the sour cream. Mix in pudding mix and beat with a wire whisk about 2 minutes or until mixture thickens. In a parfait glass, spoon in a couple of TBSP of pudding. Sprinkle a layer of cookie crumbs over. Repeat layers until glass in almost full. Repeat with other glasses (will make four large or 6 small parfaits) until all pudding and crumbs have been used. Cover the top of each glass with **Saran Wrap,** and chill about 1 hour before serving.

Both of these are fine recipes to do with children and even with the Girls Scouts themselves. Neither recipe requires much heat and is therefore fairly safe. By the way, with the parfait, it works nicely with almost any of the cookies. The **Do-Si-Does** are absolutely great. They are a little hard to break into crumbs, and you may want to help with that. Remember buy your cookies!!!

Walter N. Lambert, Noonday Chef

PASTA FOR TWO (TV 405)

6 oz angel hair pasta
2 chicken breast halves
2 TBSP olive oil
1 cup sliced mushrooms
¼ cup sun dried tomatoes in oil
1 cup heavy cream
¼ cup grated Parmesan cheese
chopped Italian Parsley for garnish

Cook the pasta according to package directions and keep warm. Grill the chicken breasts and cut crosswise into thin slices. In a heavy skillet, heat olive oil and add the mushrooms. Cook, stirring until just soft. Add the tomatoes and cream, and cook quickly until reduced by about half. Stir in the pasta and Parmesan cheese. Divide into two plates and sprinkle with chopped parsley. Serve hot.

Walter N. Lambert, Noonday Chef

TABLESCAPES, CENTERPIECES, AND EDIBLE ART
ANNE'S CHAPTER

It is so easy to add excitement and fun to any dining experience by making creative, and often edible, centerpieces and recipes. My last two chapters in **_Cooking with the Noonday Chef Volume I and Volume II_**, have been on centerpieces that are made from vegetable or fruit sculpting, which can then be recycled ("Centerpieces Tonight, Casseroles Tomorrow" or "View It, then Stew It"). The only recipe that will be repeated in this Volume is the "Onion Flowers" (often called "Blooming Onions" or "Awesome Blossoms"), which responds to the repeated requests I get for this recipe. These are onions that are used in your centerpieces and the following day dipped in batter, deep fried, and then served with Dijon mustard sauce as an appetizer. They can also be dyed with food coloring to match your color schemes. (See page 193)

I particularly like to combine sculptures, flowers, fruits, vegetables, herbs or anything else that strikes my fancy or will be appealing in a particular "tablescape" or centerpiece. While my knowledge of edible flowers is just developing, I feel they can add a lot. I am always researching and learning about edible herbs and flowers. The more I learn, the more I realize how little I know. There are literally hundreds (probably thousands) of edible interesting things, so here is a limited "short list" of the things Walter and I have tried and enjoyed. Walter accuses me of learning new things and waiting to put them in his next cookbook. Perhaps that is true, because there are endless ways to cut, prepare, and decorate, and we all enjoy trying new frontiers. Do your own thing! Needless to say, we always appreciate you sharing your discoveries with us.

WARNING: Please be extremely careful about eating or serving any produce or flowers without making sure that it has not been sprayed with poisonous insecticides. For instance, I'm sure you already know to wash **ALL** fruits and vegetables carefully before using. You may only want to use flowers from your garden, a neighbors garden, or those that you KNOW have been organically grown for serving on your elegant dining occasions.

BATTER FOR ONION CHRYSANTHEMUMS, FRITTERS, SQUASH BLOSSOMS, etc:
    1 cup flour
    ½ cup corn starch
    2 egg whites
    1 tsp. salt
    ½ cup water (approximately)

Blend flour, cornstarch, and salt. Beat in egg whites. Add sufficient water to make a batter about the consistency of thick cream. Sprinkle vegetables lightly with flour, and dip into the batter. Fry immediately in very hot oil until lightly brown. When making the onion flowers, place upside down in oil first, then turn and do the bottom side.

Walter N. Lambert, Noonday Chef

EASY DIJON MUSTARD SAUCE: Mix 2 tablespoons of Dijon mustard with 1 cup of sour cream. This is nice as fritter or onion dip as is, but Tabasco sauce may be added to taste if you just must.

CANDIED FLOWERS
(Violets, pansies, rose petals, scented geranium, etc)

> 1 egg white (room temperature, beaten frothy)
> 2 drops almond extract (or vodka to hasten drying)
> ¼ to ½ cup super fine sugar
> Wire cake rack
> Small artist's paint brush (used only for this purpose)
> Edible flowers (do not use stems)

Rinse flower petals or blossoms and dry thoroughly. Remove stamens at this point if using flowers such as Daylilies. Carefully dip or paint petals (both sides) with egg white mixture. Gently dip or sprinkle with sugar, covering both sides completely. Place flower or petal face up on parchment paper or baking sheet to dry. Separate petals if needed with toothpick. Allow to dry in a cool, dry place until sugar has thoroughly hardened. These may then be stored in an air-tight container and kept for months.

We have not given this recipe before because of the danger of salmonella from raw eggs. Now we understand that in a few months, a preventative is going to be fed to chickens that will eliminate this danger. Therefore this should be safe by the time this book is published.

Listen to the comments you receive when you top off your desserts or fancy coffee with a flower on top of your whipped cream. **NOTE:** In order to keep the flowers fresh and looking pretty, I find it easier to pick just a few flowers at a time, and after coating those, then go pick more. Try what works best for you.

CARNATIONS, DAISIES, and CHRYSANTHEMUMS: Carnations may be dyed with food coloring to fit your color themes. Any of the above may be sprinkled on top of cold dishes, such as potato salad, tuna, or chicken salad. Chrysanthemums and daisies are particularly nice used in informal settings, such as tailgate parties, pool parties, and picnics. They are nice in baskets, with checked tablecloths, wooden trays, or other casual accessories. Added to platters of deviled eggs and placed on a green leaf, with perhaps a lemon or lime cup filled with herbal dressing on the side will compliment your presentation. Top your herb butter with a daisy and a tiny leaf.

190

Walter N. Lambert, Noonday Chef

DAYLILIES: Daylilies may be stir-fried, candied, or stuffed. Try removing the centers of some fresh daylilies, and stuff with finely chopped chicken or tuna salad. Serve these on a fruit salad platter, or use a couple on a pretty green lettuce leaf as a single salad. They may also be used as a garnish for fruit plates or on a "boat" made from a cut pineapple. If you prefer not to stuff the flower, place a single blossom where the frond joins the pineapple for special appeal.

GERANIUMS: The rose and fruit scented geraniums (apple, lemon, orange and peppermint to name a few) are particularly nice to flavor or float in tea. You may also like to try in jellies (use recipe on **Sure Jell** package) or in your potpourri. These are fun flavors, so do your own thing.

APPLE, ORANGE or HONEYSUCKLE BLOSSOMS: Try anywhere you would like a sweet taste. I think of ice cream, pies, fruit salads, weddings.. Use in clusters or as single flowers on the side with a dollop of whipped topping. Make a fruit basket of a whole orange (by scooping out the inside) and fill with orange sherbert. Top with a small cluster of blossoms. What could be nicer for a bridge luncheon, bridal shower, or wedding luncheon?

VIOLETS: These are my favorites to crystallize or candy as above. Violets can add flavor and beauty to custards, fritters, salads, and sauces. Violets and fennel work nicely together.. Leaves as well as flowers are edible. Try arranging thin slices of cooked, chilled salmon on a patter garnished with fennel and violets, perhaps with thin slices of scored cucumber. Drop a pretty candied one on anything topped with whipped cream topping.

SQUASH BLOSSOMS: Recently, when Walter and I were in Santa Fe, we tried stuffed squash blossoms. The centers had been removed and the blossom stuffed with cooked ground beef, onions, rice, and seasonings. They were then dipped in a thin batter, rolled in cornmeal and deep fried. They were served on a green leaf with slivers of chives on top for decoration. It was tasty and beautiful! Squash blossoms may be used in salads or may also be steamed and seasoned with butter and herbs or stir-fried.

CHIVES: These dainty stems with light lavender delicate blossoms are especially pretty with deviled eggs or anywhere a slight onion flavor is desired. Pretty for topping soups, chowders, roasts and meatloaf. Walter and I like to use the stems in decorative patterns under clear aspic, using almonds or radishes placed on the stems for flowers. Try painting the top of a baked ham with a thick layer of clear aspic (paint it on with pastry brush), arrange your "bouquet" on top, and cover with a thick layer of aspic. Beautiful!! Chop and sprinkle over soups, potato salad, deviled eggs, cheese, or dips.

DILL: Somewhere, I read that this plant belongs to the carrot family. It flourishes in many parts of the world, and particularly in our own Tennessee. The plant is pleasant to smell, and the flowers are great for dried arrangements. Try some of Walter's recipes for dill such as Dilly Casserole Bread, dill pickles, cucumber dips, or use as flavoring for soups, salads, meats, and particularly fish dishes.

Walter N. Lambert, Noonday Chef

CARDAMOM: This fragrant spice is cultivated in the Middle East. At one time, a man's wealth was determined by the amounts and kinds of spices he possessed. (A pound of ginger might be worth a sheep, but a sack of pepper or cardamom might have been worth a man's life). Add it to curries, cookies, cakes, and tea. We recently judged at the Smoky Mountain Herb Fair, and one of the winners was a beautiful dish of <u>cous cous</u> that had just a faint, lingering hint of cardamom as a delightful aftertaste.

CLOVES: This is my favorite spice. You can use whole cloves as "eyes" for the little radish mice, use it on cheese or crudité trays, or on the "squash people" (Instructions are in your **_Cooking with the Noonday Chef, Volume II_**). A mixture of cloves and cinnamon simmering on a hot plate will make your entire house smell "feisty" and festive. Whole cloves are also nice stuck in hams, pickle jars, or for roasting fresh pork. Ground cloves are nice in cookies, spice cakes, or almost anything using molasses.

MUSTARD SEEDS: This spice is useful in pickles, herb vinegar, and I have also used the seeds as background when making seed mosaics for the kitchen. My mother, Mrs. Charles F. Wayland, Sr., once told me it was used to ward off "evil spirits", and I have not been attacked by a vampire yet! Make your own mustard: Toast, grind, and mix with a little wine or wine vinegar to make a good, strong mustard.

PEPPERS: Peppers make pretty flowers (See Volume I), but if handling the hot ones, use surgical gloves to keep hands from burning. When cutting either hot peppers or bell peppers into flowers, drop into ice water afterwards to open for use in arrangements. Slice the big bell peppers into bands, and use circles to hold asparagus or carrots. Use as cups for dips on a platter or fill with chicken salad, etc., as a side item on a salad plate.

ICE: Mint leaves, tiny bits of fruit or herbs are great frozen into ice cubes for tea or punch. Try working out a pretty pattern in an ice ring using pineapple, cherries, bits of oranges, lemon, lime, with herbs to serve in a punch bowl at a reception or wedding. Think about star fruit, strawberries, grapes or cranberries to carry out a color scheme. After your ice ring is frozen, remove it from the mold and store in baggies or foil so you may prepare several without purchasing more forms.

Ice containers are absolutely beautiful. Freeze a ½ inch layer of ice in a large bowl or half gallon milk carton. Put a wine decanter or a square gin bottle into the half gallon milk container or a smaller bowl if you are doing a bowl. The inside container may need to be taped or weighted down to keep it from floating. Arrange herbs, parsley, etc., between the two, fill with water (between the carton and the bottle over the herbs) and freeze overnight. When you remove the cardboard carton, you will have a beautiful ice container to keep your punch refilled. Gin or vodka will not freeze, so it may be used "as is", but if you are making refill containers for punch, you may want to use a nice wide-mouthed bottle to freeze empty, so you may remove the covering and have the bottle ready to refill the punch bowl or pour individually to serve punch or tea. If making a bowl, pour warm water into the inside bowl until it releases and warm water over the outside of the larger bowl until it does.

BUTTER: Almost all kitchen shops now have rubber butter molds that are relatively inexpensive. Butter is easily molded, flavored with savory herbs or spices, or given a sweet taste with honey, or honey and cinnamon, or strawberries, or many others that make a pretty and tasty spread. After you have flavored your softened butter, spread it level to the top of your mold, and place in the freezer until hard. These should then be unmolded and placed in a storage box with layers of wax paper in between. This way, you may make a nice supply and have them on hand for use when needed. It will keep for several weeks.

Earlier in this chapter, I talked about a "short list". We must stop if this list is to stay short. By now, you see the point. Learn about things about you and be open and ready to give things a try. Whether we are talking about fried squash blossoms, or squash boats, or onion flowers, or roses in the butter, there is always some new and tempting idea to try. I thank all of you who write and tell me about liking the centerpieces on the show and come to see us and say kind things. Remember, simply look at the world each day with a new eye and who knows what might end up being tossed in your salad. Enjoy!

To cut the onion flower, place chopsticks or rulers beside your onion so you do not cut through. Following the chart above, cut the heavy solid lines first, then the heavy dotted line and then the remaining cuts. You should have 16 sections when you finish cutting. Drop onion into ice water to open. If you add food coloring to the ice water, it will dye the onion to match your color scheme. You can then display the onion or use the batter on page 189 to deep fry and serve with dijon mustard sauce.

INDEX

Appetizers

Biscuit Pockets 33
Black-eyed Pea Dip 34
Cheese Ball, Almond Chutney 180
Cheese Ball, Eleanor's 180
Nuts, Quick Spicy 182
Onion Flowers, Batter 189
Sweet and Spicy Mix 182

Beans

Baked, Black and White . . . 154
Baked, Calico 107
Baked, New England 107
Baked, Quick 9
Black 103
Black Bean Soup 36
Black with Rice 18
Black with Sausage 36
Black-Eyed Peas 34
Black-Eyed Peas, Baked . . . 80
Cake, Pork and Beans 167
Chili, New Years 183
Cowboy 97
Dry Beans, Cooking 163
Lima, Baked 65
Pickled 60
Pie, Pinto Bean 167
Salad, Spicy 65
Snowy Days Soup 138

Beef

Brisket, Beer Baked 6
Burgers, All Amexican 9
Burgers, Flavored 9
Burgers, stuffed 9
Corned 6

Corned, Baked Reuben 45
Feeding Father Fast 55
Ground, Casserole 38
Halloween Casserole 120
Hot dogs, Dressed up 9
Meal in a Loaf 78
Meat Loaf, Another Easy . . . 128
Meat loaf, quick and easy 1
Meat Loaf, Special 73
Meat Pie, Mrs. O'Lamberts . . 44
Pot Roast, Savory 91
Steak, Country Style 35
Steak, Quick Swiss 35
Stew, Oven 185
Stew, Peanut Butter 185
Stew, Sweet Potato 174

Bread

Apple, Fresh 121
Biscuit Pockets 33
Biscuit, Cinnamon Roll 112
Biscuits, Apple cheese 20
Biscuits, Five Spice 141
Biscuits, Secret 21,113
Cinnamon Batter 67
Cornbread 17, 124
Cornbread Nuggets 82
Cornbread, Upside Down . . 163
Crackers, cheese 31
Crackers, Sesame cheese . . 31
French Toast, Baked 168
Herb 143
Herb Batter 67
Irish Yeast 143
Muffin, Dried Cherry 139
Muffins, Handy Bran 117

Muffins, Pumpkin 117
Muffins, Sweet Potato Nut . 176
Pancakes, Apple-Oat 121
Rolls, Quick Whole Wheat . . 46
Sculpture 132
Strawberry 4
Sweet Berry Delight 160
Butter 193
Cakes
Chocolate Pear Upside Down 86
"Glory Be" 179
Apple Pound 49
Black Forest Upside Down . . 86
Chocolate 81
Chocolate Potato 99
Crazy 55
Dirt 41
Eggless, Milkless, Butterless . 39
Fairy 54
Fruit, Fast Fancy 178
Fudge 39
Green Tomato 115
Lemon Meringue Torte 98
Lovers Torte 40
Macroon 109
Mayonnaise 50
More than Chocolate 50
Peanut Butter Pound 93
Sad 54
Spicy Molasses 71
Strawberry 52
Toffee Pound 172
Turtle 152
What's in it 167
White Chocolate 148
Casserole
Asparagus 147
Broccoli 147
Chicken Divan 151
Chicken Pie, Lemon 33
Chili 23
Cornbread, Stuffed 114
Cornbread-Chicken 38
Easter Pie, After 147
Escalloped Kraut 136

Halloween 120
Ham and Egg 47, 95
Hample 21
Hominy, Mary Clement's . . . 148
Kraut, Variations 171
Lewis Cosby's Breakfast . . . 168
Potato 19
Quiche, Country Ham 165
Reuben 136
Sausage Apple 122
Smokey's Rebel-lious
    Corn Bread 97
Summer Squash 104
Sunday Morning Souffle . . . 122
Sweet Potato with Sausage 118
Tamale Pie 23
Tamale, Diane's 42
Taste of Tennessee 66
Tipsy 21
Chicken
and Mushrooms 114
Autumn, baked 171
Baked Company 151
Baked Reuben 45
Bourbon Glazed 11
Cajun Broiled 155
Caribbean Salad 158
Chicken Lemon Pie 33
Chicken with Greens, Oriental 135
Chili, Red 83
Cornbread-Chicken Casserole 38
Curried 74
Curried Apple Salad 123
Curried Salad, Quick 82
Divan Casserole 151
Florentine, Quick 15
Fried 25
In a Skillet 100
Lemon 51
Low Fat 134
Luscious Loaf 63
Mediterranean 11
Mushrooms 164
Oriental Salad 59
Oven Baked 51

Pasta For Two 188
Poached, How to 38
Potato Casserole 19
Salad, Peachy 158
Salad, Touch of Apple 123
Scallop 63
Springtime Salad 48
Stir Fry with Vegetables . . . 186
Stir Fry, Summer 108
With Green 135
With Yellow Rice 103

Chocolate
Black Forest Upside Down
        Cake 86
Brownies, Banana 13
Cake, Lovers Torte 40
Cake, More than Chocolate . 50
Cake, Turtle 152
Cherry cheesecake Squares . 87
Coating 116
Cookies, Crazed 184
Cookies, Peanut 7
Cupcakes, Picnic 155
Dirt Cake 41
Fudge cake 39
Fudge, Sugar Free 89
Low Fat Brownies 150
Melting 13
Meringues 85, 157
Pear Upside Down Cake 86
Pudding 41
Truffle Loaf 40

Cloves 192

Cookies
Christmas Wreath 76
Cinnamon Jumbles 22
Anne's Favorites (Meringues) 98
Apple, Fresh 96
Apple, Spicy 96
Big Orange 27
Brownies, Banana 13
Brownies, Butterscotch 129
Brownies, Chocolate Chip
        Peanut 129
Brownies, Crunchy Peanut . 129

Brownies, Low Fat 150
Butterscotch Goodies 149
Butterscotch Oatmeal 149
Cheery Cherry 140
Chess Squares 16
Chocolate Cherry Cheesecake
        Squares 87
Chocolate Chocolate chunk 119
Chocolate with M & M's 119
Chocolate with Peanut Butter
        Chips 119
Chocolate, Peanut 7
Crazed 184
Crumbs 140
Date Nut Jumbles 22
Forever Amber 27
Fruit Cake 26
Glaze 96
Granola Bars, Fruity 133
Gustine 28
Holiday, Quick 177
Layered 140
Lemon, Quick 177
Meringues, Chocolate 157
Meringues, Flavored 157
Merinques, Chocolate 85
Mint Surprise 30
Miss Piggy Squares 170
Molasses, Crinkley 184
Nut Bars 76
Oatmeal-Pumpkin 29
Peanut Butter Kisses 28
Peanut Butter, Best 29
Raisin, Sugar Dip 27
Reece's Peanut Butter Cups . 76
Sugar 26
Sugerplums, Modern 79
Sweetheart Pink 85
Thumbprints, Santa's 30
Toffee Treats 116
Toffee, Quick 7

Dessert
Apple Swirls, Tn. 112
Apple Tort, Fresh 49
Bananas Foster, Classic . . . 110

Bread Pudding 78
Bread Pudding, Buttermilk . 105
Bread Pudding, Pumpkin ... 72
Cheesecake, Chocolate Cherry 87
Cheesecake, Do-Si-Does .. 137
Cheesecake, Lindy's 173
Cheesecake, Pumpkin
    Amaretto 173
Cheesecake, Variations ... 173
Chocolate Cookie Parfait .. 187
Clafouti, Lulu's 145
Cobbler, Quick Peach 56
Cobbler, Strawberry 2
Coconut filling 81
Coffee Cake, Apple 49
Cupcakes, Picnic 155
French Toast, Baked 168
Glaze, Vanilla 81
Heath Bar Variations 172
Mousse, Strawberry 2, 52
Muffin, Nut Topping 176
Peach Brown Betty 56
Peach Delight, Snappy 187
Peach, Grilled 12
Praline Topping 126
Pudding, butterscotch 41
Pudding, Easy Apple 166
Pudding, Vanilla (or Chocolate) 41
Shortcake, Original 156
Sweet Potato Pudding 118

Diabetic, Low Fat, Low Sugar
Apple Butter, Sugar Free ... 69
Apples, Baked 69
Baked Chicken Reuben 45
Brownies, Low Fat 150
Buttermilk Salad 64
Chicken 134
Chicken with Greens 135
Chicken, Cajun Broiled 155
Cinnamon Popcorn 89
"Creamed" Soup 37
Curried Chicken or Pork 74
Fructose 69
Fruit and Veggie Salad 146
Fudge, Sugar-Free 89

Green Beans, Mexican 57
Herb Batter Bread 67
Lemon Chicken 51
Oven Baked Chicken 51
Strawberry Pie 52
Sugar Free Apple Butter 69
Toufu Stir Fry 108

Fish
Florentine, Quick 15
Low Fat 134
Salmon, Lime 10

Flowers
Apple, Orange or Honeysuckle 191
Candied 190
Cardamom 192
Carnations, Daisies and
    Chrysanthemums ... 190
Chives 191
Daylilies 191
Dill 191
Geraniums 191
Onion Flowers 189
Squash Blossoms 191
Violets 191
Frozen Decorations 192
Ice Containers 192

Fruit
Apple Butter, Sugar Free ... 69
Apple Pound Cake 49
Apple Pumpkin Pie 24
Apple Swirls, Tn. 112
Apple Tort, Fresh 49
Apple, Curried Chicken Salad 123
Apple-Sausage Casserole .. 122
Apples, Baked 69
Apples, Poor Man's Pie 166
Apricots, Savory Pot Roast .. 91
Bananas Foster, Classic ... 110
Biscuits, Apple cheese 20
Chutney, Apple Cranberry ... 75
Cider, Hot 30
Cranberry Pie 32
Cranberry Salad 32
Cranberry Salsa 75
Fruit and Veggie Salad 146

Grilled 12
Grilled Peach 12
Lemon Strawberry Pie 53
Low Sugar Strawberry Pie . . 52
Orange Apricot Balls 79
Peach Delight, Snappy 187
Peaches 56, 58
Peaches, Fresh 12
Pie, Fresh Strawberry 4
Pizza, Fresh Fruit 146
Salad, Peachy Chicken 158
Salad, Special Summer 161
Strawberry Bread 4
Strawberry Cake 52
Strawberry Cobbler, Quick . . . 2
Strawberry Lime Preserves . . . 3
Strawberry Mousse 2, 52
Sugar plums, Modern 79
Sun-Maid Mixed Dried Fruit . 133

Gravy
Beef 6
Gravy, Giblet 126
Gravy, Pot Roast 91
Gravy, tomato 73
Milk 25
Red Eye Gravy 165

Holidays
Chinese New Year . 84, 141,186
Christmas . 76, 82, 131, 180-182
Easter 94, 95, 147
Father's Day 55
George Washington's Birthday139
Halloween 174
Hanukkah 131
MLK'S Birthday 135
New Years 183
New Years Day 34, 80
St. Patrick's
        Day . 43, 44, 85, 90, 143
Superbowl 82, 83, 136
Thanksgiving 77, 125, 176
Valentines Day 85, 139

Icing
Brownie 150
Caramel Frosting 170

Chocolate 50
Crazy Cake 55
Creamy Chocolate Frosting . 152
Glaze 99
Strawberry 52
Whipped cream 71
Mustard Seed 192
Pasta
Chicken, For Two 188
Country Ham 113
Fresh Vegetable Delight 57
Ham and Egg Salad 95
Macaroni, Mary Mills 169
Noodle Kugel 131
Noodles, Chinese 8
Noodles, Japanese 159
Noodles, Rice 59
Noodles, Summertime 8
Noodles, Thai 8
Salad, Cold Noodles 159
Salad, Cool Summer 159
Salad, Creamy 106
Spaghetti Sauce 55
Tamale Casserole 42
Pastry
Rich 43
Peppers 192
Pies
Chess 16
Chocolate Peanut Butter . . 144
Cranberry Surprise 32
Crunchy Peach 56
Fresh Strawberry 4
Green Tomato 115
Lemon Strawberry 53
Million $ 61
Molasses 71
Oatmeal 179
Original Million $ 61
Peach 102
Peach Batter 102
Peach Meringue 58
Peaches and Cream 58
Peanut Butter Fudge 144
Pinto Bean 167

Poor Man's Apple 166
Poor Man's Pecan 179
Pumpkin Apple 24
Raisin 68
Raisin Sour Cream 68
Sweet Potato 118
Whipped Cream PeanutButter 144
Strawberry 52
Treacle Tart 44

Pizza Party
Children's 142
English Muffins 142
Faces 142
Fresh Fruit 146

Pork
Baked Reuben 45
Casserole, Tipsy 21
chops, Autumn 171
Chops, Chinese 84
Chops, Curried 74
Ham 18, 92
Ham and Egg Casserole . 47, 95
Ham and Egg Pasta Salad . . 95
Ham and Egg Patties 47
Ham Delights 111
Ham Spread 132
Ham with Yellow Rice 103
Ham, Country 113
Ham, Country Pasta 113
Hample Casserole 21
Hog Jowl 80
Meat Loaf, Another Easy . . . 128
Sausage and Apple Quiche . . 92
Sausage Balls, Hot 109
Sausage Balls, Snappy 130
Sausage w/ Summer Squash 104
Sausage, Dublin Eggs 90
Sausage, Miss Piggy Squares 170
Sausage, Potato Casserole . 19
Sausage, Stuffed Cornbread 114
Sausage, Taste of Tennessee 66
Sausage-Apple Casserole . . 122
Sunday Morning Souffle . . . 122

Preserves
Cranberry Orange Relish . . 126

Portabella Mushroom Relish 153
Relish, Cranberry Orange . . 181
Relish, Spicy Cranberry . . . 181
Strawberry Lime Preserves . . . 3
Strawberry, Lucy C. Templeton
    Preserves 3
Zucchini Relish 169

Salads
Apple, Curried Chicken . . . 123
Apple, Touch of Chicken . . . 123
Bean, Black and White 18
Bean, Spicy 65
Black Bean 154
Broccoli 88
Buttermilk 64
Chicken, Caribbean 158
Chicken, Peachy 158
chicken, Springtime 48
Cornbread 17
Cranberry 32
Cucumber 14
Fruit and Veggie 146
Gazpacho, Molded 14
Ham and Egg 95
Macaroni, Mary Mills 169
Pasta with Ham and Eggs . . . 95
Pasta, Safe 106
Potato, Light Roasted 5
Potato, Roasted 5
Potato, Sweet and Sour . . . 153
Salad, Special Summer 161

Sauce
Dijon Mustard, Easy 190
Jezebel 130
Meat Loaf 1
Mustard-Horseradish 10
Peanut Butter, Oriental 93
Rum Sauce/Bread Pudding . 105
Whiskey Sauce, New Orleans 72
White Sauce with Cheese . . 147

Soup
Black Bean 36
Chinese Greens 70
Low Fat "Creamed" 37
Potato Collard Chowder 70

Pumpkin Ginger, Roasted . . 175
Snowy Days 138
Vegetarian Bean 138

Turkey

Chile, Tom's Turkey 110
Dressing 125
Dressing with 77
Holiday Stuffed 77
Meat Loaf 1
Stir Fry 127
Tips 125

Vegetables

Asparagus, Olive oil and
      vinegar 48
Asparagus, Poached 48
Bean, Black and White Salad 18
Beans, Black with Rice 18
Blanching, How to 106
Bok Choy 186
Broccoli Salad 88
Broccoli Stir Fry 88
Broiled, Simple 10
Colcannon 90
Collard Greens with Chicken 135
Corn Pudding with Bacon . . . 94
Corn Pudding, Quick 94
Cucumber, Dill Pickles 60
Cucumber, Salad 14
Fresh Delight 57
Fritters 162
Gold, Jade, and Ivory 186
Green Beans 57
Green Beans, Mexican 57
Greens, Assorted . . 80, 124,183
Grilled, Mixed 11
Mushrooms, with Chicken . . 100
Onion Flowers 189
Onion, Blarney Tart 43
Onion, Vidalia Pie 101
Onions, Baked 101
Parsnips 37
Peas with Yellow Rice 103
Potato Cakes, Fried 99
Potato Casserole 19
Potato Collard Chowder 70

Potato Latke 131
Potato, Chocolate cake 99
Potato, Light Roasted 5
Potato, Roasted Salad 5
Potatoes, Roasted 128
Pumpkin, Fried 24
Salad, Cool Summer 159
Spinach, Special Summer
      Salad 161
Squash, Summer Saute . . . 104
Stir Fry with Chicken 186
Sweet Potato Muffins 176
Sweet Potato, Baked 176
Sweet Potato, Savory 118
Tomatoes, Fried Green 162
Tomatoes, Sun Dried 128
Zucchini, Wanda's 62

INDEX OF INDIVIDUALS, COMPANIES, AND PRODUCTS

A Slice of Orange 97
Apple Barn 112, 166
Baxter's Apples 166
Baxters 112
Bearden Cooks 32
Bernhardt, Mrs. H. A. 63
Brabson, Mr. & Mrs. H. W. 64,69
Bridges, Shirley 149
Brunger, Scott 185
Bush Bean Company 163
Bush Golden Hominy 163
Castellaw, Betty 39
Cate, Zelma 109
Chaffins, Tom 110
Cheeze-it Hot and Spicy Crackers . 101
Chocolatier 140
Clement, Rep. Bob 148
Clevenger, Joyce 170
Clifty Farms 113, 138, 163,165
Cocke County Apples 166
Coffey, Dolores 146, 150
Colburn, David 77
Cold Stream Farms 165
Congressional Club Cookbook . . . 148
Cooper, Diane 42
Cosby, Lewis 168
Craisins 177
Cruze, Cheri 64
Cruze, Dixie 111
Cuisine for all Seasons 145
DeFriese, Ruth 60, 181
Dollywood 77
Durkee's 134
Durman, Louise 139, 152, 173

Eagle Brand Milk 140
Eagle Brand Milk, Amaretto 173
Emig, Nancy 45
Fetzer Winery Garden 65
Fitzpatricks, The 88
Forks Grove Baptist Church 179
Fritos 23
Gary, Pay 27
George Washington,s Birthday . . . 140
Girl Scouts 41,137,187
Gourley, Johnnie R. 29
Grace, Eleanor Boyd 180
Grainger County Tomatoes 113
Grandmother Freeman 143
Grandpa Jones 118
Hamblen County Schools . . . 146, 150
Harold's Kosher Foods 131
Harris, Susan 30
Hatmaker, Arie 179
Hawk, Shannon Laws 55
Heath Bar 172
Help Yourself 92
Helsley, Mary 52
Hershey's Cocoa Book 184
Highland Presbyterian Church 185
Ivey, Ellen 179
Jack Daniels 71, 166
JFG 66, 81
Jordan, Tami 61
Kalthoff, Wanda 62
Kemmer, Ann 34
Kinfolks and Custard
    Pie 16, 26, 41, 115, 120
Knox County Farmer's Market . . 64,113
Knox County Mobile Meals Program 145

Knoxville
    News-Sentinel 45, 139, 152, 173

Kroger 41-43, 66, 78,
    82, 84, 87, 88, 105, 134,
    139-142, 152, 159, 162, 163, 165
Lady Vols 97
Lambert, Howard and Anna Lee . . . 68
Lee, Penny 28
Lessons with Louise 152
Linn-Emig, Nancy 30
Logan, Dr. Nell 71
Mangan, Greg 110
Mar-Tenn Hams 165
Marco Polo 8
Mary Clement 148
Mary Starr Cookbook 148
Maryville College 185
McGrew, Pamela 26
McPherson, Hope 23
McRary, Amy 152
Millis, Jean 16, 28, 167
Mills, Mary 169
Mills, Mary Geneva 169
Mishu, Layla 24
Monte, Barbara 145
Monterey Brand Mushrooms . 114, 164
Nicely, Tanna 124
Nichols, Linda 29
Ogle, Eva 61
Owen, Mr. 58
Petros 23
Phillips, Mrs. Richard 81
Pick Tennessee Products 163, 164, 166
Plymouth Rock 94
Proffitt's 87
Proffitts Department Store 34
Prophater, Lila 109
Quillen, Cecile Cox 148
Quillen, Rep. James 148
Rudy's Farms 170
Russelville Elementary School 146
Scarecrow Inn 88
Second Presbyterian Church 39
Sharp, Diane 182

Shelton, Mrs. W. A. 39
Shersky, Addie 131
Southbound At the L & N 184
Spence, Mrs. Cary F. 39
Stout, Mrs. Jesse 54
Sundquist, Mrs. Martha 163, 166
Sweet and Low 52
Tennessee Arthritis Foundation 92
Tennessee Chow Chow 163
Tennessee Dept.
    of agriculture 66, 112, 166
Tennessee Pride Sausage 114
Tennessee Valley Fair 170
Thompson, Dawn 85
Thompson, Nell 39
Tiberio's 48
Troutt, Mrs. 29
Troutt, Stanley 66
Tyson Chicken 164
Vidalia Onions 101
Vidmar Brothers 23
Wade, Frankie 144
Warwick, Eulah 27
White Lily 17, 20,26,
    112-114, 141, 163, 164, 166
Williams, Alan 167
Williford, Helen 26

REORDER

COPIES OF <u>COOKING WITH THE NOON DAY CHEF, VOLUME 3</u> ARE AVAILABLE AT $8.95 EACH PLUS $1.00 FOR SHIPPING AND HANDLING. IF YOU WOULD LIKE THE BOOKS PERSONALIZED, PLEASE ATTACH A LIST OF NAMES. IF YOU DO NOT INCLUDE NAMES, WE WILL SIGN THE BOOKS WITHOUT A DEDICATION. COPIES OF VOLUME 1 AND VOLUME 2 ARE ALSO AVAILABLE AT THE SAME PRICE. IF YOU WOULD LIKE A REAL BARGAIN, SEND $25.00 FOR A SET OF THREE AND WE WILL PAY THE POSTAGE.

PLEASE SEND _____ COPIES OF VOLUME 3 AT $8.95 PLUS $1.00
_____ COPIES OF VOLUME 1 AT $8.95 PLUS $1.00
_____ COPIES OF VOLUME 2 AT $8.95 PLUS $1.00
_____ SETS OF 3 AT $25.00 INCLUDING POSTAGE

SEND ORDERS TO: TASTE MATTERS, INC.
                        3635 TALILUNA AVE.   B-1
                        KNOXVILLE, TN 37919

REORDER

COPIES OF <u>COOKING WITH THE NOON DAY CHEF, VOLUME 3</u> ARE AVAILABLE AT $8.95 EACH PLUS $1.00 FOR SHIPPING AND HANDLING. IF YOU WOULD LIKE THE BOOKS PERSONALIZED, PLEASE ATTACH A LIST OF NAMES. IF YOU DO NOT INCLUDE NAMES, WE WILL SIGN THE BOOKS WITHOUT A DEDICATION. COPIES OF VOLUME 1 AND VOLUME 2 ARE ALSO AVAILABLE AT THE SAME PRICE. IF YOU WOULD LIKE A REAL BARGAIN, SEND $25.00 FOR A SET OF THREE AND WE WILL PAY THE POSTAGE.

PLEASE SEND _____ COPIES OF VOLUME 3 AT $8.95 PLUS $1.00
_____ COPIES OF VOLUME 1 AT $8.95 PLUS $1.00
_____ COPIES OF VOLUME 2 AT $8.95 PLUS $1.00
_____ SETS OF 3 AT $25.00 INCLUDING POSTAGE

SEND ORDERS TO: TASTE MATTERS, INC.
                        3635 TALILUNA AVE.   B-1
                        KNOXVILLE, TN 37919